NB.S.
MARKETING TO
THE AFFLUENT

NO HOLDS BARRED
KICK BUTT
TAKE NO PRISONERS
GUIDE TO GETTING
REALLY RICH

Dan Kennedy

EP
Entrepreneur.
Press

Jere L. Calmes, Publisher
Cover Design: David Shaw
Production and Composition: Eliot House Productions

This publication is designed to provide accurate and authoritative information in regard to the subject matter covered. It is sold with the understanding that the publisher is not engaged in rendering legal, accounting or
other professional services. If legal advice or other expert assistance is
required, the services of a competent professional person should be sought.

Library of Congress Cataloging-in-Publication Data
  Kennedy, Dan S., 1954-
    No B.S. marketing to the affluent/by Dan S. Kennedy.
      p.   cm.—(No B.S. series)
    ISBN-13: 978-1-59918-181-3 (alk. paper)
    ISBN-10: 1-59918-181-9 (alk. paper)
      1. Affluent consumers—United States. 2. Marketing—United States.
  I. Title. II. Title: No BS marketing to the affluent.
  HF5415.332.A34K46 2008
  658.8—dc22   2008015785

Printed in Canada

13 12 11 10 09 08   10 9 8 7 6 5 4 3

Contents

BOOK THREE
—————

HOW CAN I GET THEM TO GIVE ME THEIR MONEY?

BOOK FOUR

RESOURCES

FOREWORD

How to Easily Attract
the Affluent

BY JOE VITALE

I was homeless 30 years ago. No job, no home, no car, no nothing. I struggled in virtual poverty for a decade after that. As I worked on my business and my self, I became an internet celebrity, a movie star, and the author of numerous bestselling books. All of this brought me increased wealth. I'm in the kindergarten category of knowing true affluence, but after paying off my debt, here's some of what I've done with my money:

- bought two exotic hand-made limited edition luxury sports cars, including one previously owned by a rock star (Steven Tyler of Aerosmith) who autographed the engine.
- bought two of the rarest guitars ever known, including one hand carved out of Hawaiian koa wood by one of the greatest luthiers on the planet (Robert Taylor).
- paid for professional auto racing instruction, which allowed me to roar around the Atlanta-Sebring racetrack in a fire suit and a helmet (and paid for a friend to attend with me).

- given a staggering amount of money to the mother of a little boy who needed a special machine to help him recover from a pediatric stroke (a boy and a mother I've yet to meet in person).

I'm not bragging or showing how frivolous I am. I can easily justify my expenses and even deduct them from my taxes. The truly affluent do far more than this, of course. They have private jets, more than one mansion, and servants to cook for them and their pets, and they spend money on diamond-enhanced cell phones.

But I'm making a point here. I'm declaring that the affluent spend money on two things. Two things that you can provide.

What are they?

Experience and Exclusivity.

As I wrote in my book on circus promoter P.T. Barnum, *There's A Customer Born Every Minute*, people will spend almost any amount of money on something, anything, that will change their internal state. They want to *feel* something. Provide it and get rich.

People also want to feel they are unique. If they can buy that uniqueness, they will. Owning something you've made—say, a collectible version of whatever you sell that few others have—is one way to accomplish this sense of individuality.

There's more, of course. That's where Dan Kennedy comes in.

Dan's book is the first one to reveal the direct route to the affluent's bank vault. He shows you how to open it and withdraw bags of loot, legally and joyfully. He talks about Experience and Exclusivity and a whole lot more. His branded No B.S. approach is a simple paint-by-the-numbers system for getting more than your fair share of the wealth the affluent are willing and even eager to spend.

Dan is a living genius at marketing, a copywriting legend, my all-time favorite marketing author, and glaringly brilliant at teaching you to think differently about your marketing efforts. He shows you how to get one thing: results.

To begin, stop thinking there are any limitations to becoming affluent yourself, and start reading this book. You'll then start to attract the affluent—*and* their money.

Go for it!

JOE VITALE, star of the movie *The Secret* and outrageous internet marketing celebrity, is the author of way too many books to list here, including *Buying Trances, Hypnotic Writing, The Attractor Factor,* and *The Key.* His main website is www.JoeVitale.com.

How to Use This Book to Get Very Rich

For many years now, I've been all about helping small-business owners transition to entrepreneurs, turn ordinary businesses into extraordinary ones, break free of boundaries and limits, and make many more millions of dollars faster than they ever thought possible. I've chronicled the strategies used and their "case histories" in 11 books, beginning with *How to Make Millions with Your Ideas*, first published in 1996, through to *No B.S. DIRECT Marketing for NON-Direct Marketing Businesses*, first published in 2006, to this book, as well as in my monthly newsletters and the PHENOMENON™ DVD, which can be found at www.InNext12Months.com. Nothing I've ever done has matched the impact of my most recent guiding, pushing, prodding, and nagging of entrepreneurs and marketers to reinvent themselves as needed in order to focus on marketing to the affluent. THIS book summarizes those five years of guiding, pushing, prodding, and nagging.

This book has three purposes.

First, to sell you on transforming your business to market to, appeal to, and attract the affluent, thereby transforming your income, security, and business life. I use the word *transform* deliberately. I try not to fool around with things of minor significance. What you can do for yourself by combining *price elasticity* with marketing to the affluent is, in fact, life altering. You will have to buy this premise before anything else here has value to you. You will have to take ownership of this idea and be willing—no, eager—to work on it every day. There's a canyon-sized gap between whatever curiosity brought you to this book and the commitment required to fully move to being a marketer to the affluent as your chief role in your business, as your personal profession, as your greatest area of study, knowledge, and expertise. Getting that commitment in just 430 pages is a tall order. But that's what I have set out to do, and I want to be completely transparent about that objective. I am here to sell you something. To sell you on making a major shift in every aspect of your business.

Imagine that you own a shop on a main street in a part of town that is losing its well-to-do residents, its closest major employers closing their doors. Poverty is setting in. Sunny days stop; gloom and doom descend. People walk stoop shouldered rather than upright, shuffle rather than stride. Studiously avoid the displays in store windows like yours. From your shop doorway, you see your entire world, and it is in decay. Only three streets away from the rear of your store, out of your sight, is a community booming with new office buildings and lots of jobs, its street's shops and restaurants busy all day with the area's workers, equally busy in evening with the residents of the shiny, new high-rise condominium complexes at the street's end. Golden sunlight makes the diamonds and gold bricks in the street sparkle.

This is exactly the position so many business owners, professionals in practice, sales professionals, and marketers are in.

What they can't see and are unaware of is not *literally* a place a few streets away; instead it is *a segment of the market* immediately before them and all around them. A unique myopia blinds so many from seeing these people so eager to spend so much on so many goods and services, with little concern over price.

If you would like to get very, very rich, you need to see where the most money is and then go there to get it. Sounds foolishly simple, I suppose, yet I daily see the vast majority of marketers wasting valuable resources struggling mightily to get money from people who have little of it to part with.

The second purpose, to give you new understanding of who the affluent customers and clients are, where they are, what they buy, why they buy, and how to get out of your own way and get in sync with them.

There is this old story of some avid hunters who seek out and hire a highly recommended guide to lead them to hidden herds of giant elk. Guns over shoulders, they hike, following this guide through woods, up mountains, through rivers, into snow, for hours and hours, until they gradually realize they've been hiking in circles. "Hey," one hunter says, "you've got us lost. I thought you said you were the best hunting guide in the United States?"

"I did, sir," the guide said ruefully, "but I believe we are now lost *in Canada.*"

To market to the affluent, you must know where they are and how to find them. In this book, I will guide you directly to them.

If you'll forgive, one more hunting story . . .

A man who regularly suits up and goes off with the other guys into the woods for days on end, suffering wet, cold weather, to hunt, leaving his wife a weekend widow, is finally confronted by her—she wants to go along and see what is so exciting. Grudgingly, fearing the worst, but wary of endless alimony, he gets her a camouflage outfit, boots, a gun, and brings her along. He stations her at the bottom of a hill, in a stand of trees, and tells her, "I'm going up the hill with Ben and Tom. If we flush deer out, they'll come down this hill right in front of you. Just point and shoot. We'll come 'a-running." He and his friends climb the hill but barely get to the top when they hear a gun blast and his wife and some other man yelling. They race back to the bottom, to find her pointing her gun at a guy standing next to a dead horse. He says, "OK, lady, OK, it's a deer. Can I at least take my saddle with me?"

To successfully market to the affluent, you must know not only where they are but what they look like. In this case, I don't actually mean just their physical appearance. I mean owning a very clear and complete picture of who they are, how they think, what they want, what they detest, and how they make their buying decisions—because they are a very different creature than what you have been accustomed to dealing with.

The third purpose is to present a collection of strategies for successfully marketing to these affluent customers and, ultimately, to put it into the context of a step-by-step system.

Let's take these three purposes in order:

First, to quote the advice given to Woodward and Bernstein by Deep Throat about the Watergate investigation: *follow the money*. As you progress through this book and subsequently go looking where directed, you are going to discover that there is an ocean of money out there, changing hands by the minute. This picture is contrary to what the media would have you believe about a slow and troubled economy and a population of broke people struggling just to buy milk and diapers. This picture may be contrary to the one you see and operate your business in, which is exactly the point. Dr. Edward Kramer, an early pioneer in success education, said that even a tiny and insignificant penny held close to the eye can block the sun. I find most businesspeople are just so myopic. Blocking their discovery of untold opportunity for extraordinary income and profit by following the money to the affluent is a picture of the poor held too tightly to the eye. Most business owners think that customers for whom price is irrelevant are as rare as unicorns trained in ballet, so they never set out deliberately to attract and do business with them. In truth, there is a giant, growing availability of such customers. Your view of the prosperity waiting for you will change with this book.

To the second, while I have been the most serious student and highly paid practitioner of direct marketing for 30 years, I have been most seriously studying and devising special marketing strategies for the affluent for the past 5 years. I write a monthly publication, the *No. B.S. Marketing To The Affluent Letter* (in addition to the regular *No B.S. Marketing Letter*), born by demand and opportunity. The explosive growth of the emerging mass-affluent and affluent populations made this specialized focus irresistible. The response to that newsletter and the information it provides led to this book. In everything I've ever done in marketing, the two things that have had the greatest positive impact for the greatest number and diversity of business owners have been educating them about price elasticity and about marketing to the affluent.

We are in the midst of a demographic revolution, with the baby boomer population peaking, the mass-affluent population exploding, and the affluent population growing richer per capita, all converging to produce a new "spending class."

Opportunities to trade up, to upgrade your clientele, to rearrange your business, its presentation of products, services, and prices to attract upscale, more freely spending consumers have never been better. The retailers' antidote to big box stores and online commoditization, the professionals' antidote to cheap-fee competitors, the service companies' antidote to cheap discounters and bait 'n' switchers, everybody's immunity to recession is: the customer for whom price is not the issue! Now the population of such customers is growing exponentially and rapidly. You need to understand them, realize how abundant and plentiful and obtainable they are (possibly contrary to your own limited perception), and learn to target and attract them. You will understand the psyche of the affluent customer and be able to market to his aspirations, values, and mind-set as result of this book.

IF YOU WOULD CHOP OFF YOUR OWN HAND WITH A DULL AXE before letting it hand over your credit card to buy a $4,195.00 cloth purse or spend $8,000.00 to fly somewhere private that Southwest goes to for $49.00, or join former Senator John Edwards at the salon for a $400.00 haircut and then the architect's office to plan a 26,000-square-foot home, or pay $6,200.00 for a hand-carved mahogany umbrella rack, then you do not understand the rich and are therefore banned from success in selling to them.

This book's mission is to introduce you to three groups of customers in a meaningful way—the rich or ultra-affluent, the affluent, and the mass-affluent—as well as three convergence groups, the ultra-affluent boomers, the affluent boomers, and the mass-affluent boomers. Here I give you six different golden keys to unlock six different doors, each leading to far greater financial rewards for you regardless of the business or sales career you are in. They are keys of understanding. Understanding the magnitude of these customer groups, their explosive growth, their psyche, their spending behaviors.

Years ago, a client tried to hire me for a copywriting assignment I foolishly rejected, for TV commercials for a home-study course teaching fishermen how fish think, based on the premise that to catch a lot of the biggest, fattest, most desirable fish, you needed to know how fish think. Knowing nothing about fishing, I thought the whole thing bunkum that no sane person would buy no matter how clever my copy was crafted. I was wrong; the commercials sold tons; I lost out on hundreds of thousands of dollars in royalties. Oh well. It is, as we rich so often say, only money. Now I tell you: you need to know how these rich think should you wish to attract them.

Finally, third, you'll be shown a *systematic* approach to converting all this newfound understanding into actual attraction of affluent customers. My life has been about building marketing systems—and I am routinely paid upwards of $100,000.00 by my private clients for doing so. Over 30 years, more than 85% of my clients have returned to me for such assistance repeatedly. You can be assured that the systematic approach I've prescribed here will work for you—in any type or size of business, professional practice, or sales career.

One of the best questions I've ever been asked, which I've taken to asking others, is: *Do you seriously, sincerely want to be rich?* If you do, you will use this book as a stepping-stone to the road paved with gold, which leads to where all the wealth is. You will go there without further delay, without hesitation, without procrastination.

Important Notices from the Author
References

A massive amount of research, tapping into more than a hundred sources as well as the experiences of my own clients and of Glazer-Kennedy Insider's Circle™ Members has gone into this book. I have not turned it into an academic textbook, meticulously footnoting each and every fact or statistic to its specific source or sources. Where only one source was used for a significant amount of information, it is footnoted. Otherwise, I have, in the "Resources" portion of this book, provided a lengthy list of websites including sites belonging to most of my research sources. The serious student motivated by this book will visit them all. Also, throughout the book, you'll find "Recommended Resource" boxes in the chapters directing you to useful sources of information and assistance. I should tell you, delays between writing and having a book published are unavoidable. While every effort has been made to verify the accuracy of the information and to list only active sites and resources, it's a safe bet that some of this won't age well—even a few months can make a difference in the fast-moving world of marketing. The principles and strategies, however, will remain valid for years to come. Some updating of the information will be provided at www.NoBSBooks.com, in the section for this book. And the best way to stay connected to my most current information on marketing to the affluent is to subscribe to my *No B.S. Marketing To The Affluent Letter,* available at www.DanKennedy.com.

Gender Language

For those of you who are gender- or political-correctness sensitive, to head off letters: I have predominately used *he, him,* and so on throughout the book with only occasional exception, rather than awkwardly saying *he or she*, *him or her*. I do not mean this as a slight to women, only as a convenience. I am not getting paid by the word.

Free Offer

I do not want our new relationship begun with this book to end as one-night stand. I have a great deal more to share with you, and it won't take you long reading this book to realize there's a lot more to be gained from me than can fit here. To make the next steps entirely risk free to you, I've made them cost free too. There is an incredible Free Gift Offer on page 429, giving you more than $600.00 in resources (at their publishers' price value), including a two-month "test drive" trial membership in my Insider's Circle, which includes my *No B.S. Marketing Letter*. During these two free months, you'll be invited to join me and other experts on Webinars and Tele-Seminars. To be sure you don't get side-tracked and miss out, why not go right now, before doing anything else, to page 429 at the back of the book and accept my offer? It will take only a few minutes. Oh, I'll remind you as we go along, but the sooner you accept, the sooner all the good stuff starts coming your way!

"LUXURY is the first, second and third cause
of the ruin of the republics.
It is the vampire
which soothes us into
a fatal slumber
while it sucks the life-blood of our veins."
—EDWARD PAYSON ROE, (1838–1888),
MINISTER, CIVIL WAR CORRESPONDENT TO *THE NEW YORK EVANGELIST*,
NOVELIST, STRICT MORALIST.

"Let the
bacchanal
begin."
—DAN S. KENNEDY

BOOK ONE

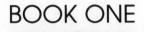

Who Are These People
Who Have All the Money?
Understanding
Mass-Affluent, Affluent, and
Ultra-Affluent Buyers

CHAPTER 1

Who ARE These People, Anyway?

"With money in your pocket you are wise,
you are handsome, and
you sing well, too."

—YIDDISH PROVERB

I have always wondered about the monkeys on monkey islands in our zoos. As we stand there looking at them, amused at their funny expressions and antics, are they entertained by looking at us in our funny clothes? Are the monkeys asking themselves, *Who* are *these goofy creatures, anyway*? I do know, from numerous conversations with my clients, that the rich are strange and odd and incomprehensible, that figuring out what motivates their behavior is as difficult as figuring out why the monkeys act as they do. While we'll never need to decipher the monkeys' thoughts and acts, we do need to decode the rich.

We can begin by organizing the population itself. Through-out this book, I'm going to subdivide the affluent population many different ways:

Ultra-Affluent

Affluent

Mass-affluent

. . . and specialty market groups, like

Affluent Boomers and Mass-Affluent Boomers

Affluent Gays and Lesbians

Affluent Entrepreneurs and Business Owners

. . . and then by gender, women and men.

These divided groups meet, converge, and also act separately. It is up to you to ultimately develop your own carefully defined target group within the affluent population that is ideally matched with your products, services, even your own personality.

Let's begin with some basic definitions.

Mass-Affluent—Household incomes of $85,000.00 to $150,000.00 and/or net worth exceeding $250,000.00. This is the fastest-growing segment of the entire consumer market. These people are younger and more diverse than any previous affluent population in history. They include families with young chil-dren; single-parent households; blue-collar, not just white-collar, employees, as well as small-business owners. Demographic groups who just five years ago, and certainly ten years ago, would have been J.C. Penney® shoppers but now make some purchases there, some *down* at Wal-Mart,® and many *up* at Saks® and Neiman Marcus.®

Affluent—Those with household incomes of $150,000.00 to $250,000.00 and/or net worth including primary and additional residences' equity, exceeding $1 million. In short, millionaires. As many millionaires bemoan, being a millionaire ain't what it used to be! The status of millionaire, once rarified, is now mainstream. We've had a two-decade millionaire explosion in America, and a similar explosion is now occurring in a number of other countries.

It is within the Mass-Affluent in move-up mode and the Affluent categories that we find what some demographers have taken to calling "middle-class millionaires;" they are of a very particular mind-set, which we'll be talking about at length.

Ultra-Affluent. Those with household incomes of $250,000.00 up and/or net worth of $3 million to $10 million. Here we find the wealthiest 10% of U.S. households as defined by net worth, according to the most recent Federal Reserve study. Their average net worth is $3.1 million, average annual income is $256,000.00. They earn 36% of all U.S. income and control 70% of the U.S. net worth. As a group, these 11 million households hold 89% of the value of all publicly traded stocks and mutual funds in the United States.

Ultra-Ultra-Affluent. Household incomes of $1 million and up and/or net worth starting above $10 million but more commonly in the $20 million to $50 million range. Private jet owners[*] fit nicely here—they have average yearly incomes of $9 million, net worth in excess of $50 million. Average age 57, 70% men. Each year they report spending $30,000.00 on wine and alcoholic beverages, $150,000.00 at hotels and resorts, $115,000.00 on clothes and accessories, $250,000.00 on jewelry, $500,000.00 on home improvements and furnishings, and they have at least two residences. As

---

[*]Based on study reported at www.MarketWatch.com.

a practical matter, their spending power is unlimited. Their ranks include Fortune 1000 CEOs, Hollywood celebrities and executives, and professional athletes, but more than half are not famous or in exotic occupations or businesses but are, instead, "the millionaire next door" who has moved up. Many have built up and sold businesses or taken their businesses public, creating lump-sum wealth.

Affluent Boomers. You'll find a very lengthy chapter devoted exclusively to this, pardon pun, booming group actively exploring and even inventing an entirely new approach to retirement and Act 3 and Act 4 of life—and funding it with an unprecedented amount of spending power.

■　■　■

These groups, and other affluent groups, offer opportunity to marketers as unprecedented as is their prosperity, spending power, and attitudes about spending. In the chapters to come, you will see this new world of opportunity revealed.

WHAT ARE THEY BUYING?

Purchases and Spending in Past 12 Months

	Affluent	Ultra-Affluent
Home furnishings	80%	84%
Women's evening apparel	43%	56%
Fine jewelry	37%	50%
Artwork, collectibles	10%	20%

Lifestyle Plans in Next 12 Months

	Affluent	Ultra-Affluent
Invest: stocks, real estate	39%	55%
Remodel/renovate	39%	37%
Trip outside U.S.	37%	57%
Buy/lease new car	25%	34%
Cruise	16%	20%
Buy new/addt'l home	9%	13%

Based on 2006–2007 research data from Monroe Mendelsohn
Research/Mendelsohn Affluent Survey, 2007 (www.mmrsurveys.com).

CHAPTER 2

The Ultra-Rich:
Different Than You and Me

F. Scott Fitzgerald: "The very rich are different from you and me."
Ernest Hemingway: "Yes, they have more money."

—DOCUMENTED EXCHANGE BETWEEN THE FAMOUS AUTHORS,
FROM *MARK MY WORDS*, COMPILED BY NIGEL REES

The *Forbes* 400 *list, compiled and published annually* by *Forbes* magazine, is a microcosmic look at the ultra-rich. In 2007, the first year that admission required a net worth of at least a billion dollars, many former multimillionaires dropped from the list. In the book *All the Money in the World*, authors and researchers Peter Bernstein and Annalyn Swan provide a terrific in-depth analysis of the earning and spending of these wealthiest people in the world. I recommend the book for those seriously interested in understanding and marketing to the ultra-rich. Here, I'll give you a thumb-sized overview of what they found out, as well as my own observations.

First of all, you should be interested in who is on this list. There are many names you know, like Oprah, Bill Gates, Warren Buffett, and the omnipresent modern-day Barnum, Donald Trump—of whom I am a very big fan. (I have appeared as a speaker on programs with the Donald; at some of the past Glazer-Kennedy Insider's Circle™ conferences, we've had the first *Apprentice* winner, Bill Rancic, and *Apprentice* competitor Kristi Frank; and our 2008 Marketing and Moneymaking SuperConference's featured guest speakers included Trump's attorney and chief negotiator, George Ross, and Gene Simmons of the band KISS, seen on *Celebrity Apprentice*. I study and recommend study of people like Donald Trump.)

You might find a variety of statistics interesting—and in some instances, useful. For example, 270 of the 400 basically made their fortunes from scratch, and another 56 made a large portion of their money even if also inheriting some wealth. Translation: 80% of the ultra-rich got there through ambition, initiative, drive, grit, ingenuity, hard work, and entrepreneurship. Their wealth has not separated them from those values. Only 74 of the 400 inherited their fortunes. Thinking of the ultra-rich as a silver-spoon-in-mouth crowd born of the lucky sperm club would be a serious mistake. This is not who they are and it is definitely not how they think of themselves.

Forty-one of the 400 attended Harvard; 28, Stanford; 14, Yale; and 10, Princeton—a total of 93 from the top-rated, most prestigious universities. But it is worth noting that a higher percentage of the ultra-rich attended run-of-the-mill universities or did not attend college at all. And, as an aside, here's a very interesting statistic about the presumed link between wealth and college: those on the Forbes 400 list in 2006 with a college degree were

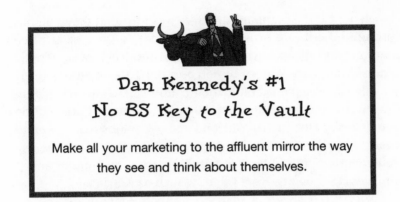

Dan Kennedy's #1
No BS Key to the Vault

Make all your marketing to the affluent mirror the way
they see and think about themselves.

worth less on average than those without a college degree—$3.1 billion vs. $5.9 billion, to be exact—making the college degree a nearly $2 billion handicap. I might mention, in the 2007–2008 Presidential primary campaigns, both Hillary Clinton and John Edwards insisted it was, quote, *impossible*, unquote, for *anybody* to get ahead anymore without a college degree as basis for their plans to provide free college to everybody, giving each newborn baby a $5,000.00 college fund, and other, similar foolishness. Of course, what they stated as fact and actual facts never meet. Further, while college enrollments have climbed from 47% in 1973, the year I graduated from high school and did not go to college, to 69% now, college graduation rates have stayed the same, 66%, according to the National Center for Education Statistics. So, while more are going, more are dropping out. Imagine what that statistic will look like if we make college free for all. *Got lousy grades, no work ethic, no ambition? Here's a free ride at Harvard. Have fun.*

That kind of talk—the criticism of the free-college plans I just provided—really resonates with the ultra-rich, by the way. They deeply resent the popular but erroneous idea that they got theirs through inheritance or luck, and they bear even greater resentment for and disapproval of handouts and freebies provided to others. Many, like Warren Buffett and Bill Gates, severely restrict the inheritances passed on to their children. As I was writing this, Barron Hilton, apparently finally fed up with Paris Hilton's being Paris, altered his will and moved billions from heirs to charity. Fundamentally, the more affluent a person is, the more vehemently opposed he is to handouts to anyone under any circumstances, except severe tragedy, such as Katrina.

The ultra-rich are a marrying bunch. Only 11 of the 2007 Forbes 400 have never been married. One hundred eighteen have been divorced at least once, but 271 have stayed married to their first spouses—a significantly better percentage than the general population. Cynics would say that has something to do with the high price of divorce. Golfer Greg Norman's divorce, in progress as I wrote this, was reportedly expected to cost more than $200 million, and he wasn't even on the Forbes list! When asked by fellow actor Arnold Schwarzenegger why Arnold was rich and he was not, Burt Reynolds answered: number of wives. Still, as many including former General Electric captain Jack Welch have observed, the reason divorce is so expensive is it's worth it. My own affluence was wounded significantly by divorce, helped by remarrying the same wife. Finally, *I* got to marry rich.

The age of the ultra-rich skews mature, as you'd expect, but it does span wide. The oldest 400 member, John Simplot, is 98; the youngest, John Arbold, 33. Average: 65. If you step away from the top of the pyramid, the Forbes 400, and look at the broader affluent population, you will still see age skew senior, pointing the ambitious marketer to the affluent toward affluent boomers.

There is geographic concentration. Out of 400, 88 have their primary residence in California, 73 in New York state—and 64 of those in New York City.

The top ten: Bill Gates, $59 billion; Warren Buffett, $52 billion. Big drop to Vegas casino entrepreneur Sheldon Adelson*, $28 billion; Oracle Software's Larry Ellison, $26 billion. Another drop to the new kids on the block, Sergey Brin and Larry Page from Google, each at $18.5 billion. Vegas entrepreneur and corporate turnaround guy, Kirk Kerkorian, $18 billion; Michael Dell of Dell Computers at $17.2 billion; Charles Koch, an oil man, $17 billion, and his brother, David Koch, also in oil, at $17 billion, both having had a head start through inheritance. Some trivia: David Koch ran as the vice-presidential candidate on the Libertarian Party's ticket back in 1980. Gates famously began his business in his garage. Buffett is legendary for his preference of investing in "ordinary" businesses like Dairy Queen®, Borsheims and Helzberg jewelry store chains, and Coca-Cola®. Adelson is the son of a cab driver and is a college dropout. Ellison is also a college dropout, started his business in 1977. The Google boys are Stanford dropouts who started their business in a borrowed garage. Kerkorian is the son of an Armenian immigrant fruit farmer. He is an eighth-grade dropout. He built his first business, TWA, the airline, from scratch, sold it for $104 million profit in 1996, and began aggressively investing in Vegas properties. Dell started his business selling computers out of his college dorm room. Eight of the top ten built their fortunes as I described earlier. This is an important point, as it speaks to the psychology of selling to the ultra-rich.

Following are some of the most interesting Forbes 400 members.

H. Ross Perot ($4.4 billion), the son of a Texas cotton broker. After his stint in the Navy, he went to work as a salesman for IBM®. The data management company he subsequently created was based on an idea of his that IBM rejected. He sold that company for $2.5 billion. His current company uses offshore labor in 20 countries and has a huge technology center in Mexico, even though Perot railed against The North American Free Trade Agreement (NAFTA) during his quixotic campaign for the presidency.

Ronald Lauder ($3.2 billion), son of beauty entrepreneur Estée Lauder, who started her face creams business in 1946, whipping up potions in a kitchen sink. She is widely credited with inventing the gift-with-purchase strategy commonly used in the cosmetic industry but having much wider application, including selling just about anything to the affluent. The leveraging of commodity consumer products to ultra-wealth is not at all unique. Also on the list as examples: Leonard Stern, who owes his $44.1 billion to his dad's Hartz® Mountain pet products; Don Hall's $2 billion has evolved from his uncle's selling of greeting cards beginning at age 18, which became Hallmark®; Hope Hill van Buren's $1.4 billion comes from inheritance, from her grandfather, the inventor of condensed soup leading to Campbell's®; John Simplot's company grows the potatoes for about one-third of all French fries sold in America; Forrest Mars Jr.'s delicious $14 billion comes from Mars® candy bars.

Leslie Wexner ($2.8 billion) is an Ohio State dropout who started his first women's clothing store with $5,000.00 borrowed from his aunt. His retail creations include Bath & Body Works® and Victoria's Secret®. Victoria's Secret is, incidentally, a clever marketing construct, a re-imagination of long-reigning then dethroned leader, Frederick's of Hollywood®.

Roy Disney˚ ($1.4 billion) is Walt's nephew, best known recently for leading the fight to oust Michael Eisner as Disney's® CEO. Roy's days on the list may be numbered, as a pending divorce promises to divide the wealth. Still, as Walt said, it all started with a mouse—and look at all that has followed.

Frank and Lorenzo Fertitta ($1.3 billion each) started out dealing cards at the Stardust. Bought a "nothing" casino way off the Strip, and parlayed their winnings to include 15 casinos and resorts. But their product you might be familiar with, a fan of, or repulsed by is the mixed martial arts fighting sport the Ultimate Fighting League, and its long-running reality TV shows and pay-per-view events, which average $30 million in revenue each.

Ralph Lauren ($4.7 billion) is the son of Russian immigrants who grew up in the Bronx, worked as a salesman in a Brooks Brothers™ store, and launched Polo with a saved-up and borrowed $50,000.00 in 1967. He sold 28% of the company, 27 years later, for $138 million and then developed other brands, expanded from fashions to furniture and brand licensing for everything from leather luggage to house paint sold at Home Depot®. In a sense, Lauren himself is the product. The strategy of a personal brand is also not uncommon in the ultra-rich category. You can arguably place Trump there. While not in this ultra-rich category myself, much of my wealth can be chalked up to my self-created status as a valuable personal brand. This is a strategy just about anyone can emulate, in any business, consumer or B2B.

Jeff Bezos' ($8.7 billion) started out simply selling books from his garage via the internet. He survived the dotcom crash and years without a profitable business model to wind up with an online mall topping $10 billion in yearly sales of everything from books to toys to tools. He is a Princeton grad and worked at a hedge fund before starting Amazon®.

S. Truett Cathy ($1.3 billion) started out selling chicken sandwiches to factory and airport workers. Opened the first Chick-Fil-A® store in a shopping mall in 1967. That chain sells a whole lot of chicken despite keeping all its restaurants closed on Sundays, honoring Cathy's strict Baptist beliefs.

Fred DeLuca ($1.6 billion) turned one sub sandwich shop into 28,000 Subway® restaurants in 86 countries through aggressive franchising, not without controversy—franchisees have filed class action litigation against him; the medical establishment has ferociously criticized the Subway diet promoted with the now famous Jared.

Michael Illitch ($1.6 billion) opened his Little Caesars® pizza shop in 1959, after an injury ended his pro baseball career, and built up a 40-store chain in ten years, then turned to more aggressive expansion, modeling Ray Kroc's McDonald's® franchising model, building to yearly sales exceeding $1.5 billion.

Ty Warner ($4.1 billion). Salesman's son who dropped out of college to follow in his father's footsteps, as an on-the-road sales rep for a plush toy company. Ty kept his thinking cap on while a road warrior and, in 1986, created Beanie Babies® and the collector-item status that fueled the craze. He's leveraged the Beanie Babies® money into ownership of a Four Seasons® hotel in New York, three luxury resorts, and the cottage where John and Jackie Kennedy honeymooned, which guests now pay $2,990.00 a night to stay in.

Rich DeVos ($3.6 billion) and his high school buddy created Amway™, after several business failures and a stint in another multilevel marketing company Amway later acquired. The company started bottling its lone product, an all-purpose liquid cleaner, in a garage in 1959. Its system of distributors recruiting distributors has led to more than three million of them worldwide generating over $6 billion in yearly sales of its own household, cosmetic, and nutrition products as well as joint ventures permitting their representation of products from Best Buy™, Amazon, and many other retailers. Rich also owns the National Basketball Association (NBA) team the Orlando Magic. And a whole lot of Amway's hometown, Ada, Michigan. I cut my teeth as a young'un in the Amway business and have both a nostalgic fondness for and deep understanding of the person-to-person selling method as a result. One of our own Glazer-Kennedy Insider's Circle's™ businesses, with local chapters, regular meetings, and mastermind groups for small-business owners, active in more than 100 North American cities, has its meeting formats and many of its person-to-person sales and marketing methods rooted in my Amway experience. This method of distribution remains viable and healthy today, including with mass-affluent customers.

What so many of these 400 members share in common is the startup of a small business, expansion of that business, then leveraging the wealth created to that point into diversified investments as well as multiplying the core business or brand through one or more means, such as franchising or licensing. These ultra-rich wind up with a unique mind-set also held in common from this experience. Among other things, they are methodical. They view everything through the prism of process. They are also deeply suspicious of anyone or anything not symbolic of hard work and methodical development. If you set out to sell them, as example, an exotic safari or fishing trip, the story of your background and how you made yourself into the reigning expert on such travel and the extent of the research, planning, and preparation invested in designing and delivering the experience is essential, and carries more influence than the most persuasive description of the trip and its amenities. This same principle applies to whatever you might sell to the ultra-rich with this startup background.

Donald Trump ($3 billion) cannot be ignored—even if you try. His retail, office, and hotel businesses are all up, thriving. Signed Gucci® to a record-breaking lease for Trump Tower. His brand-licensing business has skyrocketed in earnings and expanded just from taking "points" off the top of real estate projects bearing his name but built and sold by others to a dizzyingly wide range of products and services, from mortgages to men's clothes and even mail-order steaks sold on QVC® and in the Sharper Image® catalog. His licensing-business boom and his speaking fees from $250,000.00 to $1 million have both been made golden by his TV star status. Of late, Trump is far more in the Trump business than in the real estate business. He annually disputes Forbes valuation of him as low by half or more. For some combination of practical, self-promotion reasons and ego, Trump is representative of a relatively small part of the ultra-rich population eager for attention, publicity, and widespread recognition of his success and wealth. (Many others, if not most others, in this informal league of the extraordinarily wealthy shun media and avoid public display of wealth, although most still try to outdo and impress their peers.)

There are only 39 women on the 400 list, and generally speaking, ultra-rich women still tend to amass their wealth through marriage, divorce, and inheritance. One of the exceptions is Meg Whitman ($1.4 billion), who earned her MBA from Harvard and held executive positions at several consumer products companies, Disney®, and the big private equity and venture capital fund Bain & Company (led to its prominence by Mitt

Romney) before landing in the CEO.chair at eBay. Under her direction, the company weathered the dotcom bust, established itself as a solid leader in e-commerce, and has, of late, been broadening and diversifying through acquisitions and focusing major attention on expansion in China. To a lesser degree than Trump, but still in the same vein, Meg Whitman is the face of eBay, actively offering herself up to financial and mainstream media for interviews and having more of a direct relationship with eBay users than most corporations' CEO's have with their customers. On the current list of women in the 400, only Meg Whitman, Martha Stewart, and Oprah Winfrey have entirely made-from-scratch fortunes, and they all have self-promotion in common. (Just as this book was going to press, Ms. Whitman announced her retirement from her position at eBay.)

■   ■   ■

In many respects, the ultra-rich have the very same concerns and buying motivations as the more ordinary affluent. They are pressed for time and eager for efficiency, competence, and convenience to be provided to them—and they're very willing to pay for it. Other than those intangibles, they have few if any needs. As a matter of fact, even income is pretty much irrelevant to them; they have risen to the point of concern only with net worth. They worry about loss—of money, power, status, or security. They seek approval, recognition, respect—some only from peers, others from the world at large, all from those they conduct business with.

---

¹In interest of full disclosure, as of the writing of this book, I owned stock in the companies denoted with an asterisk.

CHAPTER 3

The Question Freud
Couldn't Answer

"No rich man is ugly."

—Zsa Zsa Gabor

I t is no secret that, as the old saying goes, "women control **the purse strings."** That once meant that the men brought home the paychecks and their wives spent the money. No longer. Many affluent households are wealthy thanks to both spouses' careers providing excellent incomes. Consequently, women have control over spending and investments based not only on the marriage but on equal—or in some cases, greater—financial contribution to it. This has erased old, traditional divisions and delegation of spending.

Surveys from the financial services industry from the 1970s, for example, showed that the married women in more than 80%

of affluent households had nominal or no involvement in the investment decisions. Similar surveys from 2000 and later indicate the 80% has moved all the way down to 40%. In mass-affluent households, women are even more likely to be actively involved in the investment decisions. In the 1960s, husbands picked out the family car. In the 1980s, couples picked out that car together. Today, the woman of the mass-affluent household most likely has her own car and chose it herself. Marketing just about anything to the affluent married household now involves the woman at least as much as the man.

In the television show *Mad Men*, about the advertising world in the 1950s, we see young women going to work for the express purpose of finding a man and getting married—they the unlucky ones who weren't able to go directly to marriage without a tour around the game board. That was then. This is now. The institution of marriage itself has fallen on hard times and disrepute. As a *career* goal, out the window. The year 2007 marked the first time there were as many single women as married women in the United States, with no sign of that trend reversing.

In 2005, single women were the second-largest group of home buyers, right behind married couples. They do *not* stay in apartments until they find husbands and get married. They bought nearly 1.5 million homes in 2005, more than twice as many as single men. Yet when have you seen any real estate advertising specifically aimed at single women? Comparable examples can be found in numerous other product and service categories, where marketers and marketing have not caught up with and are ignoring opportunities in current reality.

Some single women are single for the traditional reason— not yet (or ever) finding the right man. But there is a growing population of what demographic analysts call the "willfully unmarried," who consciously and deliberately choose to stay single. Among the willfully unmarried women are two groups of special interest to us: the particularly affluent single women and the affluent boomer single women. In these two groups, and particularly in a group composed of overlap from the two, we find untold spending power, controlled by women who are buying their own homes, doing their own investing, planning and funding their own retirements, planning their own vacations, and so on—for life. These women are permanent heads of households, and can and should be marketed to as such, and hardly anybody is. In fact, my files are lacking any good examples of advertising or marketing specific to this to show you!

Late-in-Life Divorce as a Spending Event

The majority of the divorces that occur after 20 to 25 years of marriage are instigated by the wives, not the husbands. Far from grieving quietly, many of these women quickly re-enter the dating and next-husband-hunting game, find it highly competitive, populated by an insufficient quantity of men, and full of older men seeking younger women. Consequently, a number of self-improvement investments occur within 6 to 12 months of divorce: cosmetic surgery, cosmetic dentistry, weight loss products, new and younger-looking wardrobe, new and younger-looking car. I have several clients who deliberately market to this timing sweet spot, using information compiled from public records combined with other, commercially available, rented mailing lists (see Chapter 31). In short, affluent women age 45 through 60, divorcing after long marriages, tend to go on personal spending binges and be exceptionally susceptible to certain kinds of product and service offers about four to six months post-divorce. Those identified as affluent or, in a way, newly affluent based on their own income no longer shared, alimony, or having secured the principal residence in the divorce, are the biggest spenders.

The Growing Population of "Cougars"

The older man with the much younger trophy wife has been reversed. According to AARP statistics, at least one in three women between ages 40 and 70 is dating a younger man. About one-fourth of those men are ten or more years younger. Match.com reported a doubling of older women seeking younger men between 2002 and 2005. The proof there's a trend is that the phenomenon is earning its own name. Older women expressing preference for and hunting younger men are now familiarly called Cougars. Celebrities do it: Demi Moore, Susan Sarandon, Madonna. TV shows deal with it: In 2005, Fran Drescher's show *Living with Fran* dealt with a mother of two in love with a man half her age. VH1 aired a reality show with 20-year-old men competing to date Mick Jagger's 50-year-old ex-wife.

A not yet explicitly tracked majority of these Cougars are affluent women. The theory advanced in *MicroTrends* (a must-read marketing book by Mark Penn) is that the rise of the affluent Cougar reflects "the natural instinct for people with success to trade that success for sexual attractiveness. And what was once achievable only by older men with money is now within reach of women with power and accomplishment (and money)."

The phrase "the natural instinct for" is, I think, an extremely important one. There is, in fact, a natural instinct to attempt leveraging success and prosperity into youth, sex, longevity, even immortality. Some affluent people are even prepaying to be cryogenically frozen upon death in the hope of being later thawed out and resurrected when a medical cure for what ails them is found—and laugh if you like, but companies in this field are doing quite nicely. Men are catching up to women in terms of willingness to spend money to try to buy youth and attractiveness, but this is certainly a prime area of opportunity when marketing to affluent women.

Stigmas Gone

Cosmetic surgery—derogatively called *plastic* surgery for years—was once almost exclusively for affluent women, or actresses and models. And it was not openly discussed. Today, its popularity spans age ranges from shockingly young to surprisingly old, and from mass-affluent to ultra-affluent. And not only is it openly discussed, but it is something of a status symbol. And discussed in ways that might make many people blush. For example, according to a study published in the *Aesthetic Surgery Journal*, 81% of breast surgery patients and 68% of other body surgery patients reported improvements in sexual satisfaction. More than 50% of these patients said they were able to achieve orgasm more easily following their surgery. And 56% also noted increases in their partners' sexual interest and satisfaction following the surgery. You may rest assured that the profession *is* using this information in its marketing.

This change in attitudes toward cosmetic surgery is representative of comparable changes in attitudes about just about everything, including but not limited to sexuality. Men, take a stroll through the Self-Help, Psychology, Health, and Relationship aisles at your nearest major bookstore (where most men never tread) or pick up and read copies of *Cosmopolitan* as well as the historically more staid *Redbook*. You'll probably be very surprised to discover the discussions going on.

What's most important about all this, from a marketing standpoint, is the willingness of women to confront every imaginable health, beauty, aging, and lifestyle issue head-on, and the willingness of affluent women to spend almost without limitation on themselves, their physical and emotional well-being.

Legal Discrimination

You cannot design a business to be exclusively for men anymore. But you can design any business you like to be exclusively for women. Since discrimination is one of the most powerful of all marketing strategies, this is an opportunity that shouldn't be overlooked.

The same, incidentally, is true for race. The Black Entertainment Television (BET) network and its awards, *Black Enterprise* magazine, and the NAACP are accepted and respected. Start the White Entertainment Network, *White Enterprise* magazine, or the National Association for Advancement of White Folk, and see how things go. I don't begrudge this, by the way; I merely point it out as double standard and, more importantly, as opportunity.

Smart marketers targeting women are all about discrimination. While women tend to be liberal and socially conscious, and decry discrimination in general, they respond very favorably to for-women-only products, services, media, and messages.

Ladies' nights still exist and still work, and that says a lot. It's a 1960s device alive and well 40-plus years later. Designing and presenting businesses, products, and services as "for affluent women only—no men invited" is one of the great growth opportunities of the coming ten years.

It Isn't Simple

As an example of the complexity required for success in marketing to affluent women, consider the financial services field.

In their book *Marketing to the Mindset of Boomers and Their Elders*, Carol Morgan and Doran Levy accuse financial services and investment firms of "conjuring up differences where none exist" in advertising, marketing, and selling to affluent women (investable assets, $500,000.00+) and mass-affluent women (investable assets, $100,000.00+) making their own investment decisions. Assumptions are made by many investment marketers that echo one enunciated by the head of a Charles Schwab initiative aimed at women that "women feel differently and learn differently about investing" so there's a need to "speak to women in terms relevant to their lives and in language that's appealing to them." But in one of her columns, the popular financial writer Jane Bryant Quinn expressed her distaste for financial advertising treating women as "a breed apart." Quinn describes this advertising as "condescending"—"Who," she asks, "besides women are told they need help because they are emotionally impaired?" Quinn cites market research studies confirming that there is no difference in investment patterns by gender.

So, who's right?

I would suggest they are both right and wrong.

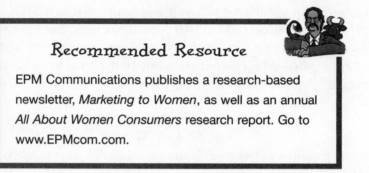

Recommended Resource

EPM Communications publishes a research-based newsletter, *Marketing to Women*, as well as an annual *All About Women Consumers* research report. Go to www.EPMcom.com.

First of all, lumping the mass-affluent and affluent women together is a serious mistake. Women with $500,000.00 and up to invest have, for the most part, been more involved with their wealth for a longer period of time. They also have, as a practical matter, access to a different level of financial advisor and choices of investment-related services. They are less likely to be paying attention to Suze Orman and *Money* magazine and more likely to be reading *The Wall Street Journal*, *Forbes*, and *Worth* than their mass-affluent counterparts. In fact, the affluent women should be separated into experience categories, such as Savvy Investors vs. Financially Uninvolveds, and then talked to quite differently. This is a distinct difference of greater significance than the affluent vs. mass-affluent tag.

Some years back, I did some marketing consulting work for Joan Rivers, the sharp-tongued comedienne turned supersuccessful jewelry, cosmetics, and fashion entrepreneur and on-air pitchperson at QVC. When Joan's husband, Edgar, died, she had the shocking experience many Financially Uninvolved women have: confronting money management for the first time, under duress. She had left it all in his hands and wasn't even sure how to balance a checkbook. Financially Uninvolveds who, for one reason or another—often the death or incapacity of their spouse—have significant investable assets to manage lack background knowledge and experience and therefore lack confidence. They are most likely to look for a single source of advice and assistance, be far more interested in safety and security than gain or yield, and be most motivated by trust. They will seek someone they can have confidence in, rather than work to have more confidence in their own judgment in these matters. Savvy Investor Women are more likely to collect and consider information from multiple sources, make at least some investment decisions independently, and have direct relationships with multiple vendors such as an online brokerage account, a stock broker, a financial planner, and one or more banks.

This means: Savvy Investor Women will respond to *information*. Financially Uninvolved Women will respond to *trust*.

The best segmentation here would be quad:

1. Financially Uninvolved, Mass-Affluent
2. Financially Uninvolved, Affluent
3. Savvy Investor, Mass-Affluent
4. Savvy Investor, Affluent

Second, Quinn is off base in denying that gender differences affecting perception of and responsiveness to advertising and overt marketing. I'm afraid she's projecting her own attitudes onto all women. Georgette Geller-Petro, an executive with the financial services giant AXA Financial,® states, "Through feedback from our advisors who work with women, we have found that women's financial goals, as well as how they articulate them, are different than those of men."

In the 2007 presidential primary elections, Hillary Clinton's campaign very successfully courted a market segment they defined as "women with needs." The label referred to mostly single, high school-educated women with children and low-wage jobs. This caused a client of mine, a business coach to mortgage brokers who noticed an increasing number of strong-minded women joining his program, and me, to coin the term "women with balls." This refers to women operating predominately via rational thought rather than emotion, and acting, at least in business situations, more like men. Quinn's comments on this topic, and much of her other writing, make me put her in this category. But it's error for her to project her woman-with-balls mentality onto a majority of other women. In fact, this is one telling if politically incorrect way to separate them: women who think like men and women who do not.

Gender difference matters. There are words and phrases— like *women with balls*—that instantly set many women's teeth on edge and make them deaf to everything else said or written by that person. I do a lot of advertising copywriting in weight loss, alternative health, and beauty categories, and I have to exercise extreme caution about "sounding male" or using instant-turn-off language. However, Quinn is right when she recoils at ad approaches or language that feels "condescending" to her. Women, especially career women, are hypersensitive to being talked down to, to not being given credit for their intelligence, knowledge, and experience. While the militant feminist of the '60s and '70s seems to be a marginalized minority, there is still a profound difference in the way women respond to language, and the way different women respond to the same language.

Consider the main characters in the *Sex and the City* HBO series and follow-up movie. Some women aspire to be like one or all of these characters. Other women are amused and entertained by them, but do not find them at all inspirational. Other women find them shocking. Ridiculous. Embarrassing. These different reactions link to age, geography, career status and experience, education, and affluence. Of course, a TV series like this has to cast a relatively wide net and try for mass appeal—thus its four different characters, including Samantha, older but also more libertine than the others and, in one long plot line in the series, a Cougar. Marketers, however, need not cast such a broad net, unless lazy. We can segment and isolate different types and groups of affluent and mass-affluent women and approach each segmented group very differently than the others.

CHAPTER 4

Boys Will Be Boys,
No Matter Their Age

"Man will do many things to get himself loved.
He will do all things to get himself envied."

—MARK TWAIN

N o man buys a Lamborghini *to get to work.*

There are Lamborghini automobiles priced from $250,000.00 to $1.4 million. Significantly, it is the $1.4 million ones that sell out fastest and for which there is the longest waiting list. But the very fact that such a thing as a Lamborghini exists reveals something very, very important about men and selling to them, which is completely contrary to myth.

Myth is that women are emotional, men are *practical.* Women buy with their hearts, men buy with their heads, with intellect and logic.

The Lamborghini is designed and built to travel at speeds illegal on every road in the United States. How practical is *that*?

Truth is, while women mature, men just get older. Arrested development.

Another myth is that men are confident. It is my experience, from selling to, dealing with, and associating with hundreds and hundreds of millionaires, that successful men are anything but self-secure. Actually, they live with an underlying anxiety that no amount of wealth relieves. As a result, they spend a lot of money on symbolic validation of their success, status, and prosperity. For example, most men aren't really clotheshorses. Symbolism aside, most I know could care less about Brooks Brothers® vs. Wal-Mart® as the source of their khakis, sweaters, or socks. But affluent men actually train themselves to appreciate fashion quality and design distinctions, and choose certain purveyors, as a means of self-validation as well as a concern about judgments others will make about them based on their apparel.

It doesn't begin or end with clothes. This same buying for validation—buying what they are *supposed to* buy from vendors they are *supposed to* patronize—extends to almost every product and service category.

Status

While status is not male vs. female, men do seek and get it differently than do women. For women, status is often a matter of association. For men, it is more a matter of competition and comparison.

A study quoted in the book *The Paradox of Choice* gave participants hypothetical choices concerning status and asked for their preferences. For example, people were asked to choose between (a) earning $50,000.00 a year with others earning $25,000.00 or (b) earning twice as much, $100,000.00 a year but being surrounded by people earning $200,000.00. In another example, respondents could choose between (a) having an IQ of 110 when the IQ of all the others is 90 or (b) having a higher IQ of 130 when the others score 150. A number of other similarly constructed a-or-b scenarios were given. More than half of the respondents chose the options that gave them the better *relative* position. That means preferring $50,000.00 to $100,000.00 because they were, at $50,000.00, earning more than others, while at $100,000.00 they were earning less than others.

This means the guy buying the 60-foot yacht may be doing so only because the others at his marina have 48-foot yachts. And, as a matter of fact, many yacht buyers freely admit their size choice was based on the sizes of their peers' or marina neighbors' yachts. A very expensive *My* _____ *is bigger than your* _____. From the locker room to the boardroom.

My highest-level Platinum business coaching groups have no members earning less than one million dollars a year. Most are in the $4 to $6 million neighborhood, and they are all in the same types of businesses (we have other mixed-breed coaching groups at Glazer-Kennedy Insider's Circle™). They are all men, not by my design. None of these members has anything to prove, nor do they have an economic need for more money. Many find it difficult to motivate themselves. But they all compete fiercely within this group environment. They compete to bring the best business breakthrough or success report to each meeting. They compete to have the highest-grossing seminar or highest-grossing new product launch. They compete based on who has bought the best new toy, who took the best vacation. They compete against each other for status within the group.

Competition for status is nothing new. But the plethora of choices has created more competition than ever before, as affluent people find themselves in more environments. If they own two homes, they are living—and competing for status—in two communities rather than just one, and status is won at the country club community in North Carolina through different choices than in the high-rise condominium community in Boston. If they are in diversified businesses instead of single, narrowly defined businesses, they compete for status in a number of different business and professional associations, professional groups, and industries.

Any marketer who finds ways to convey comparative and competitive status to his affluent male customers and clients has advantage.

Men and Their Toys

In Chapter 18, I talk at length about spending on personal passions.

A friend of mine had, for several years, a very successful mail-order business selling an $850.00 putter. *One* golf club. A certain number of its purchasers then cheerfully paid $5,000.00 to fly to Las Vegas for a putting clinic with the club's inventor and a professional golf coach. Avid and affluent golfers are possibly the most rabid and irrational spenders on their passion, willing to part with virtually any sum to shave a stroke or straighten a slice, even while insisting on turning off lights in unused rooms at home to avoid wasting hard-earned money. But golfers are not unique in this. Just about every fisherman, hunter, collector, any man with a true passion and the money to indulge it, will indulge it. I call such ideal customers "irrational, affluent buyers of the slight edge," meaning they will buy into and pay any amount for anything promising a competitive edge over their friends in a shared activity. It's important to understand that their success in business or career is tied to this philosophical approach—seeking and investing as necessary in obtaining even the slightest of competitive advantages, at every opportunity. To see it carried over into their hobbies and recreational pursuits is no surprise or oddity. Everything for the accomplished, affluent man is a competition. It's never just about having a toy; it's about having the biggest, best, newest, hottest, coolest toy. It's never about playing a game; it's about playing that game better than his buddies.

AFFLUENT BOYS PLAY DIFFERENTLY

The Alpine Motorsports Country Club features a four-mile private road course located in eastern Pennsylvania, with winding turns, long straightaways, and 220 feet of elevation change, mimicking a European racecourse. Seen from the air, it looks like the slot car track you played with as a kid, surrounded by green trees and foliage. It is billed as a unique getaway to improve your performance driving skills . . . a place to experience your high-performance automobile the way you like (without speed limits) . . . and a place to entertain a car club just as you might friends at a private golf club and enjoy camaraderie with like-minded automobile and driving enthusiasts. Professional performance driving instruction and coaching is available. In its initial advertising, $20,000.00 discounts were offered on pre-construction memberships (www.AlpineSignature.com).

Sure, anybody might buy a Porsche.® But the truly affluent Porsche owner will also buy a membership in a motor sports club with its own private racecourse.

CHAPTER 5

Marketing to Affluent Gay and Lesbian Consumers Is Out of the Closet

"When it is a question of money, everyone is of the same religion."

—VOLTAIRE

I f you are going to go to where the money is, pursue the greatest spending power, then you will be joining an ever-increasing number of companies somewhat quietly reaching out specifically to gay and lesbian consumers.

In many cases, you have a two-person household, each of its members with above-average education earning above-average incomes—with no children to raise. They have a lot more money left over every month than their heterosexual counterparts across the street, who have a tricycle and two bicycles lying in the drive-way, signifying the existence of three eating, clothes-growing-out-of, medical-emergencies-having, college-fund-needing little monsters living inside.

I'm willing to say here what hardly anybody else is: The vast majority of readers of this book—and of marketers, period—are heterosexuals who may profess having no problems with gays, but are, in truth, uncomfortable and squeamish about the very idea of designing advertising and marketing programs to attract them as customers, clients, or patients. This chapter may even be making your skin crawl. You may have religious or morality-based beliefs that interfere with tolerance, let alone acceptance. You may have a false view of gays, a mental picture of, say, disgraced Senator Larry Craig of the "wide stance" defense, arrested for trolling for gay sex in a public restroom. You may simply find "these people" foreign, incomprehensible, and unfamiliar, making you uncomfortable for no other reason than that. Some of those issues are more easily manageable than others. I am certainly not here to tell you what you should or shouldn't believe or feel. And I happen to be in favor of a business owner managing his business to suit his personal preferences. If, for your own nonbusiness reasons, you have no interest in or willingness to deliberately and specifically market to affluent gays and lesbians, and be of service to them, now would be a good time to skip ahead to the next chapter. Just know it is a bad *business* decision and, if you're running a business in which there are shareholders other than yourself, a fiscally irresponsible decision.

And, whether you like it or not, it is antiquated. In a *New Yorker* cartoon, two obviously gay men are seen in their apartment, one talking on the phone, responding to a question: "No, we're not going to the Gay Pride Parade this year. We're here, we're queer, and frankly, we're tired of making a big deal out of it." Mainstream America includes gays and lesbians. Time to get over it.

This does not, however, mean that they are a fully absorbed group unresponsive to targeted marketing and specially directed messages. To the contrary, they consistently reward those marketers who make special point of designing unique advertising to appear in the publications only they read and creating especially gay-friendly sales and business environments. The trick, as it is when appealing to any specific group, is not to be condescending or clumsy.

The Travel Industry Goes into New Territory

On November 2, 2007, *The Wall Street Journal* carried an article headlined "Las Vegas Goes All Out to Attract Gay Travelers." It reported on numerous resorts' and casino companies' marketing strategies and initiatives directed exclusively at gays as well as products and experiences designed for them. For example, it mentioned that at the trendy Palms Casino, there's a line of mostly straight men, some couples, and a few women waiting for entry

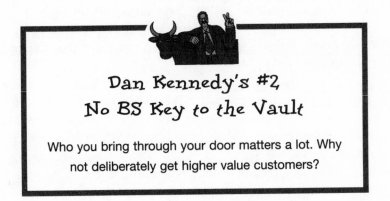

Dan Kennedy's #2 No BS Key to the Vault

Who you bring through your door matters a lot. Why not deliberately get higher value customers?

to the Playboy Club®'s party, featuring the iconic Playboy Bunnies® in push-up-bra costumes. Only steps away, there's another line awaiting entry to another club, with a dance floor filled with gyrating, shirtless men dancing with each other.

There is a very good reason that the casino industry as well as luxury hotels and resorts worldwide, cruise lines, and others in travel are, with increasing openness, catering to gay customers: Harrah's Entertainment started aggressively marketing to gays 18 months after the extensive research it commissioned revealed that gay men spend an average of 30% more than straight men when traveling. To put a bit of money math to that statistic, you could have 1,000 straights at your resort each spending, say, $2,000.00, or 1,000 gays, each spending $2,600.00. The net difference is $600,000.00. Multiply that by 52 weekends, and you get $31.2 million. As you can see, whom you bring through your doors matters a lot. This applies to you regardless of your business category—travel, restaurants, clothing store, furniture store, financial planning, whatever—both as a general principle and, specifically, regarding gay and lesbian consumers. In many categories, the gays are worth more than the straights. Marketing to the gay and lesbian population is, in its essence, taking a shortcut to a more affluent, more freely spending clientele.

Consequently, Vegas casinos, hotels, and spas as well as resorts located elsewhere are advertising themselves as gay friendly, including ads in gay publications like *OutTraveler* and *Advocate* and the cable TV channel Logo, with images of same-sex couples holding hands at romantic dinners, checking into hotel rooms together, or doing something a bit more risqué. Commitment ceremonies for gay couples are offered by such properties as the MGM Mirage and the Luxor in their wedding chapels. The popular Paris resort has a website just for gay guests, at www.GayParisVegas.com.

Just as these companies are careful to reach out to and make welcome gay clientele without turning their businesses into gay places and alienating their other, larger customer bases, any marketer must walk the same tightrope and create the same degrees of separation, including use of gay-targeted media and direct mail that remains invisible to the straight population.

Any such outreach to a particular group begins with striving for understanding of the target audience and organizing it into manageable subgroups. One method of dividing and understanding this market is by behavior. One research group (from Real World Lesbians and Gays Research Study, Asterix Group, www.AsterixGroup.com) has them divided into five categories:

1. Super Gays, 23% of the gay population;
2. Mainstream Gays, also 23%;
3. Party Gays, 14%;
4. Habitat Gays, 25%; and
5. Closeted, 12%.

One by one . . .

Super Gays are completely out, 65% are in a relationship, 66% read gay publications, and 91% consider being gay a big part of who they are. Financially, they have the highest incomes of any gay group, with 16% of this population at household incomes exceeding $100,000.00. Homeowners weigh in at 56%. There is some urban concentration.

Only 44% of the Mainstream Gays are completely out. They are equally likely to live in urban or rural areas, and they rank lower in income, affluence, home ownership, and education than the super gays.

The Party Gays are the youngest group, with 29% aged 18 to 24, and 77% out. They are the least educated and the most likely to eat out in restaurants and visit gay or lesbian clubs frequently.

Conversely, the Habitat Gays are the oldest group, with 41% of them boomers and older. The most of any gay group—77% are out, 59% live in a committed relationship with a life partner, 65% own their own homes, and 37% live in suburban areas. These are nesters at home, and as a result, they watch considerably more TV than the other groups.

To make some simplistic connections, we would find the majority of mass-affluent gays in the Habitat group and the majority of the affluent and ultra-affluent gays in the Super Gay group.

The diminishing Closeted group is next oldest, with 40% at least 50 years old. Those that are single is 52%, the most of any gay group and 47% live in small towns or rural areas, also the most of any gay group.

■　■　■

What should be obvious is that delivering the identical marketing message to this entire population is not likely to be productive. There are too many distinct economic, educational, social, life experience, and interest differences between the groups.

CHAPTER 6

Affluent Boomers'
Spending Boom

*"He's living beyond his means
but he can afford it."*

—SAM GOLDWYN, HOLLYWOOD MOGUL

Boomers represent more than 70% of the U.S. households with incomes exceeding $75,000.00 and investable assets exceeding $200,000.00. More than 70% of boomers had their wealth increase by more than half from 1992 to 2003, and another 20% had increases better than 25%. And, from 2007 through 2012, they will be inheriting an enormous transfer of wealth from their parents. It is no surprise, then, that everybody from financial services firms to Disney® can be seen frantically scurrying to build products, services, language, ad campaigns, and sales practices that will be welcomed by this population.

The Big Wave

We can argue about the exact ages or the beginning of the boomers' wave of spending and investing, fueled by lifestyle changes. We can't argue that it's here. Back in November 2005, *Newsweek* ran a cover proclaiming "Ready or Not, Boomers Turn 60," featuring photographs of the famous turning 60, including former President Clinton and President Bush, Donald Trump, Sly Stallone, Goldie Hawn, Susan Sarandon, Suzanne Somers (who is making an industry of out of being 60 herself), and Cher. In 1946, 3.4 million Americans were born—*a million more than in the entire previous decade*. This bunch has led the way in social, political, and economic change. And they are the *early* or *leading-edge* boomers, now leading a wave of enormous potential prosperity for savvy entrepreneurs, CEOs and marketers. Starting with 2006, and for the next 19 years, one boomer will turn 60 every 7.5 seconds. Of the entire U.S. population, 27% will hit 60 to 65 over the next two decades. The largest number of births in any one year in U.S. history occurred in 1957: 4.3 million; they turned 50 in 2007. In total, this is a slightly moving target; a leading edge passing 60, a huge population just hitting 50, each evolving from here. Within, all kinds of subsegments.

About one-third of boomers range from financially secure and well prepared for retirement to financially independent. About half of that third qualify as wealthy. But the amount of money they have needs to be put in the context of the very different attitudes they have about it than did the previous retirement generations. **Within the boomer population, there is a historically unprecedented percentage of affluent and ultra-affluent consumers coupled with a historically unprecedented willingness on their part to spend their money on themselves. This is a terrific dynamic for us marketers!**

There is <u>also</u> a huge generational wealth transfer occurring. In addition to their own income and accumulated wealth, boomers will inherit $7.2 TRILLION over the next 35 to 45 years.

The affluent boomer nearing, at, or sliding past 60 is a very, very different creature than was your father or grandfather at age 60.

I was 53 at this book's writing. My father and his friends at 60 were

- eager for full retirement at age 65
- considering relocation to one home for the rest of their life (Florida and Arizona were the retirement places)
- set for income shrinkage and fixed incomes
- shrinking spending
- accepting of aging
- moving into the retirement phase as a group in lockstep

In her book *Turning Silver into Gold: How to Profit in the New Boomer Marketplace*, Dr. Mary Furlong states: "Today, boomers are RE-INVENTING their lives. They are finding NEW places to work, NEW places to travel to (and NEW ways of traveling), NEW ways to spend their days, NEW ways to spend time with their children and grandchildren, and NEW ways to stay vital and connected as they age. Each choice represents enormous business opportunity." The capital letters are mine, not hers, to emphasize that all your assumptions about boomers and all history of boomer businesses are now suspect, as we are literally reinventing our third and fourth acts of life's play. In the book *After Fifty: How the Baby Boom Will Redefine the Mature Market* Leslie M. Harris even says, "Boomers see age as a lifestyle choice rather than a chronological imperative."

Today's boomers are very different from my father's generation.

They are not at all eager for classic retirement. A Merrill Lynch survey cited in the book *MicroTrends* puts three out of four saying they have no interest in retirement. In fact, today's boomers are pegging their full retirement at 80, not 65, and are looking for second, third, or fourth careers or new businesses. Career or business opportunities that do not tie them to fixed schedules or brick-and-mortar locations are gaining in popularity. As example, Glazer-Kennedy Insider's Circle Member™ Susan Berkley, CEO of the Berkley Persuasive Voice Academy in New York, tells me that two-thirds of her new students coming to learn how to make money as voiceover talent for radio and TV commercials and audio products are 55 years of age and up, many from very successful executive or professional back-grounds, and are quick to install complete recording studios in both their homes. Another Member, Brent Fogle at Options Trading University in Florida, is discovering the same sort of thing, somewhat to his surprise—the majority of his students finding him online are not young bucks trying to trade their way to a fast fortune with which to buy Maseratis® and Malibu beach houses but 55- to 60-year-old people looking for an interesting way to make some money, stay relevant and active, and have a sense of accomplishment, without being tied down to a job or conventional business. At our own Information Marketing Association (www.info-marketing.org), we track this same trend: a rising percentage of those starting writing, publishing, speaking, life, or business coaching and consulting businesses in the 50 to 65 age range, about 50% male and 50% female, for motives other than or more complex than money. This booming boomer population's interest in continuing to work well past 60 but not be tied to desk, corner office, store counter, or daily commute suggests great profit in creating opportunities to fit their preferences and capitalize on their experience and affluence.

While Florida and Arizona remain immensely popular with those in their 60s, the trend is toward split-time residences: owning two or even three homes or condos in different places and dividing time between them, not necessarily in strict seasonal rotation. Yesterday's snowbird migrating south or west for the winter is being replaced by a less migratory, more flexible splitter, who may be at his Michigan home in a university town for much of the winter, for skiing, for holiday activities with family; at his Las Vegas high-rise condo for New Year's and a number of times during the year; and at his Florida home the majority of time, making it the primary residence, but barely. Boomers are mobile.

This has all sorts of marketplace effects. For example, Glazer-Kennedy Insider's Circle™ Member Scott Tucker, one of the leading providers of turnkey marketing systems and business coaching to mortgage brokers and loan officers, has seen the reverse mortgage begin as a product of interest only to seniors typically 70 and up of modest means or even absent assets other than their home, in need of income, but now welcomed by people at the minimum age allowed, 62, as a different means of extracting money from their primary residence without going into debt in order to buy their new, second home, their gigantic RV (recreational vehicle), or their luxury timeshare membership. Consequently, he and the hundreds or so mortgage brokers he coaches across the country have begun successfully microtargeting "young seniors," that is, boomers with known interest in second or vacation homes, RVs, and so on, and probable interest in retaining their primary, current homes for life. I foresee a whole new kind of time-share, linking a cluster of homes and condos in a Midwest hometown with a cluster of homes and condos in Florida, each resident having x number of weeks in each location, and y number of weeks in neither, when on cruises and other vacations—all paid via one ownership fee and monthly service fee, all provided by one company.

Boomers are also making up an increasing percentage of the estimated four million and climbing "commuter couples," who, by choice, for business, career, or family reasons, live apart a significant percentage of time and commute to be together. Interestingly, the higher you go in affluence, the more you find this occurring.

The old ideas of shrinking income, fixed incomes, and minimum spending are out the window. My parents at 60 tended to become misers about spending on themselves, feeling obligated to preserve every penny for kids and grandkids. Even reasonably affluent retirees tended to tighten their purse strings and stop buying things for themselves. A 65-year-old couple ripping out their entire kitchen and installing a new $100,000.00 state-of-the-art, designer kitchen—unheard of! Also, the norm was a reduced income combining pension from job, Social Security, and yield from investments or savings, but IRAs and 401(k)s did not yet exist or were popular. Advertisers and marketers viewed this audience as one of rapidly diminishing value and pressed TV networks not to air programming aimed at it—and when they did, the commercials featured denture adhesives and adult diapers, not investment companies, luxury automobiles, home furnishings, or Disney® vacations. Today's boomers have entirely different financial situations and entirely different attitudes.

What Do They Want? What Will They Buy?

As you'll see, as we progress, it is dangerous and foolhardy to do what I'm about to do—generalize—yet I do believe there are overriding themes that offer us big keys to success with boomers. To quote Ken Gronbach, author of *Common Census: Counterintuitive Guide to Generational Marketing*:

> *They know what they want. They've been buying the same oil for their cars for years and they wear tan pants . . . . At this point in their lives they want only three things:*
> 1. *Life made easy.*
> 2. *Time saved.*
> 3. *Not to be ripped off.*

I'm not *sure* about the undying loyalty to a brand of oil or color of trousers—although, personally, I've happily gone from 30 or 40 different kinds, colors, and fabrics of pants to only two constituting 90% of my wardrobe (tan khakis and blue jeans)—but I definitely buy his **list of three chief wants**. If you examine most ads aimed at boomers, though, you won't find these basic appeals straightforwardly addressed. *Here's how I'll make your life easy. Here's how I'll save you time. Here are solid proof and guarantees.* And if you'd like a good copywriting checklist for a 4-by-6 card, there it is.

Anybody who has turned 50 can tell you: his attitudes, needs, desires, and priorities DO change literally with that calendar benchmark. I am closer to 50 than 60, but I'm quite sure I'll feel dramatic changes at 60 too. At 50, and even at 60, the overwhelming majority of affluent boomers are as busy as ever, even hitting their peaks of experience-based knowledge and capability, while at the same time being bedeviled by sudden and significant diminishment of physical capabilities, energy, stamina, good health, emotional tolerance for wasted time, incompetence, and hassle. When you consider all this, the first two items on Gronbach's list are obvious.

It's also worth noting that affluent boomers already own a lot of stuff. Their needs are fewer and get increasingly fewer with passing years, thus they are less interested in or seduced by *things*. Many of us now have the experience of paging through a favorite catalog or visiting a mall, able to buy just about anything we might want without second thought but finding nothing to buy. Consequently, **boomers are *service consumers* more than *product buyers*. We want nothing as a thing; we want a thing that gives us time, convenience, freedom, or ease.**

The third item on Gronbach's list is too often forgotten or misunderstood when selling to boomers. They have had more than enough life experience to have been disappointed or felt ripped off by a number of purchases and marketers. And they are not eager to repeat the experience. Boomers still think in terms of "classic credibility" while younger consumers do not; for example, brand names matter more, credible and relevant celebrity endorsements matter, years in business, professional affiliations, access to live humans for resolving problems all matter more to boomers than to younger buyers (and more to seniors than to boomers). You need to increase the reassurance for each year of your customer's age.

Beyond Gronbach's list, I would make number four that they want what is *for them*—but not if pandered to or made to feel old by the specialization or customization. Affluent boomers are, frankly, elitists. To quote somebody I can't name, "If you can't have things everybody else can't, what the hell's the point of being rich?" Further, affluent boomers, especially affluent leading-edge and aging boomers, know (but prefer not to enunciate) that they have special needs and want them accommodated without a lot of fanfare.

One of the Toughest Challenges for Marketers (The Death of Age-Based Advertising)

Age used to be a straight line, a continuum from birth to death, with benchmarks that were extremely predictive of behavior and therefore consumer spending. Many marketers still act as if this were true. People used to progress from college or military to office to family life to empty nest, retirement, and the golf course on a predictable schedule. These days, the schedule's been tossed out the window. Some 50- and 60-year-olds are starting second or third families, so a 55-year-old couple is in the market for a larger home (not a smaller one) close to a good school (not a golf course) and is a prospect for a Disney® Vacation Club time-share (not a condo in a retirement community). Instead of ending careers at 60 or 65, boomers are extending careers, starting new ones, and buying or starting businesses. **We boomers have made a helluva mess out of age-benchmark-based advertising, marketing, list segmentation, and product and service offers.**

This mess we're making requires an entirely new way of thinking about demographics, a far greater reliance on psychographics, and a much more serious commitment to such things as lead-generation advertising so boomers self-select; precise list segmentation and message-to-segment matching; sophisticated database management with the best possible tools; and smart use of response lists rather than compiled lists. It also requires literal reinvention of businesses to meet the desires of the segment(s) they choose—with the recognition that hardly any business can be all things to all boomers. Frankly most businesses—large or small, national or local—WILL FAIL MISERABLY at capitalizing on these opportunities. The fresh and creative thinking, the agility in adapting, the financial and other commitments required will be beyond their owners' or leaders' ability or willingness to provide. As a result, I believe a number of big-name companies will be bankrupt and gone ten years from today, literally driven extinct by boomers' refusal to patronize them. And most small-business owners will feel it is all beyond them.

The tiny number of business owners willing to dig in and figure all this out and adapt accordingly may find the next 6 to 12 years of boomer boom to be the greatest wealth-creating time of their lives.

A Look at the Attitudes Governing Boomers' Spending

Boomers' Attitudes toward Aging

The advertising insider term for the earliest boomers is *abbies*: aging baby boomers. But these boomers would decry the term. To say that these boomers expect to stay young isn't just a vague idea—it's verifiable through hard data from quality statistical research. Yankelovich Partners, one of America's respected research groups, found early boomers surveyed placed "old age" as *starting* three years *after* average life expectancy (82.3 years). Irrational as it may be, boomers do not feel bound by facts. They fully expect advances in health care, genomics, and other areas to have them living to or beyond 100. And the big wave of boomers behind them is even more expectant of long life. This has great significance for marketers. It means, in general, that a large number of those 60-plus are <u>not</u> thinking in terms of slowing down, aging gracefully, or retiring (as retirement has been known in the past) but instead are thinking about new options and changes. A series of TV ads for the financial services company Ameriprise featuring 60-plus actor (once wild, counterculture figure) Dennis Hopper plays to this exact point. (Dennis, incidentally, turned 70 in 2006.)

An extensive survey of women ages 50 to 64 by Dove® beauty products found that they do not see themselves as older women, and they resist such description. Age is, of course, a more sensitive issue with women than men, and the gender differences do need to be considered throughout marketing to boomers, essentially adding a female vs. male division to whatever other segmentation is done.

Boomers' Attitudes toward Health

Boomers now <u>expect</u> to be cured of all sorts of things our parents or grandparents accepted as incurable—including breast cancer and other cancers, heart disease and heart attacks, and other serious ailments. There is an optimistic faith in medical research producing more and better cures for all manner of diseases that is wholly unwarranted by reality; there actually hasn't been a new, complete *cure* for anything since polio. However, boomers still believe the cure for what ails them is just around the corner and will arrive in time to save them. This makes a segment uninterested in self-help, self-discipline, and so on regarding their diseases. As a diabetic myself, I find many diabetics undaunted,

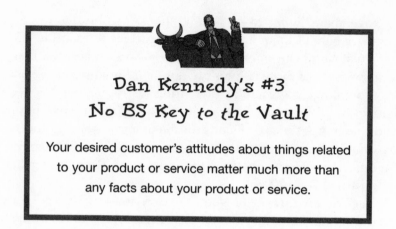

Dan Kennedy's #3
No BS Key to the Vault

Your desired customer's attitudes about things related
to your product or service matter much more than
any facts about your product or service.

talking about and anticipating easy, readily available organ
transplants and expecting other cures, so eating badly and not
exercising are irrelevant to them. Fortunately, there is a sizeable
segment who share similar hope for cures but are also extraordi-
narily proactive in attempting to influence their own health with
alternative means, thus the boomer boom is fueling the dramatic
sales growth in nutritional and dietary supplements, herbal supplements, treatments available only at foreign clinics, organic
and bio-engineered healthy foods, and so forth. On top of that,
and seemingly in contradiction to it, the pharmaceutical industry
is having a field day rolling out new prescription drugs for every
conceivable (and newly conceived) ailment, welcomed by
boomers. Viagra® may be the most age-attitude altering of all
pharmaceuticals of our time—it radically changed boomers' specific beliefs about sex lives and aging, but, more broadly, it also
changed attitudes about fixing *all* normal aging issues with
drugs. It removed stigma; it created new expectations. In short,

real medicine, alternative medicine, fake medicine, all booming with no end in sight.

The wellness industry, a new buzzword, has emerged from the fringes to be a major, mainstream business sector. It includes spas, organic foods, nutrition, exercise and fitness, and, given boomer vanities, cosmetic surgeries and procedures, beauty products and services, as well as, to a limited degree (due to the professions' own dysfunction at positioning themselves), chiropractic, massage therapy, dentistry, and integrative medicine. Given the wide range of businesses, practices, products, and services that can be classified as part of the wellness industry, determining industry size and growth is inexact. *BusinessWeek* pegged the market at $400 billion in 2005. *Hospitals and Health Networks* put it lower, at $300 billion. *Nutrition Business Journal* estimated it slightly higher, at $440 billion . . . involving 4.2% of the U.S. economy. If you take a consensus of growth predictions, you arrive at double the GDP. *BusinessWeek* projects growth to reach $1 trillion by 2020.

A wide range of big companies are trying experimental ways to enter or expand their piece of this pie. Best Buy, for example, is experimenting with a new health and wellness store. Hotel chains are putting more emphasis on their spas and spa vacations at resorts. Hospitals are also (awkwardly) trying to position themselves as wellness centers rather than just sick rooms—some getting into the fitness center business, some adding vitamin and herb stores to their pharmacies. One of the things the big corporations do not grasp about this growing consumer population is that it skews affluent, thus requiring targeted marketing and discriminating products, services, environments, and pricing. They err badly in marrying the wellness-demand growth trend with the boomer population wave as a whole. More than 50,000 corporations are currently identifying themselves as in the wellness industry, and Wall Street analysts specializing in the sector forecast that number quadrupling before 2020. This means the roughly tripled growth in consumer spending will be in play with a quadrupled number of competing marketers—and that does not factor in the much larger number of small businesses and solo practices.

Incidentally, eyeglasses and hearing aids have become fashion accessories, not just functional items. The percentage of people over 55 needing vision help is 88%. There are 60% needing hearing help—and given boomers' youthful affinity for rock concerts and rock music, that number's headed up. Innovative products that address these needs are finding success . . . from cosmetic cases with magnifying mirrors to computer keyboards with big keys and easy-to-read letters to simplified cell phones that offer no features other than the phone. A mail-order company called FirstStreet® is specializing in such products and identifies itself as "for Boomers and Beyond.™" Care has to be taken never to rub a person's face in a need brought on by aging he is loathe to admit, so, for example, advertising for a lower, easier-to-climb-into SUV with bigger captain's chairs that swivel for easy in and out access cannot say the car is for old, fat people who have trouble climbing in and out. We marketers have to give great thought to finding ways of presenting needed, welcomed products and services without triggering denial, resentment, or other negative responses from boomers.

Boomers' Attitudes toward Retirement

Classic retirement is no longer the goal of boomers. Affluent boomers who do not need to work or create earned income still

> *"Boomers have redefined every age they've moved*
> *through, so there's no reason to believe they will not*
> *define the stereotypes of what it means to be retired."*
>
> —PATRICK CONROY, CONSUMER BUSINESS ANALYST,
> DELOITTE & TOUCHE (*NEW YORK TIMES* 4/14/06)

expect to keep working—Merrill Lynch's New Retirement Survey put the total number at 81% of boomers who plan to work well past age 65. (This connects to their expectations of life span, health, etc.). A similar survey by the Wealth Institute directed at boomers with net worth from $3 million to $10 million had 62% expecting to keep working past age 65. Ken Dychtwald, president of Age Wave, says, "They want the action. They don't want to be on the sidelines." My take on this is that they fear being irrelevant, being bored, and being looked on as old or out to pasture to such an extent that even secret yearnings to relax, do nothing, travel, and golf are trumped.

From a marketing perspective, this suggests two points: first, if your products or services have anything to do with retirement, you're going to need to redefine them. (Even boomer retirees do not like the term *retiree*.) Second, there's opportunity in leveraging their fears.

Sales Strategies, Tactics, and Tools

Basically, we can never know enough. Selling, in person or in media, is about <u>connection</u>. On a primitive level, it can be completely mechanized and some, sometimes satisfactory, money can be made. But on a sophisticated level, the more we understand, the more we are understood, accepted, and trusted.

Language

One way we translate our understanding of a group of people is by the language we use when speaking to them. Far too little effort is made by salespeople or copywriters to get the language right.

Early-edge boomers are quite sensitive about language used to describe them, their options, and to describe aging.

In the 1950s, *they* used the term *old folks' home* without negative thoughts about it; today if you suggested they move into one, they'd pop you one in the nose! Then came *nursing homes*. Then, *retirement homes*. Now, *assisted-living communities*. But that industry is scrambling to again redefine itself and reposition itself to be acceptable to aging-resistant boomers, especially affluent ones, who may very well need such housing and service options but are loathe to admit it. This industry's challenge can be seen as the positioning and linguistic challenge for all businesses seeking what dare not be called any longer a senior citizen market. (If anything, that kind of language has moved up on life's calendar, to be used for and acceptable to people in their 80s and up.)

Boomers and Nostalgia

Everyone even barely conversant with NLP (neurolinguistic programming) understands the use of emotional ANCHORS in persuasion. An anchor may be a song or music, a visual image, a person, place, or thing already embedded in the prospect's mind that when recalled and linked to you, your product, or your service produces positive thoughts and warm feelings and/or a sense of common bond, thus less resistance and greater, faster trust. Mainstream, mass advertisers most commonly attempt utilizing anchors by buying rights to and using very popular, well-remembered songs of boomers' youth. The best anchors, though, aren't as simple, brief, or one-dimensional. For example Roy Rogers is an anchor for (mostly male) boomers of a certain age, but sitting on the floor in front of the TV, still in pajamas, with a bowl of cereal, to watch Roy Rogers, his superhorse, Trigger, and Dale Evans . . . that's a better anchor.

Such NOSTALGIA ANCHORS are extremely useful in marketing to aging boomers, leading-edge boomers, and, to a slightly lesser degree, boomers.

The reasons nostalgia itself is so powerful are many, and they warrant an in-depth discussion of psychology, but to abbreviate: we naturally rewrite history and memory to romance the past (in linkage to our desire for lost youth and immortality); we are dissatisfied with the present (because no reality can match imagined memory and because we are critical by nature); and we fear the future (as it links to mortality). Even false nostalgia is more appealing than present realities. As example, almost everybody likes—and buys things from—the little fake general store in Cracker Barrel® restaurants, even if the closest they ever actually got to a small-town general store with stuff in wood barrels was watching the *Andy Griffith Show* on TV. The Restoration Hardware® stores have similarly capitalized on nostalgia, real and invented. Disney's® Celebration, a planned community in Orlando (a MUST-tour) is built out of nostalgia anchors. It is the picture-perfect, quintessential American small town, appealing to those with a romanticized memory of such a place, but almost as appealing to people with an imagined nostalgia for such a place.

When marketing to boomers, you will benefit greatly from carefully choosing and using age-appropriate, gender-appropriate, geography-appropriate nostalgia anchors. But you can't overplay your hand either. Boomers are hypersensitive to being conned. They have seen a lot, have a lot of life experience, and quickly detect false, inauthentic, pandering attempts at connecting with them—and they resent them.

As an interesting example, I've encouraged my Platinum Member client and investment partner Darin Garman to increase the small-town anchors in his marketing of American heartland investment properties to investors throughout the country, including many from the coasts. Why? Because one investor enunciated for us what others have not but must be influenced by: he, a New York resident attending his mother's funeral in Iowa, saw Garman's ad, called, and bought several hundred thousands of dollars of small-town Iowa real estate on impulse, based on nostalgia for his youth. We have since seen the power of telling the story of a place where small-town values still rule, where Fourth of July parades and Friday-night games are attended by the whole town, where churches host summer picnics and neighbors meet at the ice-cream stand— even though it has nothing whatsoever to do with a numbers decision for an investor. But this has to be done gently, naturally, authentically—not waved like a big red pennant. Fortunately for Garman, it *is* authentic. It's where he lives and how he lives.

What Sets Boomers' Teeth on Edge:
How to Lose a Boomer in 60 Seconds

If you want to know what will drive boomers away from your business, here's your answer. First and foremost, it is (perceived or real) disrespect. Boomers deeply resent and often react with rage to employees who (1) call them Pops, Ma'am, Old Man, and so on, either as deliberate or accidental offense; (2) dress in ways the boomers view as inappropriate for the workplace and a sign of disrespect for the job and the customers; (3) talk down to them or are condescending, such as "I realize at your age you don't know much about the internet, so . . ."; (4) use street slang or young slang or references instead of speaking the King's English; (5) fail to clearly explain things; (6) hurry them (beyond their capability); (7) engage in impolite, disrespectful behavior, such as talking on a cell phone while ringing up their sale at a cash register.

Beyond that, boomers aren't fond of having to deal with young employees in a number of settings. SalesDesign® expert Sydney Biddle Barrows did a massive research project about consumer expectations, satisfaction, and unvoiced dissatisfaction in cosmetic surgery, and found the number-one complaint of boomer women was having to discuss their treatment, progress, recovery, or questions with *"20- or 30-year-old GIRLS who can't possibly know what I'm going through."* While it is illegal to discriminate in hiring based on age, it suggests going out of your way to recruit and hire age-appropriate staff members when you can, and to be careful how you deploy different staff members.

To do well with boomers, every person in your employ or representing you who comes in contact with your customers must learn to do well with boomers and modify his attitude,

> ### Recommended Resource
>
> SALES LANGUAGE is critical. Mark Twain said the
> difference between any word and just the right word
> is the difference between lightning bugs and lightning.
> You can fine-tune your own sales language, develop
> ultra-effective scripts, and convert ordinary selling
> into performance art—all dealt with in depth in
> Sydney Barrows' short-term tele-coaching program,
> Information at: www.SydneyBarrows.com.

language, appearance, and behavior to do well with boomers.
Otherwise your people will sabotage your marketing.

Big Opportunities and How Businesses Will Adapt to Boomers in Coming Years
Conglomeration of Services

As example of the conglomeration-of-services approach, here's
my thought about the retirement community for affluent
boomers: I think there'll be a boom in retirement lifestyle clubs
that bundle together a primary-residence condo or apartment in
something akin to today's assisted-living center with timeshare
exchanges for other such sites all over the country x number of
weeks a year, plus cruise ship weeks, car and driver transportation at all home sites, concierge travel services and concierge
medical care, all for one monthly fee or lifetime prepayment.

This may require insurance companies, doctors, hospitals, HMOs, real estate developers, and community operators to all come together in new joint ventures, or a big company from one of the involved industries—say, Marriott (already very active in assisted living and, obviously, in travel)—to be the organizer, or an entirely new type of corporation to be created. For the customer, this will offer the own-nothing, rent-everything option or the timeshare-your-whole-life-for-one-fee option. It is a quasi-marriage of today's high-end destination travel clubs utilizing mansions as well as resort properties—with buy-ins in the $200,000.00 to $350,00.00 range plus yearly dues—with retirement communities and assisted-living facilities, with full services, from a driver waiting to take you to the mall to a doctor on call to a refrigerator stocked for you. The consumers may even pay by assigning assets via their wills or transferring assets through irrevocable trusts rather than with present-day dollars, as more and more boomers feel entitled to spending it all rather than stacking it up for heirs. (Buffett has inspired and emboldened them.) This requires new and very innovative thinking about product, business models, financing models. (Charities have gotten very good at securing these postdeath payments as well as getting large sums turned over in exchange for income or benefits for life. Why shouldn't other businesses?)

The truly innovative leaders—what I'm calling *lifestyle service inventors*—will make the huge new fortunes in America. (Making fortunes from manufacturing is just about over and certainly freakish. Making fortunes from technology on the ebb. Making fortunes in any single category of business being replaced by multichannel, multimedia, multicategory businesses based on high customer value is the coming trend.)

Using this as metaphor, you have to start thinking about just how radically your industry and connected or potentially connected industries may change or could be changed, and how you can be in the lead rather than chasing—or worse, watching.

Experiences

> *"Boomers aren't likely to spend their retirement years sitting in a rocking chair. Instead, surveys suggest they'll continue to SEEK OUT REMARKABLE EXPERIENCES—whether on cruise ships, in RVs, or at hotels and gambling tables."*
>
> —*FORTUNE*, JUNE 2006

Boomers are RESTLESS. They are easily bored and in need of a lot of external stimulation. The old idea of the 60s being a time to slow down and take it easy is moving forward, to people in their 70s and 80s, and is more common to NON-affluent boomers and their elders solely because of financial limitations on their options. Today's affluent boomers want to be entertained wherever they go, whether to Las Vegas or to a neighborhood restaurant.

Boomers are unsatisfied with the ordinary. An ordinary store, an ordinary mall, an ordinary hotel or resort, all unappealing. A resort needs to provide the chance to swim with dolphins, not just a nice pool area. Vegas and Disney® set the bar for themed experiences and environments, and retailers and other businesses must follow suit. Even mail-order catalogs and websites need to provide multidimensional experiences, not just descriptions of goods. You may immediately be tempted to engage in the UNcreative "But my business is different" thinking as an excuse for not creating exciting and memorable experiences for prospects and customers, clients, or patients—but boomers will not reward you, whether as consumers or B2B buyers. In B2B, for example, my friend Steve Miller, of Adventures in Trade Shows, has been ever more prodding his clients—including owners and operators of some of the largest trade shows in America (all but one of which are suffering declines in exhibitors and attendees)—NOT to lie there dying but to re-invent the entire experience for attendees and exhibitors alike. Even a book needs to be more of an experience, with sidebars, illustrations, involvement devices, enclosed CDs or DVDs, extensions at websites (just like this one).

Service Spread Thin: A Crisis and Opportunity in Capitalizing on the Affluent Boomer Boom

Boomers are far more demanding regarding service than, progressively, members of each younger generation. A 30-year-old is not annoyed by—and may even prefer—self-serve grocery checkouts, or self-serve online banking; a 60-year-old hates it. Affluent boomers will go out of their way to go where they get exceptional service.

However, the United States is experiencing a significant and growing shortage of service-sector employees. By 2030, America will have twice as many retirees as in 2005, but only 15% more service workers to support them—and that's *with* unchecked illegal immigration. The demand for service is outpacing the work force required to provide it, now and into the future. Most businesses are reacting to minimum-wage increases, overall increases in costs per employee, and ever-increasing managerial frustrations with quality of employees by reducing the number of service employees per *x* amount of gross sales or by some other ratio; substituting automation; and substituting self-serve systems, transferring the burden to the customer. This may be mathematically sensible, but letting bean counters create policy is a consistently destructive act. (Bean counters should count beans. Period. Kennedy's First Law of Investing: never invest in a company run by the accountants.)

For success with the boomer boom, and especially with affluent boomers, **a business needs to alter its fundamental economics in order to do the polar opposite**: *increase* the number of service persons . . . pay above-average wages and offer incentives to attract and keep superior people . . . invest in *continual* training (including training on satisfying boomer customers) . . . and integrate exceptional service promises into its advertising and marketing.

My favorite business success tactic is to engineer a business to be able to substantially outspend all its competitors on advertising and marketing, customer acquisition, and customer retention. I would extend this to hiring, training, and motivating people.

Social Networks and Organizations that Attract Boomers

AARP (www.aarp.org) has 35 million members and expects to double that number by 2015. This makes it one of the largest membership organizations in the United States. It began as— and, to a great extent, is still a mask for—a business selling insurance, financial services, and other services to seniors, and selling ad media and other access to its members to companies marketing to seniors. In short, it is a marketing and media business presenting itself to a group of customers as an association working for them, serving them, even representing them politically. It is a terrific example of a tollbooth business. And of an illusion.

With its current size and success, its masquerade has become more real, but it is still not a true or classic social organization, like, for example, the Elks. In fact, AARP has no local chapters or meetings it organizes, although it does have its own speakers bureau and other support for member-organized gatherings. AARP's only official meeting for its members, its annual convention, draws more than 25,000 attendees and features speakers like Terry Bradshaw, Raquel Welch, and Bill Cosby.

AARP's media is expensive but pretty much essential if you are going to be a serious national marketer to the 55-plus, boomer, and senior markets. Many companies err by not integrating to the greatest extent possible with AARP, via advertising in its media, exhibiting at its conventions, providing editorial content for its publications, renting its lists, and offering discounts and benefits to its members. AARP is *the* big kahuna in this market, with nothing but growth in size and influence ahead.

AARP is also evidence of a "joiner bias" among boomers. Boomers are membership oriented, having grown up with many more affinity groups of influence than have younger generations. This is an exploitable bias. There is ample room for niched organizations serving boomers or only affluent boomers, largely copying AARP—for example, an association for affluent boomer travelers or affluent boomer real estate investors or affluent boomer golfers.

The **ELKS** (www.elks.org) organization has, by comparison, only one million members and is struggling with declining membership. The group's average member is 65. It has lost more than 600,000 members to old age or death since 1980 and has only recently begun serious efforts—with mixed success in different cities—to attract younger boomers. The organization does have 2,100 lodges throughout the United States. It has potential for reinvention. Unfortunately for the Elks, they do not skew affluent and tend not to attract affluent boomers . . . essentially they are trying to pump life with weak blood. They should not, however, be overlooked in developing a complete marketing plan for boomers (or seniors). They have effective and reasonably priced media and exploitable affinity.

The **Red Hat Society** (www.RedHatSociety.org) has enjoyed terrific growth since its 1998 launch, largely thanks to generous media attention. Geared to women over 50, the organization has 41,000 chapters (many very small), national publications, an online community and so on, but it revolves around local tea parties, luncheons, shopping trips, and the like. Over one million members proudly wear the trademark purple outfit with a red hat. While the organization makes no effort to attract affluent women, estimates are that better than half of its members are wealthy. The organization also has a very active licensing department, for fashions, accessories, gifts, merchandise of all kinds, books, and consumer service.

MySpace. Data was not available to me regarding the percentage of MySpace users in age groups 50–55, 55–60, and so on; however, boomer use of this and other online communities like Match.com is, by all accounts, steadily growing. Match.com experimented with TV ads aimed at boomers and at seniors, including one with a 71-year-old widow, but the company has reverted to generic advertising again. From 2000 to 2006, boomers represented the fastest-growing age group at Match.com, now 11% of its 1.7 million active members. And Match.com admits that, while losing younger members to competing hipper and niched sites, they have sustained its one million-plus membership thanks to success with older daters. *The Wall Street Journal* reported early in 2007 on Match.com's deliberate efforts to make its site easy to navigate for people who are not internet savvy.

My take is that integrating a societal or community element into just about any boomer-oriented business is, at very least, in the no-harm, no-foul category, but can be very useful. It's a way to create added value mostly from thin air, and to involve your customers with you and with each other. Ideally, you'll find a way to use it to create "pain of disconnect," discouraging departure or fickleness and encouraging continued or frequent patronage.

Some legendary entrepreneurs believe that boomers-becoming-seniors will be the wave of consumers fueling huge new growth in online community businesses. AOL co-founder Steve Case launched and is experimenting with RevolutionHealth.com, a combined health information and social networking website aimed at older Americans. Barry Diller, who owns Match.com, Ask.com, and other sites, says he is actively looking to invest in other online businesses that cater to 50-plus boomers. And Diller's no dummy. If they are right, then any boomer-seeking business ought to develop a community for its customers, alone or in concert with others who are in the same business in other locales. As example, do boomer women undergoing extensive cosmetic dentistry or cosmetic surgery want an opportunity to share with each other? Absolutely.

Boomers Buying Businesses
(and Selling Businesses)

Well over 50% of all sellers of businesses turn around and start, or more often, buy another business within 12 to 24 months. There's no indication this is less true of people in their 50s, 60s, and beyond. The franchise industry reports that boomer buyers, especially early retirees encouraged to exit their corporate careers, are a prime source of buyers. A growing number of franchisors specifically target this market. There is no reliable research I've yet located on the relationship between boomers, homebased businesses, and in-home offices, but ample anecdotal evidence suggests a major trend there.

There are three key themes.

One reason boomers start or buy businesses, franchises, or business opportunities is to prepare for and begin their next life. They have no intention of actually retiring in the classic sense, and they look to self-employment or business ownership for their sense of purpose for the years from 50 to 60 or 60 to 70. In many cases, they are pursuing dream businesses—that's how bed-and-breakfasts, small restaurants, antique stores, and the like come about.

The other reason is to make up for lost time. Several of my clients have had considerable success aiming prepackaged part-time or second-business opportunities at affluent professionals ages 45 to 55, who, while affluent, still have not amassed enough wealth to comfortably retire. They see the second-income business as a means of pouring additional income into retirement savings and/or quickly creating equity in a saleable asset. Dr. Paul Searby was very successful with this take on his dental assistant school opportunity for dentists.

A third area of opportunity is in selling lifestyle businesses to boomers, such as info-marketing or internet-marketing businesses, mobile and portable businesses, and absentee-owner businesses. The "have your cake and eat it too" theme is working well for countless promoters of businesses that lend themselves to spare and flexible time operation, outsourcing, and automation. And, claims about large income potential are not as important as lifestyle claims . . . a common mistake is focusing on the money. I have, on a couple of occasions, come close to creating a seminar-driven enterprise aimed at introducing boomers to such businesses and am convinced it's a winner—just have no time to do it.

Boomers Investing and Investing in Boomers

In the financial services industry, there is a current and likely to continue explosion of investment products, advertising and marketing programs, prepackaged seminars, sales tools, sales training, infomarketers, and coaches all aimed at reaching the boomer market. There is even a separate trade journal, *Boomer Market Advisor* (www.BoomerMarketAdvisor.com). Predictably and sadly, virtually all the ads and the editorial content in this publication is product and platform oriented, not focused on understanding and communicating with the boomer client. As is all too common, all of these fools think it is about their products. But the growing number of such products is illustrative of the size, scope, and potential of this market . . . and the need to customize for it, even if most financial companies and advisors are relatively clueless about how they ought to actually go about that.

Fact is, boomers have a lot of money invested but *also a ton of money underinvested.* Boomers, especially leading-edge boomers, have hundreds of millions of dollars parked in bank CDs, money market accounts, regular checking, bonds, and, still, in their mattresses. Those selling businesses or selling large homes and buying smaller ones; those getting paid bulk sums to retire early; executives with golden parachutes; and those inheriting money from their parents all, combined, have a boatload of investable assets and are uncertain and anxious about where to put it. (Note: Anyone going after it needs to remember the three key wants mentioned on page 49.)

There are numerous niche opportunities. As an interesting and instructive example, consider one of the Glazer-Kennedy Insider's Circle™ longtime Members, an attorney, marketing coach to attorneys, and very astute niche marketer, Bill Hammond. Within estate planning, there is an established sub-specialty called *elder law*—basically dealing with families with elder members and their various needs, from wills and trusts to rearranging assets in advance of nursing home needs or qualification for Medicare. Within that niche, Hammond created a sub-subspecialty of *Alzheimer's law*, for families with an elder diagnosed with or showing warning signs of Alzheimer's disease. Now he is using that as centerpiece of an "everything Alzheimer's" business and a contemplated national franchise for lawyers. This is a boomer business in three ways: because it is for boomers parenting their aging parents, because leading-edge boomers face or will soon face these needs themselves, and because the younger echo-boomers behind us are only ten years away from facing it with us. The end result still has an estate planning law practice in there somewhere, but you have to dig deep to find it. And it is largely about boomers' finances and investments and generational movement of wealth.

Boomers Buying Homes

According to the National Association of Realtors,® **in 2005, boomers accounted for four out of every ten (40%) second-home purchases—a record high for the age group** and a reminder that the old rules of age-based marketing are broken. The 1997 Taxpayer Relief Act, which raised the cap on tax-free profits from a principal residence sale to $500,000.00 and extended it to second homes (as often as every two years), certainly had its effect here. Boomers used to buy second homes for only one reason (preparing for retirement), and only the ultra-affluent bought vacation homes. Today's affluent boomers may have a second and a third home . . . and they have multiple buying motivations: leisure or vacation; preretirement; retirement; gathering places for geographically scattered families; and investment. (Boomers believe real estate is the safest of investments, can still quote Will Rogers on the subject, and believe it outperforms all other investments over time.) In the NAR survey, more than 90% of all second-home buyers stated it was a "good investment" (although, statistically, that's true in only about 55% of the cases, if measured as outperforming the Dow Jones basket over ten years). Since the leading-edge boomers have just hit, most real estate experts expect a flood of boomer buyers into the second-home or vacation-home market in the next few years. The "buy raw land to build on when you retire" business, a thriving and often scam- and scandal-riddled field of the '60s, is back in a big way, including successful TV infomercials, a lot of media advertising, even the dinner meetings once used to sell Florida swampland.

Affluent boomers who intend to buy new homes when they retire—59%; 45% in a different state than their current residence; 36% intend to downsize. One of the most sought-after in-home amenities: "spalike bathrooms." To me, this means the way the real estate industry works with boomer clients has to change, or the boomers will replace Realtors® with other means of meeting their needs. Boomers ready to relocate do not want hassles or uncertainties. This presents growing opportunity for real estate investors rather than agents to immediately relieve the boomer-owner of his current property, but somehow whoever is at that end of the process must also be able to support the boomer in finding and purchasing the new home, and vice versa. The opportunity here is in a seamless outcome for the boomer. Regardless, though, it tells you that this is a viable market for homes and condos—and a market less affected by price and market highs and lows then the general housing market, because when they're ready, they're ready, and they can afford the luxury of NOT waiting for better timing.

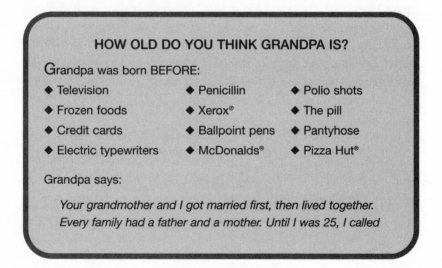

HOW OLD DO YOU THINK GRANDPA IS?

Grandpa was born BEFORE:

◆ Television	◆ Penicillin	◆ Polio shots
◆ Frozen foods	◆ Xerox®	◆ The pill
◆ Credit cards	◆ Ballpoint pens	◆ Pantyhose
◆ Electric typewriters	◆ McDonalds®	◆ Pizza Hut®

Grandpa says:

Your grandmother and I got married first, then lived together.
Every family had a father and a mother. Until I was 25, I called

> ## HOW OLD DO YOU THINK GRANDPA IS?, continued
>
> *every man older than me Sir. You could buy a new Chevy for*
> *$600.00—but who could afford one? Pity, cuz gas was 11*
> *cents a gallon. Grass was mowed; Coke was a cold drink;*
> *hardware was found only in a hardware store. If you saw any-*
> *thing made in Japan, it was junk no self-respecting American*
> *would buy. We were before dual careers, day-care centers,*
> *draft dodging, group therapy, fast food. We had 5-and-10-*
> *cent stores where things sold for 5 cents and 10 cents.*
>
> OK, now, how old do you think Grandpa is?
>
> Most I've tried this on guess from 80 to 90 to dead. In fact, he is
> but 59. (Jay Leno's age in 2008.)
>
> The younger you are, the more distant in the past you are likely to
> place Grandpa and his frame of reference, his life experiences.
> Thus, the more difficult you'll find it to connect with boomers.
> What you can't conceive of anybody still walking the earth having
> experienced we recall as if yesterday and, as we age, recall with
> increasing fondness and nostalgia. The emotional gap between
> boomers and those in their 30s is the size of the Grand Canyon.
> Boomers resent the lack of knowledge, understanding, and
> respect for their history. To connect with boomers, you must be
> familiar with, respectful of, and reference where they came from.

CHAPTER 7

Those Who've Gone from Poor to Rich

"I don't think of myself as a poor deprived ghetto girl who made good. I think of myself as somebody who from an early age knew I was responsible for myself, and I had to make good."

—OPRAH WINFREY

I've gone from rags to riches, so I think I get these rich customers better than any others.

A very significant percentage of the affluent population did, in fact, pull themselves up by their bootstraps, and they strongly identify with that cliché. Many came from stark or relative poverty or other difficult circumstances and are still very much governed by having been poor or put down. They never disconnect emotionally from this past, no matter how successful and wealthy they become. Some romanticize their past struggles. All keep them as touchstones. I doubt it coincidence that Jay Leno's star on the Hollywood Walk of Fame is located precisely at the street corner where he was twice arrested for vagrancy. Can't help but think he had something to do with that placement. Or that his massive collection of classic cars may have roots in his having to sleep in his car while homeless, when starting out. I settled for a little model of my first car, a 1960 Chevy with leaky floor and roof, bought for $25.00 on $5.00 monthly payments in 1971.

Walt Disney was once driving home from Disneyland® when he saw and stopped briefly to admire a particular new car in a showroom window. Then driving home, he said aloud to himself, "Gee, I wish I could afford one of those." It was a half hour later that it occurred to him—"Hey, I *can* afford that"—and he turned around, drove back to the dealership, and bought himself the car. This reveals a little something about self-made affluents: they may have nearly unrestricted spending power in reality, but not necessarily mentally and emotionally. Most are conflicted about money. They know they need to think, feel, and act rich to remain attractive to money, as I explain in my book *No B.S. Wealth Attraction for Entrepreneurs*. But they also battle guilt, fear, anxiety, abhorrence of waste. Those who have worked for their wealth, rather than inherited it or gotten it in some amazing windfall, as a movie star or athlete signed to a $50 million contract, can be self-indulgent and profligate, but are not casually so. A yacht salesman told me, "I always show them an outrageously pricey one first, a very expensive but slightly smaller and less luxuriously equipped one second, and a stripped-down bargain model third. They buy the middle one and are able to feel good about not spending as much as they could have. They feel like they acted responsibly."

Selling to the Self-Employed Affluent

A very valuable subsegment of these self-made affluents is business owners and entrepreneurs. Here you may very well find your best customers, clients, or patients.

Self-employment is one of the most reliable paths to first-generation wealth, supplemented by real estate investment. All the research into the rich done by Dr. Thomas Stanley, summarized in his books like *The Millionaire Next Door*, shows that self-employeds make up a slightly growing 20% of the U.S. population, yet account for about 70% of the affluence. The net worth of a U.S. household in which its head is self-employed is nearly 500% greater than one in which the number-one breadwinner works for somebody else. Frankly, we business owners tend to pay ourselves a lot better than we do anybody else! And among the ultra-affluent, just shy of 50% own a business that is their primary source of wealth. The other 50% is fragmented, with wealth amassed from inheritance, marriage and divorce, pedantic investment over time, and a number of other sources.

The personality of these affluent business owners and entrepreneurs is sharply drawn, with little ambiguity, so they can be the easiest of all affluents to market a wide variety of goods and services to.

One of my multimillionaire clients owns a large pest control company. He grew up in a house with no indoor plumbing. He started in business with a spray can of chemicals and hard work. Another multimillionaire client was divorced by his first wife and shunned by his own family for being a wild-eyed dreamer who refused to get a decent job. Only when his brother, a doctor, saw an article about my client in *Forbes* did the family make overtures to patch things up. Another multimillionaire client now traveling around in his two private jets and living in what can only be described as a palatial estate in Florida was once working as a car mechanic, and recalls having to explain to his wife that they could not afford to have the clothes dryer repaired and having to borrow the money to go to his first seminar on real estate. These examples are more typical than atypical of the affluent entrepreneur profile. They have never been handed anything. They've worked and sacrificed for everything they've gotten. They got it by "taking no shit" from anybody and have no intention of doing so now.

Won't Take No for an Answer

First and foremost, they view themselves as fiercely independent. They chafe at rules and tend to exit, stage left, immediately upon hearing rules language from anyone marketing to them. The fastest way to repel this customer or client is tell him "no, you/we can't do that," and when asked why not, say, "policy."

I have stayed at every imaginable kind and brand of hotel, from the much-lauded bastion of service, Ritz-Carlton, to the orange-roofed Howard Johnsons; top-rated resorts, city business hotels, rural motels. I and my companies have spent millions of dollars putting on meetings, conferences, and conventions for groups of 20 to 20,000 in these same facilities. Since this is self-described as the service and hospitality industry, you might expect service and hospitality. But you'd be wrong. In 30 years of this patronage, I have been in only two of these places where, no matter what I asked, I never heard the word *no* or *can't*. Ironically, one is not a luxury property—Trump Plaza in Atlantic City. I took a small contingent from my wealth coaching group there for a theme meeting coinciding with the airing of the first episode of a season of *The Apprentice*. There were only 18 of us, an inconsequential pimple on the butt of this big hotel and casino. Throughout the two days, our every request was met with "Yes" or "I'll be back to you within *x* minutes," which was always followed by "Yes." Says something, I think, about from-Trumpdown. The other properties where this occurs are Disney's® in Florida, notably Animal Kingdom Lodge® and the Grand Floridian.® Everywhere else, you get no's. I've stayed in a lot of resorts once. I take a vacation at a Disney® property nearly every year. If not already, I'll certainly generate a million dollars in lifetime customer value for Disney.® Only $10,000.00, give or take, for just about every other resort I've ever stayed at but will never stay at again. That's the value of being able to say yes to the affluent.

If They Admire You, They'll Reward You with Their Business

Second, the self-made affluent are great admirers of the qualities that got them where they now are. Every one of them is doing business with somebody who reminds them of themselves when they were starting out. I got my first bank loan from a 70-year-old entrepreneur who owned the small-town bank outright, and the mill, and the main street restaurant and hardware store, and most of the real estate as far as the eye could see in any direction. I met him for lunch at his diner on a Wednesday, not knowing his bank was closed on Wednesdays. Afterward, he unlocked the bank, found its checkbook in a drawer, wrote out a check to me for $50,000.00, and told me he'd have somebody draw up the paperwork and mail it to me to sign. He said I reminded him of himself when he was a young buck too dumb to know what couldn't be done and tough enough to do it. I regretted not having asked for $100,000.00.

These people reward ingenuity, drive, persistence, and salesmanship. They have a *spiritual reverence* for these virtues.

An axiomatic example was given me by a fellow who was charged with selling a new kind of pizza-making conveyor oven to New York restaurants. In the city of pizza, only fixed ovens with real pizza stones were acceptable. To crack the market, he determined he would need the number-one restaurateur as a reference, the owner of a couple famous, high-end restaurants as well as five different franchise chains. It just so happened this entrepreneur had just secured the area rights to a new pizza franchise and would soon be opening dozens of locations. The salesman sent him a letter requesting an appointment. Then he sent him one of his business cards with a handwritten request, along with some brochure or article about the ovens or the restaurant business in general, every day. Every day for two months. Finally, his phone rang and the famous restaurateur asked—in good humor—"What do I have to do to get you to stop sending me your business cards?" The salesman told him he'd bought the cards by the thousand, so there was a long way to go, but a brief appointment would put an end to it. The ending is happy. More than 100 of those pizza locations have the "odd" ovens.

On the other side of this coin, the self-employed affluent genuinely detest sloth, weakness, wimpiness. They are hustlers who not only respect hustle but find those lacking it pathetic and untrustworthy. That does not mean they respond well to *desperate* hustle; they don't. But aggressive hustle, they do.

They Are—More Often than Not—Searching for Value,
as They Define It

Third, they know the value of a dollar, and tend to pride themselves on being smart about money, getting good deals and bargains, negotiating successfully, even being seen as frugal.
Donald Trump likes telling the stunts of buying the bankrupt billionaire's oceanfront manor as a foreclosure bargain, of recouping his investment in his famous Mar a Lago resort by replacing all of the antiques, antique furniture, and art that came with it with reproductions and selling the originals, and of buying his huge 727 airplane rather than a smaller private jet because there was less of a market for 727s so it could be had at a bargain price. The late Sam Walton and Warren Buffett, famously, symbolically frugal: old pickup trucks, off-the-rack suits, even brown paper bag lunches.

When you step down from these ultra-affluent business leaders to the merely affluent, you find even more serious frugality. While they all have one or two things they will spend wildly on, most abhor waste and have an emotional need to buy smart with most things they buy. I believe this is rooted in two things: (1) a patch of thin skin about others' perceptions of the rich as drunken-sailor spenders who are fools about money, reinforced by the news stories featuring those who are, from Britney Spears to the former Tyco CEO now in jail, made famous for $50,000.00 gold-plated umbrella stands and toilet seats and such, and (2) a vivid memory of and residual paranoia about from whence they came, when spare change from the couch cushions was needed to buy dinner. Most affluent entrepreneurs harbor a nagging fear of losing it all or having it all taken away from them and winding up broke. This anxiety is always there, like a low-grade infection. If they feel they are wasting money, that anxiety flares up.

It's important to know that the price these people will pay for something has to do with how right and justified or queasy and irrational they feel about it. Not about intrinsic value or their own ability to pay.

I'll use myself as example. For a while, I've been thinking about buying myself a classic car. There are two that interest me, both cars I had as a kid: a 1964 suicide-door Lincoln Town Car or a 1973 AMC Javelin. The Town Car is out; it won't fit in my garage. I found a Javelin in a car auction catalog, called, and learned—to my horror—its minimum selling price would be $43,000.00. I believe I paid about $4,000.00 for mine, new, in 1974. It's not the $43,000.00. I could spend it and not miss it. A new luxury car would cost the same. I buy racehorses that cost this much with no hesitation. But I just can't wrap my head around blowing that much on a damn American Motors Javelin. I wanted it but couldn't bring myself to pay the price. My point is that you can't assume that because an affluent entrepreneur can easily pay your price, he can do so without having to justify and rationalize it.

In marketing to the affluent, you will mostly be marketing to these people who have made themselves affluent through ingenuity and initiative—*not* rich heiresses roaming Rodeo Drive between two-martini lunches and hours at the spa, *not* rappers and rock stars or superstar athletes draped in bling. The way you present yourself to them must be in sync with *their* values.

HOW A BUSINESS-TO-BUSINESS MARKETER SELLS SUCCESSFULLY TO AFFLUENT BUSINESS OWNERS

Too often, B2Bers deny the applicability of my marketing strategies to their situations, erroneously believing there is great difference between marketing consumer products and services to consumers and marketing business products and services to business owners. There is, of course, no opportunity in this. The only opportunity is in looking at everything in this book from the perspective of how you can use it—not how you can't!

Chris Hurn is CEO and co-founder of Mercantile Commercial Capital, the nation's leading 90% loan-to-cost commercial loan provider specializing in serving owners of small- to medium-sized companies and purchasers of franchises. In 2007, his firm was named to the *Inc.* 500 list of fastest-growing privately held companies in America. Here is an abbreviated edition of my interview with him, from my *No B.S. Marketing to the Mass-Affluent Letter*:

DAN: Chris, I want to spotlight what I view as the five main reasons for your outstanding success in your field and the dramatic growth and expansion of your company. Let's start with your understanding of your clientele—and, of course, your emphasis on marketing your services to the affluent.

CHRIS: In many ways, we've been marketing to the affluent from day one, as they are the small-business owners best able

BUSINESS-TO-BUSINESS MARKETER SELLS, continued

to purchase their own commercial property, rather than renting and sacrificing buildup of equity. Consciously and strategically, however, we started marketing to a more affluent client late in 2006, and in the ensuing 12 months, we've seen that make a huge, positive difference. Our market includes the 26.8 million owners of small- to medium-sized businesses, spanning industrial-type companies, restaurants and hotels, and professional practices, such as medical and dental. We do a great deal of work with independent restaurant owners and franchise purchasers. Interestingly, baby boomers are a prime client group for us. They are hitting a time of realization that they have not created sufficient wealth for retirement, and are turning to real estate ownership tied to their businesses as a means of accelerating wealth, and converting rental payments that enrich their landlords to equity for themselves. So **we do not talk to our clients just in terms of properties and loans; we talk about the four American dreams:** owning your own home; becoming your own boss; owning your own commercial property; and living a carefree retirement. In fact, we have a trademarked tagline: Fulfilling Dreams with Smarter Financing. **We strive to connect with our clients on personal, psychological, and emotional levels, not just factual and practical.** This is foreign to all the bankers we theoretically compete with. And, as you've taught us, the more affluent the client, the more he is looking for expertise, for relationship, and most of all, understanding.

BUSINESS-TO-BUSINESS MARKETER SELLS, continued

DAN: Your understanding of your clients has led you to do a number of things very unusual in the commercial lending world. Rattle off a few . . .

CHRIS: We provide a broad array of valuable information to our clients and prospective clients through newsletters, teleseminars, monthly audio CDs where I interview famous authors and experts on business, finance, marketing, and sales topics. You can see much of this at www.504Experts.com, and readers of this book will find a special business report for them, free of charge, at www.504 Experts.com/DanKennedyMarketingToTheAffluentBookSpecial.

By being an information provider, we separate ourselves from ordinary lenders. What do you say? Banish the ordinary! We have also built special programs just for our affluent business owners, such as our Commercial Loan Concierge,® which relieves our client of all the work in securing SBA [Small Business Administration] loans and requires completion of only one form. On his behalf, we then collect information from his accountant, real estate agent, general contractor, attorney, and office manager rather than asking him to play fetch. **We also go out of our way to be one with the client. I call myself America's entrepreneurial banker, and I write, talk, and present myself as an entrepreneur dealing with all the same frustrations, challenges, hopes, dreams, and daily experiences that my clients are. They feel like we are on the same side of the desk, working together. This is a**

BUSINESS-TO-BUSINESS MARKETER SELLS, continued

very different experience for the client than dealing with typical bankers and lenders, who usually have little or no entrepreneurial experience, do not understand the entrepreneur, and treat him with suspicion or disdain.

(More about this in Chapter 37.)

DAN: I think it's very important for people to grasp that you are not selling money and interest rates.

CHRIS: Price is the lowest common denominator, and it is what most lenders sell. It is the way clients choose unless they are given other criteria. By acting completely different, **we are able to change the client's thinking from** *lowest price* **to** *best opportunity*. We sell time; by relieving the client of all the work and jumping through hoops common with most lenders, we enable the business owner to invest his time in his highest-value activities, doing what he does best. We sell expertise, relationship, service. We're selling the most in-depth and extensive experience, fastest turnaround, best service—and entrepreneurial bankers. And we sell bigger ideas: our impact on our clients' wealth, our assistance with their aspirations. As a result of our choice of clientele and our unique presentation of ourselves, we do not compete on price, and we do command fees, on average, twice that of competitors—although we are also extremely effective at securing excellent financing for our clients due, in part, to a unique business model I won't discuss here, so we're usually within 25 basis points (a small margin) of the least expensive option available any-where. We very, very, very rarely lose a deal to price.

BUSINESS-TO-BUSINESS MARKETER SELLS, continued

As you know, a secret most marketers do NOT know is that affluent clients or customers are very willing to pay one person a significantly higher fee or price than another person, for what is essentially the same product. If you connect with them, in a way that speaks directly to them, and offer optimum service and privilege, price becomes virtually unimportant. From a business standpoint, this successfully selling at higher prices and margins than competitors permits delivery of a better client experience, spending more to acquire clients if necessary—a competitive advantage, faster growth—which put us on the *Inc.* 500 list, and still better profitability, so the business owner can get wealthier faster. Selling by price to price-conscious customers does exactly the opposite: restricts the quality of the client experience, creates competitive disadvantage, inhibits and slows growth, and forces the owner to accept a lower income. If I may, I'll tell you an instructive story about this . . . .

DAN: Absolutely.

CHRIS: A couple years ago, we financed a commercial property for a very well-known financial planner in our base city, Orlando. We structured his transaction so that he had more square footage than he occupied himself (different from his original thought), and he was able to lease out about 35% of the space to three tenants, who covered 100% of his mortgage payment. For him, free rent, an expense eliminated, and free equity, wealth creation. But we also structured his deal to include not only the building's purchase price and interior build-out, but even furniture, fixtures,

BUSINESS-TO-BUSINESS MARKETER SELLS, continued

office equipment, and closing costs, so everything was paid for by the tenants. His out-of-pocket was only 10% of the total project, something he would never have received anywhere else. In all probability, elsewhere, he would not have received the advice and planning leading to the wealth creation from tenants, but even if he had, he would have gotten the building financed with 20% or more down, then separately had to pay for improvements, and separately pay for or lease furniture and equipment. Now **here's what's revealing:** A couple years later, he joined one of my business mastermind and coaching groups, where I disclose many confidential aspects of my business. This made him aware of just how much we made on his transaction—and we made a large profit. Most would fear his discovery of that and expect him to be aggravated. But he was so pleased with what we did for him, he proceeded to tell me and the others in the group he only wished we had made double, because we more than deserved it. This is typical of how affluent clients think, with the right perspective; they expect professionals who work with them to be highly compensated and successful, and as long as they get what they want, and get great value, they are never disturbed by your fees, even if higher than competitors' or perceived as outrageous by others. There is a formula in this story.

DAN: Chris, thanks for your time. You obviously have a thorough understanding of marketing to your selected clientele that's going to keep your company on the fast-growth and high-profit tracks for years to come.

BUSINESS-TO-BUSINESS MARKETER SELLS, continued

CHRIS HURN is a multifaceted entrepreneur. In addition to captaining Mercantile Capital and its team of entrepreneurial bankers serving business owners nationwide, he also has a nationwide network of affiliated lenders and a coaching program for commercial mortgage brokers and lenders. And he is the Glazer-Kennedy Insider's Circle™ independent business advisor in the Orlando, Florida, area, conducting monthly local chapter meetings and coaching groups (information and complimentary guest passes for chapter meetings are available at the advisor directory, at www.DanKennedy.com). All business owners, especially those with brick-and-mortar businesses, can benefit from his special report, free to readers of this book at www.504Experts.com/DanKennedy MarketingToTheAffluentBookSpecial.

CHAPTER 8

The ¾-Full Glass

"In all likelihood, world inflation is over."

—THE MANAGING DIRECTOR OF THE INTERNATIONAL MONETARY FUND, IN 1959

A very important thing to understand about the psychology of affluence is optimism.

In the very same month late in 2007 that Gallup released and publicized a poll showing some 92% of the population purportedly in a state of angst and depression over the state of the economy, Rush Limbaugh sent factoids out to his newsletter subscribers saying, "Here are the facts about the actual robust economy, a continual surprise to mainstream reporters":

❖ **The GDP grew by 3.9% in the third quarter—<u>faster than expected</u>, according to the *New York Times*.**

❖ Productivity surged 4.9% in the third quarter, <u>the fastest pace in four years.</u>

❖ Since January, 1.25 million non-farm jobs have been created, 8.4 million <u>since the Bush tax cuts.</u>

❖ The GDP is up 18.5%, about $1.8 trillion since the start of the Bush presidency.

❖ The deficit has fallen to just 1.2% of GDP.

❖ Discretionary income for U.S. consumers grew to <u>a record high</u> going into the fourth quarter.

Limbaugh presented these facts in the context of a two-page "lesson in Economics 101," debunking the gloom and doom being spread at the time by Democratic presidential contenders and complicit media. You may or may not think he cherry-picked his facts of the moment, to fit his own consistent premise that the economy is strong, the gap between poor and rich is good news of expansive opportunity, and good times are ahead. But it really matters less what you think than what his gigantic audience, featuring mass-affluent and affluent business owners, entrepreneurs, and professionals, think. And they think Limbaugh is right. And they reward him by tuning in for hours every day to hear this optimistic message. No one spreading a pessimistic message can boast of an audience even a fraction of his. They also reward his advertisers, and his program has been a market maker for companies ranging from builders of pre-engineered commercial and industrial buildings to hardwood floors to computer software.

In September 2007, the American Affluence Research Center conducted its yearly fall survey of affluent and ultra-affluent consumers and investors. This was immediately after a very volatile August in the stock market, amid much negative noise about the subprime mortgage crisis, and a slowing, weak housing market. The media was a gloom-and-doom machine turned on High. Still, the survey respondents were "cautiously optimistic" in their outlook for the economy, and expressed a "positive outlook" about the stock market and their own personal incomes. The percentage expressing no plans for major expenditures in the next 12 months was neither up nor down from the previous five surveys. And about two-thirds of the wealthiest of the households reported plans for major expenditures in the coming 12 months, including automobiles, home remodels, and cruises.

This is but one illustration of the optimistic attitude of the affluent. The cynic might think it's easy for the affluent to be optimistic because they have so much money, but that ignores the fact that the majority of the affluent got to this point through their own initiative as entrepreneurs, business owners, and investors and, themselves, cite optimism as a cause rather than

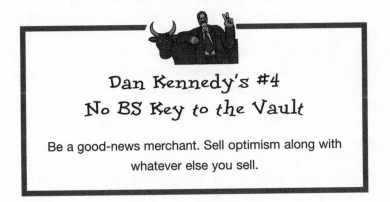

Dan Kennedy's #4
No BS Key to the Vault

Be a good-news merchant. Sell optimism along with whatever else you sell.

effect. *At their core*, they are optimists. And they tend to be most responsive to optimistic messages.

In my own survey of millionaire entrepreneurs, I found that the overwhelming majority ranked Ronald Reagan as the best President of our lifetimes and ranked John F. Kennedy as second best. The title of worst went to Jimmy Carter. If you carefully examine the speeches, addresses to the nation, interviews, and overriding themes of these three men and their presidencies, you can easily see Reagan and Kennedy as representatives of optimism, Carter as a representative of pessimism. Because of the time required for my words written here to get published in book form and then into your hands, much will have changed, but I wrote this the morning after the 2008 Iowa caucus, where the winners were Governor Mike Huckabee and Senator Barack Obama, who respectively whipped the entrenched, institutionalized, old guard candidates, such as John McCain and Hillary Clinton. It's difficult to define exactly what was being rejected and rebuked by these voters, but I do not believe it is coincidental that the victors had the most optimistic messages, admittedly light on specifics and heavy on inspiration. Having done a bit of consulting and advertising copywriting for presidential and senatorial campaigns and 527c organizations, I can tell you that fear and rage—that is, attack messages—work in short-term sprints, but that the marathons are consistently won with positive, hopeful messages. Think Ronald Reagan's shining city on the hill and morning in America, Bill Clinton's man from Hope. This need for expressed optimism is especially true when reaching out to the mass-affluent and affluent.

I have several clients in the investment real estate field, who have been largely unaffected by the troubles that began dominating the news from mid-2007: the mortgage meltdown, tightening of available credit, slow housing market, drops in values. Many of their competitors have seen their investor clients freeze new investing. Not my clients. Why? Because they quickly became passionate preachers of a positive message. Citing John D. Rockefeller's famous "buy when there is blood in the streets" advice, they have beaten the drum of now as the best time ever to find bargains and buy, buy, buy. A copy of one of those client's advertisements to this effect appears at end of this chapter (page 98). This is from Rob Minton, who's *Income for Life Program* for independent (and often beginner) investors is provided through more than 100 Realtors® nationwide, reaching over 25,000 investors.

Most affluent entrepreneurs are very familiar with Napoleon Hill, author of *Think and Grow Rich*, and his admonition that "in every adversity lies the seeds of equal or greater opportunity." This is a belief already in place that any marketer can link himself to when his industry, product, or service category or clientele are actually facing difficult times, or are being told they are by the media.

Optimists are naturally attracted to other optimists. If you seek to go where the money is, you will find yourself unwelcome if you lack and fail to express an attitude of optimism. I have long told my clients, "Whatever else you are a merchant of, be sure that you are also a merchant of good news."

"BUY WHEN THERE'S BLOOD IN THE STREET"

By Rob Minton, broker, author, and consultant

The statement above was made by John D. Rockefeller, the richest man in history. In fact, a study of the ten wealthiest people has uncovered one striking commonality.

This commonality is that they invested into assets when everyone else told them to sell. As markets spiraled downward, these wealthy individuals invested significant sums of money to acquire assets at discounted prices.

When the markets eventually rebounded, as they always do, their wealth escalated significantly.

Consider J. Paul Getty's purchase of the Hotel Pierre for $2.35 million in the midst of the Great Depression. When the economy rebounded, this hotel shot up in value to between $25 and $35 million.

Getty bought when there was "blood on the streets"—when everybody else was selling—and he profited enormously.

Right now, there is blood in the streets in our real estate market. Smart investors are using a unique investment strategy to acquire nice homes in nice areas at discounted prices. These nice homes are providing monthly income and locked-in future profits.

You can learn more about this unique investment strategy by requesting a free report from the real estate information center. Call 1-888-845-9670 and enter ID 246. Leave a message with your mailing address and the package will be shipped to you. Or visit www.QuitWorkSomeday.com.

WHAT THE WEALTHY AND SUCCESSFUL BELIEVE THAT THE POOR AND UNSUCCESSFUL DO NOT

If you roam the libraries and bookshelves in any ten affluent or ultra-affluent individuals' homes and offices, you will find at least seven well stocked with what I call the literature of the rich. Books like *Think and Grow Rich*, *The Power of Positive Thinking*, *The Magic of Thinking Big,* and other classic, perennial bestsellers of similar theme. If you visit the homes of any ten poor people, you will likely find none of these books in none of the homes. It is not coincidence. It is causative. The possession of such books reveals a very particular and specific mind set on the part of the affluent—that there is a profound and direct link between their thoughts, attitudes, and beliefs and their prosperity.

Consequently, the affluent of this belief are conscious, even forced, optimists. They deliberately resist their own pessimism or pessimism delivered to them by others. The poor, on the other hand, are extremely pessimistic and welcome delivered pessimism as proof that their lack of success is rooted in circumstances beyond their control. The rich explain the poor as "poor of mind, poor in purse." The next logical extension of this is that the rich tend away from skepticism, the poor tend to it. Pessimism and skepticism are close cousins. Because the rich strive not to permit themselves to be pessimistic, they automatically tend not to be skeptical.

So, whom would you rather be selling to—a skeptical and pessimistic person, or an accepting and optimistic person?

CHAPTER 9

Peer Deep into
Their Souls

*"I do not wish to be in any club that
would have me as a member."*

—GROUCHO MARX

The affluent are segregationists. Even those loudly
proclaiming their liberal or socialist politics and social
consciousness. Segregationists all.

In the old South, white people didn't want to drink water
from water fountains used by blacks. In the new *Richistan*, rich
people do not want to drink the same water or use the same
entrances or, God forbid, sleep on the same sheets as ordinary
folk. *Richistan* is the "place" described by Robert Frank in the fascinating book *Richistan: A Journey Through the American Wealth
Boom and the Lives of the New Rich,* a must-read for every marketer
to the affluent. Among other things, it gives insight to the tiered

and aspirational elitism of the mass-affluent, affluent, and ultra-affluent, each group emotionally validated by its purchased privileges that those one level lower are denied.

First of all, segregation has been the NATURAL order of things since cavemen. We form tribes. In elementary school, junior high school, high school, and college. At work, at the office, within our professional and trade associations. In our cities and neighborhoods. We form tribes. We form tribes more to exclude than include. We seek separation, differentiation, and disassociation from unlike as well as association with like.

In an episode of *Mad Men*, the outstanding AMC dramedy about the advertising agency business—and life—in the 1950s, a new woman moves into the suburban community, and she is, horror of horrors, a mother of a young child, divorced, without a husband. All the other women are married, of that tribe, and quickly close ranks to protect their husbands and themselves from the dangerous influence of this foreign, exotic creature. It reminded me of an episode of the old *Andy Griffith Show*, when a stranger comes to Mayberry, and everyone becomes convinced he's an international spy, just because he is a stranger. This speaks to the fear, paranoia, loathing, dislike, and disdain we have for the different even as we seek to feel different. The tribes we form try to reinforce our differences as superiority by excluding a majority of those we can label as inferior.

Assimilation has remained a theoretical goal but never realized. Each tribe voluntarily segregates. If this were not the case, there would be no BET or NAACP, there would be no gay pride parades or gay and lesbian magazines and websites, no Italian or German neighborhoods, no Chinatowns, no women's health clubs like Curves,® and, in economic examples, no private schools or colleges. No one would want such things. Everyone would want only to be fully and completely assimilated with everyone else. But this is not what you want or what I want. Nor is it what liberals want; if it were, their kids wouldn't be in private schools and there would be affordable public housing in zip code 90210. It is certainly not what affluent people want—they have worked very hard to arrive at the financial ability to segregate themselves.

As a political exercise in America, we keep trying to desegregate society in terms of race, ethnicity, gender, economic status; we have geographic redistribution schemes like forced school busing and wealth redistribution schemes engineered into tax code. Just about as fast as we democratize something, the people affected resegregate themselves. Hotels were once used only by the rich and by business travelers; they democratized prices, but then added concierge floors, then higher- and higher-priced hotels, even to the point of putting a Four Seasons inside the Mandalay Bay. When I started flying on business in the mid-1970s, I was the young oddball in first class. With very rare exception, it was all 50-year-old white guys in suits and ties, frequent business travelers—the riffraff could not afford sitting there, and the divider was firmly policed by the stewardesses who brought us drinks, food, and even *Playboy* magazines and on long flights sat and played cards with us. Today many flights have no first class, and those that do have seats dispensed at cheaper prices than 30 years ago (inflation adjusted) and often to people getting up there with frequent flier points. Air travel has been price democratized and desegregated, and even the crowd that used to go Greyhound® now flies the unfriendly skies. What happened? A giant boom for private aviation, featuring fractional jet ownership. You can't stop segregation. And you damn sure can't stop those with money from segregating themselves from everybody else.

What the Gates Really Are

A gated community is not really about protection from thundering hoards of criminals, as was a drawbridge and alligator-infested moat for the affluent tribe's early predecessors. You are, of course, at far more risk of home invasion, burglary, and other crimes living in an inner-city ghetto than in a suburban gated community. Today's gates are symbolic far more than functional. They are the grown-up version of the boys' tree house with rope ladder pulled up after only the chosen few in the club have climbed up. A symbol of exclusion. *We are in, you are not, nah, nah, nah.* The gates are symbolic of exceptional achievement, accomplishment, and status. Symbolic of the very existence of an elite tribe. Mostly, this is simple economic segregation. But as another example, consider the Florida city envisioned by Domino's

Dan Kennedy's #5 No BS Key to the Vault

Create the tribe your desired customers are eager to be a member of.

Pizza® founder Tom Monaghan, into which he has poured hundreds of millions of dollars, his intent to create a *Catholic*-gated community devoted to Catholic life. As a legal practicality, he can't ban heathens or Baptists or Jehovah's Witnesses; he can only design every brick, every cultural icon, every tribal activity to make them feel unwelcome. Gate at community's entrance or cross in its town square, symbols of tribalism.

As a marketer to the affluent, it is vital you fully understand tribalism in general, and the affluent's devotion to membership in smaller and smaller, seemingly more and more elite and therefore profoundly exclusionary tribes.

The affluent tribalism is simply an extreme variation of all tribalism. The most important thing to understand about it is its emotional driving forces, so that you fully incorporate those same forces into your marketing. Those forces include those common to all tribalism: acceptance, recognition, peer approval, like-mindedness, elitism. But **the overriding driving force of affluent tribalism is validation of superiority.** The affluent believe—whether through heritage or achievement—that they are inherently and profoundly superior to all others. The majority have arrived through accomplishment born of ingenuity and innovation, discipline and persistence, work ethic and related behavioral characteristics, as well as philosophy they see lacking in the masses, so they do not view their affluence as luck or gift but as product of and then as proof of their superior character. In short, their affluence is a special form of *moral* authority and superiority.

This is the belief system that gives affluent liberals and socialists their moral authority to dictate to others how they should live: Barbra Streisand telling people to dry their clothes on clotheslines rather than wasting energy on electric dryers, although it's doubtful she has James Brolin out on the Malibu beach with laundry basket and clothespins. Al Gore preaching energy conservation to save the earth from global warming while flitting about in gas-guzzling private jets between giant, energy-inefficient homes. Warren Buffett insisting "the rich" should pay more income tax while virtually all of his income is not subject to it, but instead taxed as capital gains. Nothing new here. Limousine liberals have been with us since first wealth. And, for the most part, they do not perceive themselves as disingenuous hypocrites. In their minds, they possess their special moral authority as superior beings.

This is the same belief system that gives affluent conservatives their moral authority to dictate to others how they should live: Limbaugh, of whom I'm a fan, but still, Limbaugh railing against drug offenders from his radio pulpit while indulging his own addiction to pain killers not just by doctor shopping, but allegedly by sending his housekeeper out to buy stolen drugs from back-alley dealers. This is the belief system that keeps the rich's reaction to the homeless fellow in the doorway "Get a job" rather than "There, but for the grace of God, go I." Affluent conservatives believe their affluence is result of superior initiative and discipline, certainly not luck of the draw.

If you are an affluent by accomplishment yourself, this may seem an unflattering glimpse in the mirror. Be that as it may, accurate, honest, realistic, and pragmatic assessment of the deep-seated beliefs of those you seek to sell to is valuable beyond price. Even the price of turning one's self-portrait to face the wall. We are what we are.

So, what do Superior Beings want? It's really quite simple. Recognition as Superior Beings. The sort of segregation that kings and queens have always had, that is *appropriate* for kings and queens. Special privileges. Fawning service. Products, services, and places inaccessible to anyone but kings and queens.

CHAPTER 10

The Affluent E-Factors

*"There is perhaps no feeling more acute
than being left out."*

—MARK PENN, IN HIS BOOK *MICROTRENDS*

E-Factors are the emotional drivers of buying behavior.
For years I have taught sales professionals and marketers
a generic list of E-Factors and done my level best to get
them to rely on that list, whether selling to the CEO in the boardroom or Mom 'n' Dad in the kitchen at home. The most common
mistake made by marketers is an egotistical belief that *their* customers are smarter, more rational, and more sophisticated than
others, thus not controlled by E-Factors. It's a costly egotism.
Everybody's buying behavior is driven by emotions, justified as
necessary, after the fact, with logic.

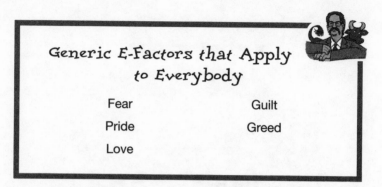

Generic E-Factors that Apply to Everybody

Fear	Guilt
Pride	Greed
Love	

In addition to the E-Factors affecting everybody, the affluent have a particular set of E-Factors to consider, some of which may surprise you:

❖ insecurity

❖ fear of being found fakers

❖ desperate desire not to commit a faux pas

❖ today, not passe

❖ feeding emotional emptiness

❖ giving selves gold stars

❖ after all, what's the point of being rich

The affluent are insecure in many ways. They certainly worry about going backward, about losing their money, status, or privilege. If you've never been rich, you have no frame of reference, but if you've been rich then poor, you know what you're missing! They are acutely aware of the aggravations, inconveniences, and financial difficulties endured daily by ordinary mortals that they have left behind—and lose a few winks every night worrying about waking up *back there* again.

More importantly, they are concerned with being *found out*. Affluents who have gotten there largely or totally on their own become keenly aware that everybody else thinks of them as profoundly smarter or more talented or privy to special information or otherwise superhuman. Many actually use this in the attainment of career or business success, making themselves into and being accepted as wizards. I've been in the wizard business myself for three decades and have wound up hanging out with an entire community of them. (We even have our own trade association! The Information Marketing Association, at www.info-marketing.org.) Yet we know wizardry is more illusion than reality. I often say if ordinary people realized how ordinary in capability most millionaires are, there'd be a lot more millionaires—what holds most back isn't lack of opportunity or lack of capability, but the illusory belief that millionaires possess some special abilities they do not. The affluent are also very sensitive to judgment by their own chosen tribe of other affluents and are worried about "using the wrong fork" one way or another, showing up in an out-of-fashion dress, not knowing what the others know and converse about during cocktails at the club. Think of the whole thing as a high school clique, and everyone in it as desperate for acceptance by the others and secretly feeling the others may be superior.

These anxieties actually spur a lot of productive behaviors and ironically contribute to the successful becoming more successful, the rich becoming richer. They may eat healthier and exercise more to look better as a path to status with peers. They may read more, read more eclectically, and stay more abreast of political and financial news, leading to more successful investing. They may contribute to charitable and civic organizations and activities as a means of self-validation and validation within the tribe. These anxieties can obviously be used in selling to them, and both for-profit and nonprofit marketers should pay heed.

Then there is the matter of emotional emptiness—the long-standing debate, and joking about, whether or not money can buy happiness. People without money like making themselves feel better about their situation by insisting that the rich are no happier and may be less happy than the nonrich. Having been poor and now relatively rich, I can assure you that money buys a lot of access to opportunities, experiences, comforts, and conveniences that can lead to happiness, but I don't think it directly and itself buys happiness. Other than Disney's® character Scrooge McDuck®, I don't know of anybody who gets joy from going into his vault and playing with his money like a child playing with toys. But I know quite a few affluent adults who buy some very expensive toys and enjoy playing with them very much. There is, however, an underlying level of disappointment in most affluents with the fact that their affluence isn't a true Easy Button™ that works without fail or a crown everyone recognizes and bows to. When I switched from driving old, bad, cheap, beater cars to my first shiny new Lincoln Continental, it was a supreme disappointment to discover that birds crapped on its hood with impunity, just as they had my bad cars. You'd think the birds would show some respect! And it is true that a lot of affluent consumers' purchasing is done as a means of showing themselves respect and giving themselves recognition for their hard work and accomplishment they don't feel they are getting from others.

Dan Kennedy's #6
No BS Key to the Vault

Make owning your product or being your client
signify something.

Being told, subtly, that "you deserve this (and most others don't)" and "owning this signifies accomplishment and status and commands respect" is extremely persuasive to the affluent.

Recognition Does Matter

Should you, for a moment, think the affluent are not motivated by this seeking of recognition, you should familiarize yourself with the fundraising modus operandi of the Republican and Democratic parties and candidates. Much of it revolves around motivating affluent individuals to be bundlers and bring together groups of maximum donors, thus raising $50,000.00, $100,000.00, or more in clumps, for which the bundler is rewarded with invitations to special events like cocktail receptions at the Vice President's home or dinners with a Congressman seated at every table of eight, photos with the politicians, little trinkets like presidential seal cufflinks and suitable-for-framing parchment certificates. I have seen it as a donor myself and used it to help political candidates as an advisor. It is every bit as pin and medal driven as is a direct-selling organization like Mary Kay® or Amway,® except money is being raised rather than made, and it is millionaires and multimillionaires vying for the emerald or ruby or diamond pin, rather than cosmetic, vitamin, and soap sales agents.

The mass-affluent also have their own special E-Factors:

- ❖ the aspirational acquisition

- ❖ I own therefore I am

- ❖ knowing the secret handshake and having those who know it know you know it

This is all about being part of the clique. It once was all about having stepped up. Having visibly arrived. In the post-World War II era, when the suburbs were becoming both a place and a way of life, it was called "keeping up with the Joneses." Auto, TV, home improvement, and similar industries—as well as credit companies—benefited by this force of nature; if one driveway on the street suddenly provided home to a new station wagon, a fleet of station wagons was sure to follow. But today, there is a more complex collection of emotional drivers behind the purchases of the mass-affluent. There is some of the "Look, we've arrived" going on, but a lot of purchases are made as a forward statement of "where we're going." I call these *aspirational acquisitions*. The woman with a full-time career and two kids who is too exhausted to cook anything you can't microwave in its own dish still buys a $75,000.00 custom kitchen with a cooking island and state-of-the-art equipment, as she aspires to be more Martha than Rachael, and intends to devote more time to the art of cooking very soon. If you carefully tour the typical mass-affluent's home, you'll find ownership of all sorts of things bought because his peers have them, other things bought with strong intention of investing time and energy in them sometime soon—from nearly empty home wine cellars to rarely used home gyms and saunas.

The affluent seem to mature in their attitudes about owning things, and the longer they are affluent and the more affluent they are, the more they choose and buy luxury goods and services for practical and functional reasons regardless of symbolic statement made. But for the mass-affluent, the things they buy and own and their self-images are tightly linked. "I own, therefore I am" is a powerful driving force. *If the most popular and perceived-as-sophisticated mom in the neighborhood wears x, drives x, enrolls her child in x, and I do the same, I am as sophisticated as she.* Ownership equals being.

You can profit significantly by giving serious thought to how you may present your products, services, and business in sync with these E-Factors.

BOOK TWO

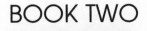

What Are They Spending
Their Money On?

CHAPTER 11

"They" Are Trying to Figure It Out

"If anthropology had devoted a branch to the study of modern shoppers in situ, a fancy Latin way of saying shoppers out shopping, interacting with retail environments, including but not limited to every rack, shelf, counter and display, every sign, banner, brochure . . . entrances and exits, windows and walls, the elevators and escalators and stairs and ramps . . . in short, every nook and cranny—that would be the start of the science of shopping. But anthropology didn't pay attention to those details."

—PACO UNDERHILL, AUTHOR OF *WHY WE BUY: THE SCIENCE OF SHOPPING*

I f you want proof of the significance of the mass-affluent explosion, you need look no further than the biggest retail monster loose on the planet who, so far, has prospered without these customers' love and affection. Wal-Mart® has built its empire on grinding down suppliers' margins, favoring goods manufactured overseas at dirt-cheap costs, and mastering superefficient distribution so as to bring a wide variety of goods into a plain, decidedly unstylish store environment where they can be sold at everyday lowest prices to customers who care a lot about cheapest prices. The store's only lure has been low prices, and it has naturally attracted nonaffluent customers.

Friend of the low-wage workers (except, arguably, its own), big blue-collar family, and workin' folk, and enemy of the nearby small-shop owner, Wal-Mart® has dominated.

This company is run by very smart people. These smart people have seen the writing on the wall, and what is written there is a growing, pressing need to somehow attract a fast-growing population of customers far more valuable per capita than those they have, a customer they ignored for decades. In the past few years, Wal-Mart® has gone to work on what it privately calls its "mass-affluent problem" with fervor. The owners have invested and are investing in a variety of experiments, including a yet unsuccessful addition of better-quality, celebrity-designer apparel, an introduction of organic foods and produce and pricey wines into its super-stores, even the building and opening of different prototype stores designed from ground up with different merchandise to better appeal to the mass-affluent. The most productive experimentation has, maybe ironically for this brick-and-mortar giant, been online. The Sam's Club® holiday gift catalog and website have mimicked Neiman Marcus® and offered $30,000.00 Jimmy Buffett concert packages and trips to the NFL Pro Bowl in Hawaii, even a New Zealand wine country trip at $48,000.00, as well as plasma and HD TVs from $2,700.00 to $3,300.00, gift baskets with Godiva® chocolates, the Dyson® high-tech vacuum cleaner at $500.00, an $8,998.00 Hummer® golf cart, and real diamond jewelry from $567.00 earrings to $9,000.00 tennis bracelets to a one-of-a-kind $263,000.00 necklace. This is Sam's Club, home of five-gallon tubs of peanut butter and three sweatshirts for $5.99! For the 2007 Christmas shopping season, Wal-Mart® abandoned its smiley face character and "low prices every day" for new, classier TV spots and the "Save money. Live better/"™ slogan, and emphasized picking out and ordering high-end home electronics and other products at its website, for pickup at the local store.

Whether Wal-Mart® can navigate these waters or not remains to be seen. It's not easy for such a huge ship to rediscover agility, nor for such a successfully branded company known to all for one thing to create a second identity. It is the fact that it is pouring financial resources, time, energy, effort, and newly recruited talent into the attempt that must be listened to. The message is loud and clear.

Wal-Mart® far from alone. At the time I was doing most of the work for this book, Sears® took a 13% stake in Restoration Hardware® and was contemplating outright acquisition, as a connection to more affluent consumers. It previously acquired the Lands' End® clothing company for the same reason. Sears® effectiveness at overtures to the affluent has been, to date, unimpressive. But that's not the point. The fact that the company feels compelled to try is.

For a variety of reasons, Martha Stewart is shifting her attention and allegiance from K-Mart® to Macy's® One reason is to go where the mass-affluent are. When Donald Trump put his brand name on steaks, they weren't sold in grocery stores but in the Sharper Image® catalog and on QVC. QVC is Macy's® HSN is K-Mart® For the ad campaigns that ran in late 2007 and into 2008, Dunkin' Donuts® dumped its blue-collar appeal with the John Goodmanesque workin' man voice in favor of popular food celebrity Rachael Ray, in my mind an improbable choice evidencing desperate desire for a mass-affluent customer.

I could fill this book with comparable examples from every field: historically low-end merchants, service providers, and manufacturers waking up to the smell of Starbucks® coffee instead of Denny's® and envying the merchants, service providers, and manufacturers that sell successfully to the no-price-limit crowd. Recognizing it as *the* growing crowd.

Of course, most big, dumb companies try to effect this kind of radical change by buying rather than building businesses. They don't really know how to build. They think they can manage something already built. Sometimes they're right about that, sometimes not. But if you watch or start watching who's buying whom these days, one of the key trends you'll see is big companies trying to buy a quick pass to the affluent market.

The fact that they are having these meetings, trying these experiments, making these acquisitions, frantically fumbling for the door handle in the dark, to get to the mass-affluent and affluent customers they've largely ignored until now speaks volumes. It tells you that the starter has fired the gun and the race is on, and it is no longer just a few runners competing in some obscure mountain region—it's more like the Boston or New York Marathon, with thousands elbowing each other right down main streets.

If you give them all too big of a head start, you'll never catch up. If you sit on the sidelines as a spectator, to those who compete and win will go all the spoils.

CHAPTER 12

What Are You a Merchant Of?

"To be an Imagineer, it's important to keep reality at arm's length."

—CHRISTIAN HOPE, CONCEPT DESIGN DIRECTOR, QUOTED IN *THE IMAGINEERING WAY* ABOUT DISNEY'S IMAGINEERS

There was a time when coffee was coffee. Ice cream was ice cream. A phone was a phone. Even a pair of shoes was, well, just a pair of shoes.

At one level, at the lowest price and profit level, there are still merchants stuck in this time warp, continuing to conduct business as if people still bought products.

Today, that cup of coffee comes with more options than a Lexus.® Would you care to add . . . vanilla or caramel syrup? A double shot? Foam? Cinnamon sprinkles? Thus, the $5.00 price for the $.50 cup of coffee. But even that is only half the story. Ordinary products morphing into complex arrays of choices, options, add-ons, brands, and luxury brands is one way prices have been inflated and margins inflated even more. The profit margin of the double shot of extra something or other far exceeds the profit margin of the cup of coffee itself. The designer-name bag selling for $11,000.00 does not cost 100 times more to make than the similar-appearing bag sold at Target® for $110.00. This is a path to profit—and to greater acceptance by affluent consumers. But, as I said, it is only half the story.

Starbucks® does not define itself as a coffee shop or even more elegantly as a coffeehouse. The company describes itself as being in the "third-place business"—home, office, Starbucks® in between. It is not a merchant just of jazzed-up coffee drinks. It is a merchant of place, of feelings, of status, and maybe most of all, of experience. Its inspirations are more Disney® than Denny's® One of the many students of the Starbucks® phenomenon, Ken Herbst, assistant professor of marketing at Wake Forest University's Babcock Graduate School of Management, makes the obvious point: "If you walked up to someone about to buy a pound of coffee at the grocery store (at about $4.00 a pound) and tried selling them just a cup for $5.00, they would tell you that is too expensive. But if you are at the coffeehouse, you are going to pay for the experience."

This means that price is not tied to product. As soon as you disconnect those two things in your own mind about your own products and services, you'll be liberated to make a great deal more money and to have much greater success appealing to affluent customers or clients. To be redundant for emphasis, most business owners are severely handicapped by keeping price and product linked in their own minds. What I call the *Price-Product Link* is as restrictive and antiquated as the *Work-Money Link* that I take apart in my book *No B.S. Wealth Attraction for Entrepreneurs*.

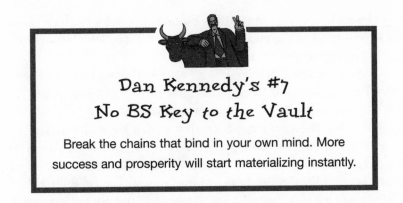

Dan Kennedy's #7
No BS Key to the Vault

Break the chains that bind in your own mind. More
success and prosperity will start materializing instantly.

These links are imaginary. They exist only in your mind, not in
the marketplace, yet they are ties that bind as if real, physical,
1,000-pound chains.

The Price-Product Link becomes ingrained religious belief in
most business owners, beginning with textbook formulas for setting price. Retailers are taught the doctrine of keystone pricing,
meaning double their own cost. If you buy it for $1.00, it should
be priced at $2.00, then, at times, discounted from there. In my
line of work, direct marketing—what was once called mail
order—we're also taught formulaic markup as doctrine,
although ours is eight times rather than two times. In businesses
where raw materials are converted to finished products, like
printing, there is a plethora of price-calculating software to do
the thinking for you, using standardized markup formulas. In
every case, the price is chained to the product. There is the fun-
dament that a particular product is worth only a certain multiple
of its cost and not a penny more, period, end of story.
Unfortunately, this widely and deeply held belief is completely
and utterly stupid.

The two biggest chain cutters that de-link price from product are who is buying the product and the context in which the product is presented, priced, and delivered.

The *who* is what this book is all about. The simple act of selling whatever you sell to more affluent consumers may allow its price to rise, with no other modifications.

Price for the same product also varies by context. This is easy to see with commodity items like food, even though many restaurant owners still never grasp it. When is a third pound of peanuts not a third pound of peanuts? In a jar, on the shelf, that's all they are, unless dusted with Starbucks® mocha latte powder and packaged in a fancy tin. But when served hot, from a vendor's cart in the park, scooped into the bag and sprinkled with cinnamon by a handlebar-mustached man in red-and-white striped jacket and straw hat, with calliope music playing from the CD player in the cart, they are not peanuts at all. They are an experience that evokes emotional feelings. Even as you read my words, your mind may have flashed to Mary Poppins in the park or a trip to the circus as a child. While it is not so easy for most to transfer this idea to other businesses, it does, in fact, transfer to any business. Context alters or liberates price. Move the exact same product from one context to another and its price can easily be altered.

What It Is Needn't Determine What It Is

A visit to the dentist can be just a visit to the dentist. Cleaning and checkup, a routine experience and a routine price. Or it can mean being picked up at your home by the dental office's gleaming white limousine, brought to the elegantly appointed office with grand piano playing itself in the lobby, neatly uniformed staff rising to greet you at the door and escort you to a comfortable chair, get you a fresh-brewed latte, offer you a choice of magazines (just like what stewardesses used to do for first-class passengers on airlines a decade ago) . . . then, only a few minutes later, escort you to the spa room for your complimentary manicure and hand massage . . . then to the dental hygienist for your regular cleaning, plus a whitening treatment, while you relax in a dental chair with a full-body massage pad and gentle heat and listen to your favorite music, *not* piped-in elevator music or, worse, the radio . . . then back to the spa for some anti-aging skin treatments . . . and back to the limo, carrying a complimentary gift basket of little soaps and skin lotions along with your tote bag containing your next three months' supply of specially formulated toothpaste, whitener, and breath freshener. The charges for the cleaning, whitening treatment and products are all evened out during the year as a monthly membership fee automatically charged to your credit card, so there is no plebian act of standing at the front desk at the end of your visit, reviewing charges and writing out a check nor any such bill arriving in the mail.

We can give just about anything a comparable makeover. A meeting with the financial advisor or tax accountant, a visit to the sporting goods store, a stay at a hotel, even a true business-to-business experience, like buying and receiving printing from the printer or industrial parts from a manufacturer. Somewhere in the process there is opportunity to alter the experience and the way the buyer feels about it. It begins with determining the feelings you want to create for the buyer: security and peace of mind. Being pampered like a queen or king. Nostalgia. Whatever. It is this that unties price from the anchor of product and allows it to float upward like a helium-filled balloon on a slightly breezy day.

Different buyers want different experiences and the feelings they invoke in different circumstances.

Michael Silverstein, author of *Trading Up: Why Consumers Want New Luxury Goods—and How Companies Create Them*, says that affluent consumers want goods, services, and experiences that make them feel special. True enough, as far as it goes. But even "special" is subjective and multifaceted.

I choose to fly private rather than commercial, at substantial expense, with practical rationalization tied to the extremely high value of my time and the urgency with which I need to get where I'm going or to get home and get to work. But, as confession, it is at least as much about being and feeling special. For one person using private aviation, that might mean status lorded over others. That's not it for me. For some, it might be about the pampering. Not for me. For me it is—after 20 years of suffering the ever-worsening indignities, inconveniences, and stresses of ordinary air travel—about escape from the way ordinary folk must travel, to a better experience. The feeling to me is similar to the one I get going downstairs to my basement office and being at my chosen work in minutes, in comfortable clothes, knowing that outside, thousands of ordinary people are slogging through snow, waiting for cars to warm, enduring bumper-to-bumper traffic in hourlong commutes. In short, it is about a feeling of superiority.

Yet I get my hair cut at a walk-in, no-appointment hair cutting place. There's nothing about it that makes me feel special. To the contrary. I prize the in-and-out speed and simplicity more than anything else. But someone else my very same age and income might profoundly prefer a trip to a very upscale men's salon with mahogany paneling, plasma TVs playing sporting events, and relative quiet that takes four times as long and costs ten times the price. Not because the haircut is any different. Because the feeling he gets from the experience is meaningful and therefore valuable to him.

Affluent consumers do not simply choose the priciest option of everything in every category. Different affluent consumers value different experiences differently. It's up to you, the marketer, to find the group of affluent consumers you can match up with an experience you design and can deliver, that disconnects price from product.

CHAPTER 13

Value in the Eye of the Beholder

In a 60 Minutes *story broadcast in 1973, an astonished Morley Safer was told that a Saudi prince and his three bodyguards were traveling to Syria aboard the Orient Express "to shoot swans with a chromium-plated submachine gun."*

I n response to an article of mine in my No B.S. Marketing *to the Affluent Letter,* a Glazer-Kennedy Insider's Circle™ Member sent me this note:

> I have to confess, we **worry** a lot at our company about pricing. So I was **astonished** to find out about Williams-Sonoma's prices: for Halloween Caramel Apples . . . mini-apples, no nuts, set of four, "only" (!) $29.50 plus $7.50 shipping and handling. Or a larger single apple, with or without nuts, $19.50. For ONE apple! Plus $6.50 s/h. Or your own personalized Halloween cookies, 3 cookies, $24.00. You could combine the apple and cookies at $43.50. For a discount on shipping, buy $150.00 worth. Though **I am appalled,** it appears that there is a large enough set of people for and to whom these things appeal, as

> Williams-Sonoma does a very good business. Reaffirms the adage that "you are not your customer," or perhaps more accurately, "you are not *necessarily* your customer."

That you are not your customer is an astute observation and brings me impetus for a very important discussion.

First, note that Williams-Sonoma® is a cataloger focusing on the mass-affluent, __not__ ultra- or super-affluent. Its products are *routinely* purchased by hundreds of thousands of households with annual income in the $100,000.00 neighborhood. The $19.00 apples are NOT being nibbled only by a few eccentric multimillionaires who also clean their eyeglasses with hundred-dollar bills. It is VITAL that, through this book, from catalogs like Williams-Sonoma's, and as many other sources as possible, you get, accept, embrace, fully internalize that the Continually Emerging and Expanding Mass-Affluent Class of Consumers in America is spending like crazy on premium-priced luxury goods and services, buying all manner of things that will shock you. (I recently reserved a suite at a Disney® hotel—where *families* go on vacation—at $1,800.00 a night, and it was the last of two remaining rooms in the entire hotel in January.)

Second, of all possible reactions to discoveries like these, being appalled is *least* appropriate. Let's consider the reasons somebody might be appalled (my subscriber didn't enunciate his). One would be the "children are starving somewhere" idea, that if people didn't pay $19.00 for caramel apples, somehow starving urchins somewhere would be fed and cared for. Gee, if it really were that simple to solve poverty and world hunger, I'd give up my $19.00 apples and my luxury SUV and my $800.00 cowboy boots tomorrow. But that's just not how money really moves around, how wealth or poverty is caused or affected, and I'd refer anybody wrestling with that idea to my *No B.S. Wealth Attraction* book. Until you come to grips with the truth about prosperity NEVER being a zero-sum game, where one person's wealth or, by your judgment, waste deprives someone else, you are hamstrung, handcuffed, hog-tied mentally, emotionally, and practically in your own attraction of wealth. The supply of wealth to which all have ready access based exclusively on their own chosen behaviors is not a debit-credit system at all. This is contrary to what 95% believe to be true about money, but it is not coincidental that 95% have comparatively little while 5% have most of it.

Or somebody might be appalled at the wretched excess, the foolish spending. I've been broke; I have a gut-level, visceral reaction to what I judge as waste. But that imposes your value judgments or mine on others. A devout atheist opposed to all religion might very well view your $20.00 put into the church collection plate enroute to the Vatican with just as jaundiced an opinion as your critical view of his purchase and enjoyment of a $20.00 apple. One man's wretched excess is another's highest and best value.

There are better (more profitable) reactions than being appalled. One is to use this information as fodder for your own continuing inner thoughts, dialog, and (probably, hopefully) reorientation of your understanding of price, value, consumer behavior. Another is to be inspired and motivated, to re-examine your beliefs about your own customers' or clients' attitudes, spending, interests, passions, and to search for opportunities to (1) design and offer premium-priced goods and services (options or levels) to your present clientele and/or (2) seek out a clientele that places price very low on its list of Buying Decision Factors. (As example of that, imagine how many restaurant owners, grocers, gift shop owners, and so on will read this chapter but will never bother to go to www.SRDS.com, find the Williams-Sonoma mailing lists, contact the list manager, and rent the best Williams-Sonoma buyers they can in their area, to promote their businesses to! Refer to Chapter 31, "We Know Where They Live.")

Back to **understanding value**: no, a $19.00 apple a day won't keep doctors at bay any better than a $1.00 apple, at least as a result of its nutritional properties. (It might, based on its effect on the consumer's positive attitude. But that's not my principal argument here.) <u>The value that motivates the Williams-Sonoma buyer to pay $19.00 for the apple is not in the apple at all.</u> It may be in the impact of it given as gift or served at a party. It may be in the feelings of success or prosperity or of rewarding oneself with indulgence that come with making the purchase (even before ever taking a bite of the apple). It may be a sense of superiority, of buying or serving the best or something unique and unusual. Bragging rights: it's a trophy apple, because, after all, we can't really frame and hang our bankbooks on the wall for all visitors to see, so instead we opt for other visual representations of our achievement and success: trophy car, trophy house, trophy watch, trophy wife, trophy apple. It may be the time saved and convenience of ordering from the catalog rather than schlepping off to a gourmet store across town. It may be all those things. It is certainly, mostly emotional and psychological, not practical. Thus, the $19.00 apple may very well contribute to the person's emotional well-being in ways a grocery-store apple cannot.

When I was young and poor and insecure, just starting in business and routinely asking older, more successful people to give me money, I bought and drove fancy Lincoln Continental Town Cars. And I always flew first class—at the time the only young kid up front, surrounded by 50-year-old executives. I didn't drive the car or fly first class for its impact on others; I did so for its impact on me, for its programming of my own psyche. Neither the value of the car nor that of the first-class tickets for me had anything to do with getting from place to place. The value to me was purchased confidence and feelings of parity and belonging, of having arrived where I was actually trying to get. I never paid $19.00 for an apple, but I did always order Chivas Regal.®

Personally, I don't wear a watch at all. Years back, I owned and wore a Rolex® and a Tag Heuer,® but such things no longer interest me. But I pass no judgment on the fellow who wears one or ten and proudly flexes his cuffs at every chance in order to display them. I also understand that the different motivations different people have at different times of their lives for paying $5,000.00 or $50,000.00 for a wristwatch have nothing whatsoever to do with their need to know precisely what time it is. For that, of course, a $50.00 Timex® will do just fine.

The most successful marketers learn <u>not</u> to question how the public or their customers get value—only to strive to find out about it, recognize it, and capitalize on it. To be of service means offering and delivering what customers value; that's the role of the businessperson. Should you feel a need, instead, to impose your value criteria on others, you ought to exit business and enter politics or ministry.

CHAPTER 14

Stop Selling Products
and Services

"Any fool can make soap. It takes a genius to sell soap."

—MR. GAMBLE OF PROCTOR & GAMBLE

A cloth bag is not worth $4,000.00 without the Gucci®
logo, or some other designer's logo.

You may feel that it is not worth $4,000.00 with the
logo either. But that reveals you remain hung up on what a product is, instead of what it symbolizes and represents, what status
it confers on its owner, what emotional reactions it evokes, how
it feels to purchase and own it, how others important to its owner
feel about it.

Few things are intrinsically worth their price. We have all
accepted that a diamond engagement ring priced at least equal to
two months' salary is a requirement. But the diamond may be far,

far, far more artificially inflated from its actual cost of materials than that Gucci® cloth bag. Diamonds are, in essence, polished dirt.

A Great Ad Campaign Can Last Forever

While most businesspeople think of De Beers's dominance in the diamond industry as a result of controlling supply, truth is, it is more the result of creating and manipulating demand, thanks to brilliant advertising delivering a consistent theme for half a century.

Finding rocks is easy. Selling rocks, tough. In the last 50 years, only two markets have opened up for stones. You wear them on your fingers when in love; you put them over the head of a loved one after death. The second was mastered by the Rock of Ages Corporation. The first by De Beers and its holding company, a near monopoly. The product itself—diamonds—was a loser. If you apply ordinary supply and demand, every diamond dug diminishes the value of those already dug because, in fact, diamonds *are* forever. Further, they are plentiful. De Beers recognized the problem with its mundane commodity, so it took the radical move of ignoring inherent value altogether. Instead the company made the product ritualistic and metaphoric, its purchase mandatory, without practical purpose. This required the use of advertising to create demand where there was none, and no reason for any. This defies, of course, one of the oldest, most tired business axioms: find a *need* and fill it.

Before the first ad ever appeared, some of the most extensive market research in advertising history was conducted, including direct questioning of thousands of men and women. The researchers determined that women had to be convinced that the diamond was *the* ritualized representation of love, commitment, and marriage. For women, the "diamond is forever" positioning began in advertising in 1914 and has continued unchanged to this day. And, to solve the forever problem, De Beers created the 10th anniversary ring, 25th anniversary ring, and similar products.

The researchers also determined that men had to be helped past confusion about how to buy this polished rock. For men, the industry's voodoo about carat weight, color, clarity, and so forth was created to provide logic where there was none. Men wanted to know what it was worth. Since it was arguably worth nothing, a logic had to be invented to assign worth to it. But in the cleverest of all gambits, a simpler shortcut for buying decisions was also created, stating the price in the frame of the buyer's own wages: "How can you make two months' salary last forever?" Today, the two-months'-salary-rule is widely accepted by the public.

In truth, what De Beers did for diamonds, anyone can do for anything.

You're aware there are wines that sell for hundreds of dollars per bottle. But there is a Samuel Adams *beer* that sells for $140.00 per bottle. How can beer be worth such a price? You may answer: It can't. Or answer: Why not?

To make a giant income marketing to the affluent, you must erase your own deeply ingrained insistence at connecting price to worth and worth to function.

A business associate told me how her neighbors paid a local architect $67,000.00 to draw up plans for a new house to be built on their beachfront lot. She found an architect to do what she judged to be identical work—if not better—for her new house to be built on her beachfront lot, paying just $7,000.00. And she questioned her neighbors' sanity at failing to shop around, at paying such an outrageously inflated fee. She was proud of her bargain. But, contrary to protestations of the psychiatric community, there is abundant evidence that, in our society, insanity is subjective. My kudos go to the architect commanding his $67,000.00 fee. In all probability, he secured it for things other than a tube of blueprints. My associate may very well be correct in judging her $7,000.00 blueprints just as good as the ones delivered for $67,000.00. But her $7,000.00 ones didn't come with the pride, status validation, bragging rights, and other emotional benefits her neighbors derived from searching out and hiring the biggest name, purportedly the most sought-after architect in the tri-state area, an architect, in fact, who had done the plans for a famous celebrity's new beach house and who had three homes he'd designed featured in *Town & Country*.

On closer examination, this little story reveals even more. It shows two people's very different values, and why what I call

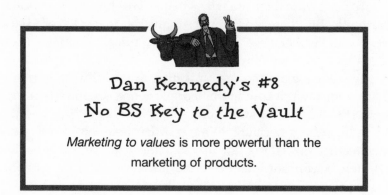

Dan Kennedy's #8
No BS Key to the Vault

Marketing to values is more powerful than the marketing of products.

marketing to values is so much more important and powerful than is the marketing of products. My business associate is a woman who, her whole life, has competed with men, has made herself successful in a field difficult for women, has fought being taken for granted as a blonde beauty, and prides herself on her mental toughness, shrewdness, and won't-take-no-for-an-answer-ism. One of her highest and most important personal values is that "nobody pulls the wool over my eyes." Her neighbor is the second, younger wife of a wealthy doctor from a wealthy family— but she came from a poor family, grew up on the wrong side of the tracks, and, in her first marriage, lived a blue-collar life. Her beauty got her the trophy wife position, but she found herself thought of and gossiped about as a classless bimbo rather than accepted into the rich wives' sorority. She has been a relentless social climber ever since, by donating to charities, sponsoring charity balls, patronizing *the* hairstylist, *the* cosmetic surgeon, *the* personal trainer, and being seen in the most current designer fashions, in an orchestrated effort to force her husband's peers' wives to accept her into their circle. One of her most treasured values is their acceptance or their envy. In reality, neither her payment of $67,000.00 to her architect nor my friend's payment of her negotiated $7,000.00 to her architect had much to do with the comparative intrinsic or actual value of the work reflected in the two sets of blueprints.

Another way to look at this, as a marketer, is a choice between selling things with ham-handed, brute force, typically against resistance, or selling aspirations and emotional fulfillments with finesse, typically with little resistance. Which seems like it might be more pleasurable? More profitable?

YOUR OWN FRESH CATCH—WITHOUT THE SMELL, SALT WATER, OR WORK

For $2,995.00, you can buy all rights to all the lobsters caught in a single designated trap off the rocky Maine coast—about 40 a season—pulled from the trap for you and shipped to anybody, anywhere you like by John and Brendan Ready of Ready Seafood. But the lobster's just the commodity. You can go to www.CatchAPieceOfMaine.com and meet your lobstermen, read their biographies and blogs, see pictures of their boats, and vicariously live the life of the man of the sea—as one writes in his blog: "Where else can you see majestic whales, jumping bluefin tuna, and seals when you go to work?" You can even track your catches on the internet.

Industry insiders are, of course, skeptical, expressing doubt that anybody'll spend $75.00 a lobster, wondering who would want to do this. A bank executive forked over his $2,995.00 for his trap, so he can have his lobsters from his trap sent to clients and potential clients—and have a great cocktail party story to tell about the lobsterman working his trap for him. The owner of an outdoor adventure company in Florida bought a trap after visiting Portland on vacation and going out on a lobster boat; he likes staying connected to the experience. The brothers have a total of 400 traps to sell, 50 from each of 8 lobstermen. If accomplished, they'll enjoy a total gross revenue of $1–2 million! They have already quickly sold 30 traps, then got an article about them published in *USA Today*, which undoubtedly has moved them closer to their goal.

CHAPTER 15

Products and Services for the
Affluent Go Mainstream
Mass-Affluent

"All animals are equal, but some are more equal than others."
—FROM *ANIMAL FARM* BY GEORGE ORWELL

For a number of years, a very pricey, personal matchmaking service called Valenti, aimed at affluent men who might hire professionals to find them their perfect mates, ran full-page advertisements in only a few very upscale magazines. Matchmaking as a profession has historically served only the most affluent of clientele, quietly and discreetly. Today, you will see the Valenti full-page and even two-page advertisements in dozens and dozens of magazines, notably including ones not targeted only to the ultra-affluent or even the affluent. You'll find the ads in, for example, the *DuPont Registry*, a magazine for buyers and collectors of very expensive classic cars, but you'll also find them in *Entrepreneur* magazine, read by white collars and blue collars, small-business owners, mass-affluent job holders who aspire to start or buy their own businesses. (If curious about Valenti, go to www.Valenti.com.)

For several years, I took note of a full-page ad for a $14,615.00 home exercise device called the ROM (Range of Motion), which appeared only in a handful of magazines read by affluent men. After all, $14,615.00 ain't your late-night infomercial's ab chair! Today, that very same full-page ad appears in dozens and dozens and dozens of different magazines ranging far afield from just ultra-affluent or affluent readership. Personally, I know of one of my millionaire clients who owns one. But I also know of a $75,000.00-a-year midlevel executive who saw the ad in a mainstream sports magazine, ordered the free DVD, and then spent 20% of his entire year's gross income buying one. (If curious, visit www.FastExercise.com.)

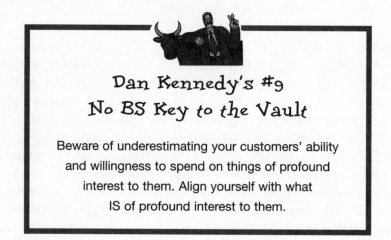

Dan Kennedy's #9 No BS Key to the Vault

Beware of underestimating your customers' ability and willingness to spend on things of profound interest to them. Align yourself with what IS of profound interest to them.

These are just two of hundreds of examples of pricey products and services that have recently migrated from small, elite markets to the mainstream, as evidenced by the widening range and diversity of advertising media being used. Their success in doing so suggests a number of things. First and foremost, that most marketers grossly underestimate their clientele's willingness and ability to spend on things of profound interest to them, and then to underprice their own goods and services based on this misunderstanding. Second, that the number of affluent buyers per capita has increased and is increasing within the readership of a large number and wide diversity of publications. For marketers to the affluent, this is a mandate to test media outside the obvious, even media that may have proved unproductive if tested three to five years ago. Third, that there is an exciting convergence of mass-affluent and affluent customers, growth of those customers, increase in their discretionary income and spending power, and our ability to reach them.

How Dare the Uncouth Heathens Invade Our Citadels

This mainstreaming of luxury brands, goods, services, and status symbols has created some dissatisfaction among the ultra-affluent, which presents yet another new area of opportunity for marketers. The more luxury brands are democratized, the less psychological satisfaction the rich get from owning them. There are 379 Louis Vuitton® stores and 227 Gucci® stores these days, so possession of a Vuitton® or Gucci® bag is not nearly so special as it was only a handful of years ago. In fact, a mind-blowing 94%

of Japanese women in their 20s own a Vuitton® item, according to *Fortune* magazine. In case you're slow with math, that means only 6% of all Japanese women do *not* own a Vuitton® item. As columnist George Will observed in one of his newspaper columns, "When a yacht manufacturer advertises a $20-million craft—in a *newspaper*, for Pete's sake; *The Financial Times*, but still—cachet is a casualty!"

As the luxury that once was theirs alone becomes mass owned, the ultra-rich seek new differential or positional goods that only they can afford. As Adam Smith wrote in *The Wealth of Nations*, for most rich people, "the chief enjoyment of riches consists in the parade of riches . . . when they appear to possess those decisive marks of opulence which nobody can possess but themselves." Or, as John F. Kennedy reportedly said to Sinatra: "There is little point in having sex with a woman any man can bed. Even less point in being seen with her."

This offers up fresh opportunity to marketers of all sorts of products and services to create and offer even higher-priced, more elite goods. The way many companies who've democratized their brands are handling this is with limited edition versions of just about everything. Hennessy® produced and sold a limited edition cognac(!)—only 100 bottles, at $200,000.00 per bottle. Another approach is the platinum level, expressed one way or another, to which only the most elite customers gain access. As American Express abandoned all pretense of exclusivity for its once-prized green card and even took steps down with its plum card, it also strengthened the cachet of its platinum and black cards, now carrying on very public mainstream advertising for green and plum and, invisible to the masses, carefully targeted solicitations for platinum and black.

There are great opportunities for nonluxury marketers to move up and for luxury marketers to move down, as luxury mainstreams to the middle. Every marketer has to consider levels, tiers, or differential deliverables so these opportunities can be fully exploited.

GIVING THE CHAUFFEUR THE DAY OFF

The Phantom sedan by Rolls-Royce is 19 feet long, sells for more than most houses, has a sound system with 15 speakers, and features sheepskin carpets—and is driven for you by your chauffer. In 2008 or 2009, Rolls promises coming to market with a smaller, leaner, cheaper Rolls you would drive yourself. The company's design chief calls it "your everyday Rolls." The Phantom sells for around $350,000.00; the you-drive-it-yourself model is expected to come in around $100,000.00 to $150,000.00 less. Experts predict Rolls successfully selling as many as 3,000 of these "baby Rollses," on top of the nearly 900 Phantoms sold per year. Volkswagen,® which quietly owns Bentley, sells about 750 of its Phantom-comparable model but about 10,000 of its Bentley lite, the Continental GT, at about $170,000.00 each. Rolls is attempting growth in both directions, trying its hand at both opportunities discussed in this chapter.

In 2007, it introduced a new Phantom Drophead Coupe convertible at the higher price of $412,000.00 and a new, expanded set of options for the Phantom that can take its price above $500,000.00 to as high as $2 million. The Drophead Coupe,

GIVING THE CHAUFFEUR THE DAY OFF, CONTINUED

incidentally, is magnificent: a full-sized four-door convertible with classic suicide doors for ease of entry, a trunk cleverly designed to open into top and bottom sections to create a picnic table for tailgating at polo matches or your kids' Little League games, and a yacht-like teak-and-brushed-aluminum hood available as a $3,500.00 option. This is an all-new standard of luxury for convertibles. At the same time, the company is pushing forward with the everyday Rolls models, with two buyers in mind: first, its regular customer, who may now buy both. Rolls' CEO says: "Most of our buyers have a car for each occasion." Second, the upwardly mobile mass-affluent or ordinary affluent customer willing to stretch into the $200,000.00 range but no further, who lives somehow without the services of a chauffer.

In the sports coupe category, other luxury car makers offer lower-priced models: Mercedes® at $138,000.00, Aston Martin at $126,000.00, even Maserati® as low as $115,000.00. Of all luxury car makers, Mercedes® has led in moving down, to appeal to mass-affluent customers, now able to buy a Mercedes® for as little as $29,650.00. Presuming success with the baby Rolls, is it only a matter of a few more years before there will be a Rolls-Royce® for everybody?

Sources: BusinessWeek magazine, November 5, 2007, www.BusinessWeek.com; *Trump* magazine, Winter 2007; *Condé Nast Portfolio*, November 2007.

CHAPTER 16

How the Mass-Affluent Trade Up

"Kids in Beverly Hills 90210 put on their own unique Christmas pageant, and the first scene, in particular, was fascinating. In it, Mary and Joseph are going to Bethlehem to pay their taxes. One little girl was Mary, one little boy was Joseph, a fat kid was the donkey, and a kid with thick eyeglasses was their CPA."

—Bob Orben, TV comedy writer and director of White House speechwriting during the Gerald Ford administration

One of the most important facts about the mass-affluent is that they do not trade up across the board.

In his research, Michael Silverstein, author of *Trading Up: Why Consumers Want New Luxury Goods—and How Companies Create Them,* found that the typical mass-affluent person seeks little steps up in a lot of things, makes major steps up in only one to three things, and remains unmoved by luxury, brand, experience, or other factors in many other purchase categories. To put that in a frame of example, Mrs. Mass-Affluent may indulge in little things like going to Starbucks® rather than Denny's® or to Cold Stone Creamery® instead of Dairy Queen,® may buy luxury-brand drop-downs like the line of Vera Wang®

designer duds sold at Kohl's;® may have one category of purchase where price is literally out the window—perhaps the care
and feeding of her poodle—but may also still buy whatever coffee is on sale at the supermarket absent brand loyalty and recoil
at the price for a Lexus,® preferring a Toyota®

She is a complicated creature.

This makes marketing to the mass-affluent a complicated thing.

Luxury-goods merchants have caught on, and are very much
engaging in what I just referred to as luxury drop-down. The
makers of old-line luxury goods like Mercedes® automobiles or
Coach® bags have created lower-priced products—usually smaller,
with fewer features, but of the same quality and bearing the brand
name—enabling the mass-affluent consumer to cross the luxury
line without qualm. Some luxury merchants have found enormous leverage in leaving a huge chasm between their top-priced
items and their new luxury-for-the-masses merchandise. Women
who can't afford one, and even those who can, might blanch at a
$10,000.00 Vera Wang® dress but be quite happy to pay $99.00 for
a Vera Wang® blouse at Kohl's.® But without knowledge of the
$10,000.00 dresses, they'd balk at such a high price for that blouse.
Some marketers, including several of my clients, even go so far as
to create and promote red-herring-priced goods or services they
hope no one buys, only to set a standard that makes their actual
prices seem imminently reasonable by comparison. I talk more
about this in Chapter 39, "Price, Profits, and Power."

Their Little Indulgences Equal Big Profit Improvements

Let's go back to the Starbucks® and Cold Stone Creameries® of the
world. In these businesses, almost any marketer can find practical

inspiration. While many mass-affluent consumers easily able to afford high-fee cosmetic dentistry, luxury cars, first-class travel, or designer fashions may find the price tags too big to swallow, they are easily wooed by little luxuries. For what seems like a small uptick in price—yet is a very big increase in profit margin for the merchant—the consumer can feel affluent yet not like somebody just throwing money around, can feel special without guilt. A $70,000.00 sticker on a car, a $35,000.00 fee quoted by the dentist, a $2,000.00 airline ticket—these are all so in-your-face. On the surface, the difference between the $70,000.00 car vs. the $35,000.00 car isn't so great; a car may feel like a car. On the plane, all the seats arrive at the same time. But the fact that you can pick up a half gallon of ice cream at the supermarket for about the same price as a tiny cup of ice cream at Cold Stone Creamery® is more disconnected. The experience is dramatically different. At the creamery, you pick out your flavor, your ground-up pie crust and candy bars, and watch your dessert being made for you on a granite slab. The company, with 1,400 stores, bills itself as "The Ultimate Ice Cream Experience.®" The price is still easily found in pocket or purse. It requires no thought, is done on impulse, feels good, and is easily rationalized if need be—*I've had a hard day, I deserve it.*

These little indulgences do add up. It is frequently pointed out by Scrooge-like, annoyingly practical financial experts like David Bach, author of the *Automatic Millionaire* books, Suze Orman, Dave Ramsey, and their ilk that, were someone to forego all the Starbucks® and Cold Stone® and Omaha Steaks® purchases in favor of coffee brewed at home and carried in a thermos, ice-cream bars bought at the grocery and kept in the office freezer, and so on, he would quite easily save from $25.00 to $50.00 a week, $1,300.00 to $2,600.00 a year, and, if it were all wisely invested even at modest interest rates, could add well over a quarter of a million dollars to his retirement fund or pay off his home mortgage during his working-life years. It is a wildly unpersuasive argument. As Pamela Danziger, author of *Shopping: Why We Love It and How Retailers Can Create the Ultimate Customer Experience,* puts it: "We want our little pleasures and we want them now."

Danziger has termed this inching up of price "luxflation." A form of self-induced inflation, experienced by consumers willing to pay what seems little more for much better experiences—when, in fact, that little more may be a 500% to 5,000% premium. It's ironic that the government, economists, and the media sweat bullets and display great angst over inflation creeping up by a half of a percent or a percent while consumers cheerfully accept 500% inflation in dozens of purchases every day. This is important to grasp, as it affects every business. Mass-affluent consumers may complain about inflation in general or many items'

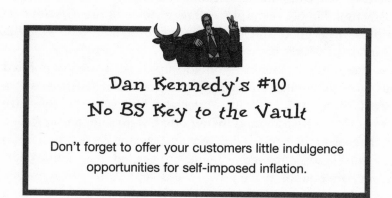

Dan Kennedy's #10
No BS Key to the Vault

Don't forget to offer your customers little indulgence opportunities for self-imposed inflation.

prices in particular, yet that can have zero impact on their response to your prices.

These little indulgences can really add up for you.

This is not really new. The story is now legend of how the dime-store soda fountains survived the Great Depression with the point-of-sale strategy, where the counterman responded to the milk shake order by asking, "Do you want yours with one egg or two?" What hasn't changed is that ATS (average transaction size) is one of the most important numbers to know, manage, and work at improving in many businesses, whether you sell milkshakes to frequent customers or farm tractors to very infrequent repeat customers. To continue the milkshake example, let's say we own an ice-cream stand where the cashier responds to each order by presenting the offer of a double flavor shot and an extra scoop of fresh fruit. If half say yes to the extra $.55, and they serve 50 shakes a day, that's $.275 added to every transaction. If the shake itself sells for $1.50, we have increased the average transaction size by 18%. But we may have increased the profit margin, invisibly, by much more. Of course, if we can alter the whole experience to support a higher price, still add the extra fruit, and add a big chocolate chip cookie, well, we might take our $1.50 average transaction to $3.50. On a grander scale, we may turn our ice-cream stand into a much-talked about, much-preferred destination of the mass-affluent rather than just one of a dozen same-as, same-as places in town. Being in the little-indulgence business in a big way can lead to much bigger profits, but even to something more valuable: sustainable unique positioning in your customers' minds and lives.

CHAPTER 17

Thanksgiving Dinner Grandma Doesn't Make

"There is at least one respect in which the rich, the really very rich, are different—they understand vegetables . . . . Have you ever noticed how, in the homes of the very rich . . . they always serve the most beautiful vegetables, and the greatest variety? The greenest petit pois, infinitiesimal carrots, corn so baby-kerneled and tender it seems almost unborn, lima beans tinier than mice eyes, and the young asparagus! The limestone lettuce! The raw red mushrooms!"

—Truman Capote, "La Côte Basque"

To give readers a look at something affluent customers do that might be foreign to you, I decided to use the Thanksgiving dinner—something just about every reader has experienced every year of his life.

So it's Thanksgiving and you're hosting.

Most people go to their local supermarket. Some get all raw materials and build everything from scratch. They get a turkey, they get the ingredients to make stuffing and then stuff the turkey, they get ingredients to make gravy, they get ingredients to make that green bean and onion crisp casserole, they buy pie dough, apples, and so on. This is the way your grandmother did it, unless she raised, shot, and skinned the turkey and grew the vegetables too. This is probably the way your mother did it. It's probably not quite the way you're doing it. You may get close. You most assuredly buy some things in cans, bottles, and bags, from pre-cut celery sticks to pie filling to gravy. Either way, if you're serving eight people, you probably spend as little as $100.00 to no more than $200.00. Or, you might get totally prepared foods. High-end grocery markets, some restaurants and delis, and catering companies will sell you very nicely prepared, complete Thanksgiving feasts: the turkey, all the fixin's, three side dishes, pie, the works. Done for you. No shopping, no messy preparation, and if you like, no cooking. For eight at the table, you might now spend $200.00 to $300.00. Or, on the cheap, you could get a fully assembled and cooked Thanksgiving meal from a chain like Boston Market® and spend less.

Or you could order everything from the Dean & DeLuca® catalog or website and have it delivered to your door. This is a gourmet foods mail-order company dealing with the affluent. It sells caviar. So, here's what your Dean & DeLuca® Thanksgiving feast will be like: The Heritage Turkey Feast that serves eight includes a Bourbon Red Heritage Turkey or a Bronze Free-Range Turkey. These are not mass-produced turkeys. There is, as you might imagine, a story about them. The turkey is stuffed with whole porcini mushrooms, shallots, leeks, celery, herbed breads, and toasted pecans. There is also gravy made from sautéed shallots, leeks, and thyme. There is sweet potato corn soup, yams in a casserole with bananas, rum, and slivered almonds, cranberry sauce with cardamom, and fluffy biscuits. That'll set you back $420.00, plus shipping. You will also want one large pumpkin pie and one large sour cream apple walnut pie, $52.00 and $54.00, respectively. You might go big and add a Cornucopia Cake, made of dark chocolate wrapped around almond cream cake with raspberry filling and a display of marzipan fruit on top—$135.00. A couple bottles of the recommended Mount Carmel Pinot Noir, $70.00 each. Grand total has now snuck up over $800.00.

The temptation, of course, is to think: *I would never pay such prices. Who would pay such prices?* as if no one would. But plenty do. And further up the food chain, pardon the pun, people hire cooks and caterers to round it all up, prepare it, cook it, and serve it, thereby spending from $1,000.00 to $3,000.00 to stuff the eight people with stuffing made of mushrooms and pine needles.

The first moral of the story is that there is a price for every person and a person for every price. And there is a difference of experience in serving this fancy, gourmet feast procured from Dean and DeLuca® vs. one gotten at the supermarket. The price is far more a function of the person buying this feast and his feelings about the experience of buying it and serving it than it is about the turkey, gravy, and pies. To refer to an earlier discussion, this is price de-linked from product and re-attached to experience and feelings about the experience, and therein is an extra price strategy tossed in: to de-link price from product, you must attach price to something else. Make a note.

The second moral of the story is that you can pretty much sell anything to affluent consumers, absent boundaries. They buy a lot of things non-affluent consumers would never dream of buying at all. They buy things from sources, in ways, and at prices that non-affluent consumers can't even imagine. And they buy many things at a distance or delivered or done for them that non-affluent consumers would never consider buying unless standing in front of it, loading it up, hauling it home, or doing it for themselves.

Returning to Dean & DeLuca® for a moment, you aren't limited to calling the company once a year at Thanksgiving. For Christmas, it offers a three-pound Candy Cane Cake: chocolate cake layered with mint mousse, then covered with red-and-white striped frosting, with candy cane and edible red bow on top—$135.00. And, why make a gingerbread house when Dean & DeLuca® will deliver an artfully decorated gingerbread house cake for $175.00? Caviar options range from $325.00 for one ounce to $5,200.00 per pound. Mother-of-pearl serving spoons, set of 6 for $65.00. And you can join cheese-of-the-month clubs for $500.00 per year, plus $174.00 shipping and handling. Oops, I meant formaggio of the month. All these choices and many more are at, of course, www.DeanDeLuca.com.

CHAPTER 18

Money Spent on Passions

"All the things I really like to do are either illegal, immoral, or fattening."

—ALEXANDER WOOLLCOTT, IN HIS PLAY
THE KNOCK AT THE STAGE DOOR (1933)

I make this point numerous times in this book: few affluent consumers and even fewer mass-affluents buy premium goods and services or spend freely *across the board.* The greatest dichotomy I personally know of is a person who routinely buys and enjoys expensive, imported caviar but also frequently parks her Mercedes® in the parking lot behind the bread company's store and there, furtively, buys day-old bread. I know a former Fortune 500 CEO who will pay virtually any price without thought for a round of golf, and fire up the private jet to get there, but buys his khaki slacks at Target,® and has been known to pull out Val-Pak® coupons at restaurants. Just getting the more affluent customer is not necessarily the golden key to far greater income. Getting the more affluent customer passionately interested in your category of product, service, expertise, or experience is.

One certain way to connect with affluent consumers is to connect to their passions.

Visit www.ILikeCigars.com, read *Cigar Aficionado* magazine, and you will discover a subculture where people passionate about cigars spend sums shocking to all others on rolled-up weeds you set fire to. As example, consider the elegant yet practical Zino Platinum Cavern Humidor, featuring a cedar tray with palladium plated brass handles on a wooden case finished with 15 coats of lacquer, safeguarding up to 60 stogies. Price: $2,800.00 (www.ZinoPlatinum.com). You might also like a little novelty item, the official James Bond 007–logo laser-fire lighter, a mere $190.00 (www.StDuPontLighters.com).

In the book *Turning Silver into Gold: How to Profit in the New Boomer Marketplace,* researcher Dr. Mary Furlong writes in-depth about what she calls "the passion and play market," where companies and even entire industries are, pardon the pun, booming thanks to boomers' and especially affluent boomers' willingness to spend without budget and buy without price resistance.

The average homeowner is in his mid-50s. Homeowners ages 55 to 64 already spend more on horticulture than any other age group, but with the rise of the mass-affluent boomer homeowner, spending in this category could as much as double in the next five years. Gardening is a $38 billion industry ready to blossom. This same growth of affluent boomers promises positive impact on every passion and play business category, from books to golf to cooking. However, what once was age progressive—meaning you worked to retirement age to then begin indulging, finally playing golf twice a week or finally devoting time to your garden or photography or whatever—is now disconnected from age for the affluent. We have to look at these passion and play businesses as being for the affluent at any age, as their philosophy is to enjoy as you go rather than defer gratification until later. In fact, all age-based marketing thought must change. The idea of seniors on fixed incomes being penny-pinching, reluctant buyers is as inaccurate as is the idea that certain hobbies and pursuits are the province of retirees. Furlong describes the years ahead of boomers as "regenerative" rather than retirement and points out they have plenty of spending power; they earn more than $2 trillion in yearly income and control over 75% of the financial assets in the United States. She writes: "And they are going through more transitions now than at any other time in their lives. Each of those transitions is a tipping point for product and service decisions." Maybe the biggest of those tipping points is the opportunity to indulge their interests and passions as never before. The boomers' kids, though, populate the mass-affluent and have a "no waiting attitude" quite different from their parents. So they are *all* spending freely on passions and play.

Consider the wine business. Once, a rather narrow, elite, and quite limited customer base predominantly populated by the affluent and ultra-affluent supported a closeted industry largely invisible or mysterious and intimidating, thus of little interest to the mass public. Today, the major wine aficionado magazines are sold on newsstands, and the huge public food shows attended by tens of thousands in each city have become wine and food shows. AARP has its own wine club, wine events, newsletters, and programs, but the buying of fine wines, expensive wines, the installing of home wine cellars, the joining of wine clubs have moved from affluent to mass-affluent, from 50-plus down to 30-plus. This is luxury democratized. A special interest becoming a widespread interest.

Passion and play is the surest way to de-link price from pragmatism. The mass-affluent who will grumble about the total change rung up at the grocery-store checkout counter for a week's groceries will separately sign up for Gevalia's® limited edition coffees of the world at $36.95 per month plus shipping and handling, which translates to spending approximately $20.00 a pound(!). And the coffee aficionado will buy pricey coffees everywhere she goes, without second thought.

I once knew a very successful optometrist who complained frequently and bitterly about the costs of supplies for his practice, a year-to-year increase in the cost of his Yellow Pages advertising, his home's property tax, even the local deli's nickel and dime price increases. But, an obsessed Ohio State fan, he had purchased a giant, gas-guzzling motor home painted in Ohio state logos outside, decorated in red and gray furnishings and carpet inside, equipped with satellite dish, big-screen TV, and bar, to travel to and tailgate at every game, home and away, every season. He also purchased season tickets and bought away-game tickets from ticket brokers and scalpers at sky-high prices—all without a peep. Every Friday and Saturday during season, his office was closed, sacrificing whatever income might have been produced, so he could stock the motor home and go to Columbus or wherever the team was playing. Without a thought.

THE MARTHA STEWART OF MOTORCYCLES

Motorcycles aren't just for tough-looking women with tattoos and bulging muscles displayed with sleeveless leather vests anymore! In the past ten years (1997–2007), the number of women motorcycle owners has grown by 36%, but given the wave of mass-affluent boomer women, many analysts predict a growth rate of two to three times that over the next ten years. There are nearly five million women motorcyclists in the United States. In 2006, 12% of Harley-Davidson motorcycles and 15% of Kawasaki motorcycles were sold to women. One out of every four people taking motorcycle instruction classes is a woman. The average age is 42, 28% are college grads, 35% are in professional careers, and their incomes or their household incomes skew affluent. Kathleen Steele Tolleson, the president of ROAR Motorcycles Inc., sees mass-affluent women buyers as the greatest growth opportunity in the motorcycle industry, and she has set out to become the Martha Stewart of the field. Her company, launched in 2007, builds custom and semi-custom motorcycles just for women, designs and offers apparel, jewelry, and even its own cosmetic line, Windblown.®

ROAR clients can order a DreamBike,® individually tailored to the client. There is pragmatism: Tolleson is quick to point out that women bikers' physical needs are different than men's. Women have better lower-body strength; men tend to have greater upper-body strength. By lowering a motorcycle's suspension and center of gravity, ROAR builds a motorcycle a woman can easily pick up

THE MARTHA STEWART OF MOTORCYCLES, CONTINUED

off its stand by shifting her hips and legs, preventing common back, neck, and shoulder pain, especially for boomer-age women riders. ROAR designers are also paying close attention to details, like clearing the handlebars of objects likely to break a fingernail. But the practical aspects take backseat to the exclusivity appeal. "These are designer motorcycles," Tolleson says, "and women are happy to pay more for them, just as they are for designer fashions. In fact, a DreamBike® designed and built for the client is a personal fashion statement." Bike colors are custom and can be matched with everything from the requisite leather jacket to a shade of lipstick. The client experience is a far cry from walking into a showroom and dealing with an ordinary salesman, a situation most women find off-putting. ROAR has a team of highly experienced, master builders, designers, and male and female consultants collaborate with every client in the designing and building of every motorcycle.

Guys, if you're looking for a unique gift for that special lady in your life, you may want to skip the jewelry department at Neiman's and forget the custom-fit bikini. Get her a custom-built motorcycle. You can't ride a diamond ring. However, most ROAR clients are women who treat themselves, so you might come home from work Friday and find a turquoise-and-lemon-mint motorcycle with diamond-encrusted pinstripes parked in your Lexus's® spot in the garage.

The average price of a DreamBike® is about $30,000.00, with models as low as $20,000.00 and as high as $100,000.00 or

THE MARTHA STEWART OF MOTORCYCLES, CONTINUED

more. These prices are, of course, substantially higher than those of off-the-rack motorcycles. ROAR's ability to sell at prices from 200% to 500% higher than competing manufacturers and products is the result of a combination of many of the strategies discussed throughout this book, including niching and microtargeted marketing (the *who* is more important than the *what*), customization, creating a unique experience, membership and affinity concepts, and, of course, effective marketing and promotion.

The company's marketing programs include the ROAR Sisterhood Motorcycle Association and Little Sisters for younger riders or riders-to-be; a charitable foundation focused on women's issues; online and offline publications; an aggressive internet strategy including ownership of highest-searched domains (such as www.MotorcyclesForWomen.com); even strategic location of ROAR's design center and showroom in Daytona Beach, Florida, home of Bike Week and Biketoberfest, which, combined, draw 600,000 motorcyclists each year. Some sort of reality TV show is on the drawing board. Tolleson, a petite 5-foot-tall, 54-year-old church pastor, speaker, radio personality and author is the company's chief publicist, spokesperson, and rainmaker. She grew up racing cars, snowmobiles, and motorcycles in Minnesota and has been an avid motorcyclist her entire life. Will this conversion of personal passion to business venture resonate with its intended market? It certainly has all the makings of a huge success.

You can see it all at www.RoarMotorcycles.com.

CHAPTER 19

Money Spent Collecting

"Shopping is the museum of the 20th century."

—The Dalai Lama

*S*hould you wish to add a life-sized, real, fully drivable antique fire engine to your portfolio of vehicles, you can find bargains in the $10,000.00 to $12,000.00 range. Buying one of the authentic George Barris Batmobiles at a car auction will set you back considerably more. People collect both. And antique motorcycles, lawn mowers, vacuum cleaners, pocket watches, grandfather clocks, medical devices, board games, toys, dolls, jukeboxes, fountain pens, and anything and everything else you have ever seen. They haunt estate sales, flea markets, and auctions, pay brokers, roam the internet, and respond to countless ads in countless magazines and newspapers in search of an elusive item. When they find it, price is pretty much irrelevant.

I have, in my basement, an antique gambling machine, combining a pinball machine and roulette wheel, with a horseracing motif—horseracing being my passion. It requires old-fashioned picture tubes to function and is frequently on the fritz. I bought it *on a whim* for, as I recall, $8,000.00. Some whim. The antique dealer who sold it to me has since kindly alerted me every time any item with a racehorse on it finds its way to his shop.

Classic car auctions are a great place to see a big population of affluent collectors for yourself. In a magazine promoting one such auction, attended by 200,000 people and selling 5,000 cars in four days, I found an old car I'd want: a 1973 AMC Javelin AMX, a near replica of the 1974 Javelin that was my first ever new car. Inquiring, I was told it had a reserve tag on it of $36,000.00 but would probably sell for more. This is an American Motors i.e., *Rambler* sporty car. Good grief. The extremely knowledgeable and helpful lady on the phone with me was quick to point out that bidding live from a distance was possible (they would assign an agent to act on my behalf, with whom I'd speak via cell phone), I could watch via the internet, and 100% financing by a major bank could be arranged in 15 minutes. Or, if coming to the auction, I could buy a Segway® and have it waiting for me or pre-arrange a golf cart rental, to roam the acres of cars comfortably. This is but one of dozens of major auctions and hundreds of lesser auctions for classic cars occurring each year all over the United States.

Such collectors are passionate about this one thing and most willing to spend on it, but often, collectors are collectors, so they collect more than one thing. And, of course, are willing to spend liberally on many other things (although not everything).

Consider the lowly pen. I have a habit of losing good ones as soon as I get them, so I stopped buying even ordinary Cross® pens years ago. My office is littered with Bic® pens bought by the gross and Flair® markers. Nowhere to be found, the designer-name or antique pen on its own display stand. But visit www.FountainPenHospital.com for a look at some very pricey pens—and repair services.

It seems that everybody collects something. Affluent people simply have the wherewithal to collect pricier things or to pay more in pursuit of the things they collect. They can and do also spend money on information about what they collect, association with others who collect the same things, travel to places where they can find or show off the things they collect, storage facilities, insurance, and care and maintenance for their collected things.

Beyond these specific interests, affluent customers are particularly in tune with the very idea of collectible value. So collector's editions and limited editions of just about anything you can think of—book, artwork, wine, home furnishing, golf club, fishing rod—have added cachet and value.

PRICES OF SOUGHT-AFTER FIRST ENGLISH-LANGUAGE EDITIONS OF RARE BOOKS

The Fat Man is no longer in pursuit of the actual Maltese falcon—today he wants a copy of the first edition of the book! Here are a few first editions' market values (based on being in their original dust jackets and in mint condition).

Author	Book	Market Value
Dashiell Hammett	THE MALTESE FALCON (1930)	$85,000.00–$100,000.00
James Joyce	ULYSSES (1922)	$75,000.00–$90,000.00
Ernest Hemingway	THE SUN ALSO RISES (1926)	$65,000.00–$70,000.00
J.D. Salinger	THE CATCHER IN THE RYE (1951)	$25,000.00–$30,000.00
Tennessee Williams	A STREETCAR NAMED DESIRE (1947)	$15,000.00–$20,000.00
Harper Lee	TO KILL A MOCKINGBIRD (1960)	$15,000.00–$20,000.00

Source: The Executive's Almanac, by Milton Moskowitz.

INTERESTING COLLECTORS CLUBS

Aladdin Knights of the Mystic Light, founded in 1973, for collectors of Aladdin lamps and memorabilia. Approximately 1,000 members.

American Lock Collectors Association, founded in 1970, for collectors of old locks, padlocks, and handcuffs. Members receive a newsletter and information on upcoming events and lock shows. Number of members not known.

American Pencil Collectors Society, founded in 1958.

Circus Historical Society, founded in 1939, for collectors of historical materials related to circuses. About 1,400 members.

Count Dracula Fan Club, founded in 1965. Research library with 25,000 books, trips to Transylvania, and support for collectors of Count Dracula films and memorabilia. About 5,000 members.

National Fishing Lure Collectors Club, founded in 1976. Newsletter, trading meetings, annual convention. It has 3,000 members.

Source: Organized Obsessions, by Burek, Connors, and Brelin.

CHAPTER 20

Money Spent on Kids and Grandkids

"You can get very hungry while waiting, if your livelihood depends on someone's disease. Death does not always listen to the promises and prayers of those who would inherit."

—MOLIERE

I recommend a visit to www.LilliputPlayHomes.com as instructive. This company advertises in publications read by the affluent, such as *Billionaire* magazine, an offshoot of the *Robb Report*. In the issue on my bookshelf, their company's quarter-page ad appears next to one from a law firm specializing in asset protection featuring a John D. Rockefeller quotation, and above a half-page ad for a mergers and acquisitions and commercial financing broker. On the facing page, ads for waterfront homes priced from $2.6 million to $11.9 million. Here, an ad for incredibly pricy backyard *playhouses*?

The perfect place.

Don't leap to the conclusion there's such a tiny market for such things that there can be only one odd company in the business. Visit www.PoshTots.com, where you can have a completely custom-designed backyard playhouse built for your kids or grandkids, replete with lofts, decks, and skylights, or designed to a theme, such as a Pirates of the Caribbean-esque ship. Prices from as little as $2,449.00 all the way up to $52,000.00. This company's offerings were featured on the same page in *Upscale* magazine as fractional jet ownership package priced at $415,000.00 and a unisex, diamond-encrusted wristwatch at $25,000.00.

It is but one demonstration of thousands of demonstrations in my files and among my clients of this valuable fact: many mass-affluent and affluent parents and grandparents set price entirely aside when buying things for their children and grand-children. This is true for all sorts of reasons. Status and showing off. The opportunity to delight somebody, when all the adults in their family including their spouse are thoroughly jaded and very undelighted by the luxury lifestyle they enjoy. Guilt, over shorting the little ones on time or attention. Having been deprived as children themselves. The psychology is complex but the reality is simple. In this case, you can sell a child's playhouse for more money than a storage shed, garage, or room addition.

It is also demonstration of another very important fact: marketers of products for the lil' ones are not limited to—and are, in fact, advised not to limit their advertising to—media specifically for parents, about parenting.

A friend of mine selling a very expensive children's product who asked not to be named in this book said that his best clients are the guilt-ridden affluent parents, and he'd discovered the best place to find them is in magazines read by those flying private jets. He says the frequent business traveler, executive, or entrepreneur, with young children at home, in his second marriage to a younger woman; the very affluent couple leaving the kids at home with nanny, baby-sitter, or grandparents while on luxury vacations; and the wealthy grandparent competitively vying for attention with other grandparents are, far and away, his best customers—and that the best time to catch their attention is when they are jetting across the country.

A Member of one of my coaching groups, Ron Caruthers, has a thriving practice as a consultant and coach to Southern California parents eager to win the competitive battle to get their son or daughter into the top university of choice, and to do so at lowest out-of-pocket cost or debt possible. He generates millions of dollars of fees annually, and his best clients are mass-affluent and affluent parents. It's something of a secret, but affluent parents can arrange their personal finances and children's assets so that they can qualify for a considerable amount of financial aid from the universities and scholarships from other sources, as well as make whatever contributions they do make directly as tax advantaged as possible. But a lion's share of Caruthers's income is not derived from the specific college planning services and fees, but from transition of these clients into full-fledged financial planning clients for life. His approach is so successful he has developed a second business, assisting other financial planners in entering this field. The model here is to find a relatively narrow, specialized, and extremely attractive *first thing* to put in front of your main services and use to attract affluent clients. For example, carpet cleaning is a rather ordinary and commonplace service, as is generic financial planning; expert stain removal from expensive Oriental and handmade rugs is a much less common, more promotable service to affluent owners of luxury homes, as college planning is a more specialized expertise promotable to affluent parents.

CHAPTER 21

Money Spent on Pets

*"The Don CeSar hotel is overly pet friendly. Ridiculously pet friendly.
They have a pet concierge that comes to your room and describes
the services they offer your pet. . . .They said they had
aromatherapy for dogs. I'm like, 'Do you have a candle
that smells like another dog's ass?' That's what he likes."*

—COMEDIAN RON WHITE, CHARTER MEMBER OF THE
BLUE COLLAR COMEDY TOUR (WWW.TATERSALAD.COM)

You might want to come back as a dog in an affluent
home in your next life. Their future looks bright.
Designers have discovered pets, so, for example, you can
buy a Gucci dog bowl for $900.00. At ww.PostModernPets.com,
affluent owners can buy an Italian-designed doghouse or a
Cabitat cat condo, a leather dog bed ($1,450.00), or a Jonathan
Adler designer dog dish. One of the humans behind this website
says it is "for people who are serious about incorporating their
pets fully into their lifestyle."

There is a fast-growing population of such people. In his
book *MicroTrends*, author and political pollster Mark Penn called
them "pet parents."

My wife and I are admittedly among them. The little dog who lives with us is considered when we choose hotels and resorts to visit—with rare exception, they must be pet friendly. Preferably *very* friendly. We prefer her with us rather than left behind, so shopping center, store, and similar choices are also made based on whether or not she is welcome. She has her own little couch, her own fur throw, her own blanket. She commutes between our two homes with one or both of us uncaged, relaxed in the private plane, which she greatly prefers to traveling with the peon pets on commercial airlines, where she must be stuffed in a small cage that fits under the seat. And yes, she knows the difference between driving toward the regular airline terminal and turning off to the private terminal. She is spoiled. I call her our Million-Dollar Dog. And our Million-Dollar Dog has a bone to pick with you, if you aren't accommodating her as one of the family.

In one city you'll find a Starbucks®-like, upscale coffeehouse for humans under the same roof as the Whole Pet Café, serving healthy meat, vegetable, and whole-grain meals and designer waters to dogs, at $4.00 to $10.00 per item. Next door, a fancy veterinary clinic and a high-end pet fashions and accessories store. In another city, a pet day spa featuring not just grooming and nail clipping, but fur-beautifying blueberry facials, massages, saunas. Classical music is played exclusively in the fur stylist's salon. Another city boasts a pet hotel with private suites, complete with comfortable beds, heated floors, and plasma TVs. None of these businesses is in Beverly Hills or Manhattan, although businesses just like them are there, as you'd expect. The ones I just described are in Dallas, Texas; Long Beach, California; and Charlotte, North Carolina. In Alexandria, Virginia, near one of my homes, the entire community of Main Street merchants wisely caters to pets and their owners. A local hotel has a happy hour for dogs. The bakery features birthday cakes for pets. There is a dog apparel store.

Pets are the new children and grandchildren. Boomers' kids are grown and gone. Families once staying in close geographic proximity are now spread out to different and distant locations. Spoiling grandchildren is made more difficult by this separation. So affluents, especially affluent boomers, dote on their dogs, cats, and other pets. And spend truly astounding sums doing so.

In fact, 27% of people now take care of their pets in their wills. Hotelier Leona Helmsley made national news with the multimillion-dollar estate left to her little dogs, guaranteeing them their own staff and exceptional care for life. Posthumous care of pets is but one of the evolving and emerging new businesses catering to the affluent.

No affluent pet owner does the math. The gourmet dog food he purchases in little containers costs more per pound than the steaks he eats himself. The Burberry dog coat at $200.00 costs more per square inch of plaid than his own Burberry overcoat. It does not matter.

Pet products are now one of the top ten U.S. retail segments—a bigger industry than toys or candy or hardware. Currently, more than $38 billion is spent each year on pets, double the amount spent just ten years ago. This staggering number may again double within the next ten years. About 63% of American households have pets, up from 55% roughly 20 years ago, and an all-time high. That's double the percentage of households with children. In the past 20 years, the drop in households with kids mirrors the rise in households with pets. As baby boomers become empty nesters, household spending on children is declining while spending on pets is rising. Over a three-year term, spending on toys, games, tricycles, and children's clothes fell by more than 20%; spending on pets rose by 23%.

The fastest growth segment: luxury pet products bought by affluent pet owners. About 40% of all the dollars spent buying things for pets deliver them to only 1% of the pets, the most pampered of the pampered pooches and kitties. Louis Vuitton,® Chanel,® and Burberry® sell designer dog collars and leashes, Gucci,® Tiffany,® Coach,® L.L. Bean,® and Harley-Davidson® are all in the luxury dog accessories business.

The love of dogs drove the book *Marley and Me: Life and Love with the World's Worst Dog* to the top of the New York Times bestseller list—a lofty place this book will never see—and kept it there. If you haven't read it, and you like dogs, you must. It even made Howard Stern weep aloud while reading its end, as he told the author in a note. It made me cry. It has made everybody I know who has read it, including those I bought it for as a gift, cry. That speaks to the poignancy of the book, but also to the extreme connection pet lovers have to pets. Even if this is foreign emotional territory for you, it isn't for the majority of your affluent clients.

YOU GOTTA SEE IT TO BELIEVE IT!

www.FetchDog.com
In FetchDog's collection of luxury and designer beds and throws for dogs, you'll find one made to look like a convertible sports car

---

YOU GOTTA SEE IT TO BELIEVE IT!, CONTINUED

with an open top, windshield, side mirror, rims, door handles, roll bar, embroidered Furcedes logo, and "L.A. Dog" license plate: $279.00. A Furrari is also available. If you'd like something less flashy and more classy, consider the Sniffany & Company bed, a plush, oversized replica of that famous little blue box with the white ribbon: just $129.00. Add a Chewy Vuitton® toy shaped like a purse for just $15.00.

www.ScootersFriends.com
This site features dog coats. Almost endless choices of dog coats. Pink and brown snakeskin with faux fur . . . reversible wool and camel hair . . . multitextured pink wool with pearl trim . . . quilted velvet coat . . . glen plaid raincoat. Separate collection of evening wear. No excuse for your dog to suffer the embarrassment of a fashion fur pas.

www.Muttropolis.com
This company has physical stores that "delight pet parents with the community feel of a friendly dog park," as well as an online catalog with categories covering every need:

Be My Valentine Shop	Eco-Friendly Dog Products
All Things Pink	Shop by Size/Age
Beds and Furniture	Bowls
Carriers	Clothes and Accessories
Collars	Grooming and Spa
Toys	Training & Behavior
Treats and Supplements	

INVESTMENTS IN PETS' CARE

Expense (Per Year)	Dog	Cat
Food	$ 241.00	$ 185.00
Treats	68.00	43.00
Vitamins	123.00	3.00
Toys	45.00	29.00
Grooming	107.00	24.00
Boarding/Pet-Sitting	202.00	119.00
Veterinary Care, Routine	211.00	179.00
Veterinary Care, Surgical	574.00	337.00
AVERAGE Yearly Cost	$ 1,571.00	$ 919.00

Pet owners in households identified as affluent help bring this bell curve way up; they spend, on average, four times the average on their dogs, double the average on their cats. There is substantial variance between those in urban vs. suburban vs. rural geographies as well. If you are a national or local marketer of pet products or services, it is obviously to your profound advantage to target affluent pet owners. If you're a dog or cat, it's advisable to choose an affluent owner!

Sources: American Pet Products Manufacturers Association; Global Market for Luxury Dog Products and Accessories Research Studies; *The Economics of Pet Ownership* by Jim McWhinney.

PUT AWAY YOUR LITTLE DIGITAL CAMERA. IT'S EMBARRASSINGLY MIDDLE CLASS.

New York's Julie Skarratt is a famous leader in the profession of pet portrait photography. You get print and digital versions as well as an internet-based slide show set to music. You can, if you wish, be included in the images—as long as you're well behaved and don't bite. Fee, upwards of $10,000.00.

Source: Town & Country magazine, January 2008.

CHAPTER 22

Money Spent on Women

"If women didn't exist, all the money in the world would have no meaning."

—ARISTOTLE ONASSIS

The Brown Card, nicknamed "the ecstasy card," was sold by Michel Cluizel Chocolat of Paris, actually located in New York, for $50,000.00. Cardholders enjoy limitless access to a private bar with fine wines paired with chocolates, exclusive tasting events, limited edition chocolates, and even a personal introduction to Cluizel himself, be still our beating hearts (www.ChocolatMichelCluizel.com).

Is there any sum some men will not spend to attempt impressing, delighting, or seducing women?

No, and many marketers grossly underestimate this sexually stimulated price elasticity. I am constantly dismayed at the unimaginativeness of gift certificate or gift card packaging and pricing by spas, hair salons, jewelers, resorts, stores, and others. Pay attention to Michel Cluizel. He's selling a $50,000.00 gift card, but with a unique and exclusive collection of products and privileges attached.

Shortly before Christmas, several years ago, a cosmetic surgeon, Dr. Stephen Greenberg, appeared on ABC's *Good Morning America* and explained how happy husbands were to purchase his Million Dollar Makeover gift certificates for their wives, unmarried significant others, mistresses, and girlfriends. Yes, they were paying $1 million for the ultimate gift for their honeys: a tune-up from tip of lip to toes and everything in between. It occurred to me that in some marriages, this gift might not be oohed and aahed over with as much enthusiasm as, say, a new car with diamonds in the glove box. Nevertheless, Greenberg said he was responding to men who were coming to him and asking for the *ultimate* package. His *ordinary* $100,000.00 Silver Package and $200,000.00 Gold Package just weren't good enough. The patient on the show with him, an attractive mother of four, a recipient of the Million Dollar Makeover gift, was set to get an eye lift, face-lift, neck lift, tummy tuck, butt lift, laser hair removal, enlarged lips, and, of course, breast augmentation. She still missed something; according to a report in *The Wall Street Journal*, hymenoplasty is the ultimate surgical gift—tightening of the vagina or even restoration of virginity, itself starting at only about $5,000.00. Dr. Edward Jacobsen, a Greenwich, Connecticut, OB-GYN, offers vaginal makeover packages for international patients that include airfare, limousine travel, and luxury hotel accommodations. Cosmetic surgery of all kinds has long ago emerged from hiding and become popularized by celebrities and more something to brag about than be quiet about. And there is a clientele for the million-dollar gift of it, raising as one question what ultimate package or ultimate gift you ought to sell in your business?

I can recall a time not that long ago when TV commercials aimed at men at Christmastime touted buying perfumes and jewelry. It's a relatively recent phenomenon that, with perfectly straight face, many car companies run commercials suggesting surprising the wife with a new car. Dealers even furnish big red bows. "He went to Jared®" pales in comparison to "He went to Lexus.®" The ante is upped.

However, an excellent lesson in selling a gift of any kind comes from the mail-order jeweler Karats & Facets, which target markets to the mass-affluent. A page of outstanding sales copy from the company's catalog appears at the end of this chapter (page 188). It is headlined "Guaranteed Gasp or Your Money Refunded." This company clearly understands it isn't in the jewelry business, but in the gasp business. Or, as the catalog puts it, assisting you with an "investment in your relationship." In selling anything to men for women, this understanding should be yours as well.

Think you've seen it all at Victoria's Secret®? Go to www.Fabriintimo.com for a look at Antinea Paris lingerie and ID Sarrieri lingerie. Or peruse the better-known La Perla® lingerie, like the Black Label bustier and slip priced at $37.00. (www.laperla .com). It's salient that the La Perla® lingerie is advertised in *Million-Air* magazine, published and provided only to people flying in private jets. The Fabri Intimo® lines, in *Billionaire* magazine. Victoria's Secret's® advertising is conspicuously absent in these periodicals. I can give you my most confident personal assurance that few men know the difference between one bustier and another, but affluent men will buy what they perceive to be the prestige lingerie as a gift. And how will they know which is which? By where they see it advertised.

GUARANTEED GASP OR YOUR MONEY REFUNDED

Here is jewelry to capture her heart.

Unique gemworks that make her feel unique. This is jewelry you won't find in department stores (many are one-of-a-kind estate pieces). Nor will you spend hours shopping for them. Just make your choice(s). Dial 800-260-4987, ext. 500, on your phone, and a gift to make her gasp is on its way.

You expect only the finest quality when you purchase Karats & Facets jewelry, and you surely get it. We choose our gems for their immaculate cut and clarity. We use only solid, high-karat gold for our gem settings. Bracelet links are pin-hinged for super flex-strength. And we add not one but two locking clasps to make them vault-safe.

Karats & Facets jewelry is more than an investment in your relationship. Its intrinsic value is one that sustains with the years.

Yet we offer these beautiful pieces at amazing values, unmatched elsewhere. How can we? We buy our gems directly from abroad, eliminating agent and middlemen costs. We smith our own gold in our own workshops (you're welcome to visit anytime). Then we market our jewelry directly to you to avoid distributor, broker and retail markups.

Finally, there's our airtight Satisfaction Guarantee: If you're not 100% satisfied, you have 30-days to return it for a full refund.

CHAPTER 23

Money Spent on Bling

"You asked 'what time is it'? It's three diamonds after noon."

—Sammy Davis Jr.

Tdhere is a special population within the ultra-affluent **who buy bling**. This group of bright, shiny-object lovers tends to include a lot of people who make a lot of money suddenly or without much effort or through talent and celebrity or mere celebrity. Think Paris Hilton. Michael Jackson driving himself to brink of bankruptcy with wild spending and shopping sprees. Hollywood and music celebrities, sports stars. You might identify these as the affluents with more money than brains. Personally, I like getting such stupid money just as much as I like getting smart money. It seems to spend the same. So affluents with stupid money deserve your consideration.

Some have, in their jeans pocket, a Swiss Army knife made of gold or silver and bejeweled with 800 diamonds, for which they paid as much as $100,000.00 (www.Bonfort.ch).

Traveling to Las Vegas recently, I thumbed through a magazine found in the private air terminal, a magazine I'd never seen before, totally devoted to buyers of pimped-out rides. High-priced sports cars, luxury cars, and SUVs given customized makeovers. I discovered more than 30 full-page and multipage ads for wheel covers. Wheel covers. Most priced from the bargain of $995.00 to more commonly $1,495.00 to $4,000.00 per hubcap. Per hubcap. The most expensive, a set of four inset with diamonds and rubies, priced at $2 million. Extra costs: $100,000.00 a year for the two guys you hire to guard your wheels—and each other—at all times, $50,000.00 for trips to your therapist after seeing your extremely busy, compliant, and talented girlfriend's dog lift his little leg and pee on one of your wheel covers. Talk about emotional conflict.

The more common bling, ultra-expensive wristwatches for men and women and high-fashion jewelry for women, is all quite different for the affluent and ultra-affluent than that on display in the glass cases at your local shopping malls. There is, for example, a Limited Edition Grand Complication Audemars Piguet men's watch priced at $743,600.00 or the more affordable Master Minute Repeater in Platinum by Jaeger-LeCoultre at just $241,000.00. I recommend an investigative tour of the websites listed on the full-page jewelry and wristwatch advertisements in magazines like *Elite Traveler*, *Town & Country*, and *Trump*. Some jewelers' and watch companies' websites to visit for an eye-opening education:

www.DavidYurman.com

www.Vacheron-Constantin.com
www.AaronBasha.com
www.deGrisogono.com
www.RosenbergDiamonds.com

Bling means different things to different people. The affluent person who can't fathom paying $4,000.00 for a hubcap will pay that much or ten times that much for a particular wristwatch that will be recognized by his tribal peers as a symbol of wealth, status, and significance. But even the most conservative individual has something he's bought as bling. And there may be yet-unseen opportunities to inject some bling into your products.

A LAPTOP WITH BLING

The original IBM ThinkPad was the first laptop with an integrated CD and DVD-ROM drive. For a time, it was the fifth appendage of the executive road warrior. It celebrated its 15th anniversary in 2007. So 5,000, and only 5,000, commemorative ThinkPad Reserve Edition units were being offered for sale—at $5,000.00 each. The ThinkPad Reserve Edition was clad in hand-stitched, saddle-grade premium French leather. The ThinkPad logo was engraved into the leather. It boasted a 160 GB drive (vs. the original's wimpy 250 MB) and came with its own concierge; for 36 months, the owner had direct access to his very own around-the-clock tech support specialist, who could instantly help with file backups and, if need be, dispatch a technician to the owner's location within four hours. So there was, arguably, a practical defense for the $5,000.00 price tag. But really, it was about the leather. Information may still be at www.ThinkPadReserve.com. Yes, it even has its own website.

CHAPTER 24

Money Spent at Home

When the Seiberlings—he, a tire magnate—built their home, Stan Hywet Hall, an 80-room Tudor mansion in Akron, Ohio, in 1915, at a cost of $3 million (in 1915!), Mrs. Seiberling ordered workmen to cut scuff marks into the hardwood floors so the home wouldn't look "ridiculously new and unlived in."

Between 25% and 30% of affluents own multiple homes for personal use, with the majority of these owning two such homes. Ownership of three or more homes for personal use is concentrated among those with the highest net worth and is more common with ultra-affluents. For those with multiple residences, the average value of the second residence or vacation home is $865,000.00; the average value of the primary residence is $1.3 million to $1.4 million. About half of the second homes are within a day's drive of the primary residence and tend to get frequent weekend use. The more distant second residences tend to get seasonal use. What this means to the marketer of products and services for the home is that one in four to one in three affluent customers have opportunity to buy for more than one residence. This is another reason to think globally rather than locally (see Chapter 28).

The owner of two or more homes is in a near constant pattern of spending on one or the other. In the fall 2007 surveys of the affluent conducted by the American Affluence Research Center, plans for major home remodeling were up slightly from the previous survey. Their calculations predicted 2.7 million home remodeling projects and 605,000 purchases of new primary residences or additional secondary or vacation residences by affluents and ultra-affluents, from fall 2007 through fall 2008—even while mainstream real estate and home improvement spending was expected to be in a slump.

As an aside, the dual- or multiple-residence owner is an outstanding target customer or client for marketers of a wide variety of goods and services beyond home furnishings, home decorating, home improvement, and home services such as maid service and landscape maintenance. For example, for insurance, financial services professionals, CPAs, and attorneys, these clients have more complicated needs and interests and tend to respond to professionals' advertising in the national magazines and journals they read more so than local media.

But, to return to the home itself, as a quick education, you might visit www.DesignerDoors.com to see "picture-perfect, hand-crafted architectural accents crafted by skilled artisans for the re-visioning™ of your home." Should you dare call them garage doors, they dispatch a tough nanny to wash out your mouth with soap. This is a nice lesson in the fact that no commodity product bought solely as a necessity for its function need remain such a mundane thing when sold to the affluent.

Brian Maynard at KitchenAid, quoted in Pamela Danziger's book *Let Them Eat Cake,* says he views true luxury today "as being an expert at something. It's being a wine expert, a cooking expert, a golf expert. Luxury is about personal transformation . . . . In terms of our brand, KitchenAid is for people who love to cook, who have that expert knowledge and love to use it. If it has anything to do with a cooking passion, we provide a product for that. We talk about the brand by communicating why someone would want convection cooking or a wine cellar with temperature zones."

A key part of the KitchenAid marketing program is the sponsoring or creating and hosting of "experiential events," such as Book and Cook events, where the company brings in influencers like celebrity chefs, cookbook authors, food writers, and kitchen designers to complement product demonstrations and displays. KitchenAid has very deliberately and strategically worked at moving itself from mass marketing of ordinary and utilitarian products to marketing to the affluent, with unique products. Once known for dishwashers, it now strives to be a purveyor of premium-priced kitchen products for true cooking aficionados. It is significant that Maynard is talking not so much about his products as about his customers—people with cooking passions, expert knowledge, and a love for showing it off.

Maynard is also aware that his customers are both affluent and mass-affluent, with more in common psychographically than demographically, so he even took the very unusual step of using half-hour TV infomercials to sell the company's $370.00 mixers, a price point typically thought too high for direct-response TV. At the time, Maynard said: "Our customer loves to cook, her home is very important to her, she's on a never-ending journey to make her home her showcase and the kitchen is the heart of her home. There are a lot of people who fit that profile who make less than $50,000.00 a year, so if we just used demographics and cut ourselves off at above $50,000.00, we'd miss a lot of customers."

Kitchens, of course, are big business. A friend of mine recently had hers re-done, and commented, "Apparently anything not made out of *granite* no longer has a place in the kitchen." You probably know someone—if not yourself—who has recently put from $25,000.00 to $100,000.00 into a complete kitchen makeover. As with all big-ticket purchases made by the mass-affluent and affluent for their homes, whether kitchens, theater rooms, meticulously landscaped and lit backyards with grill areas rivaling the kitchen, and so on, it's not about utility, but about a variety of emotional issues.

AND WHAT MIGHT THEY BUY FOR THEIR HOMES?

If your family loves pizza, then you may have considered getting a pizza oven. But is an oven that cooks only one pizza at a time enough? A double-deck pizza oven equipped with real pizza stones (the secret of great crust) can be yours for just $180.00 from Brookstone.®

If you've always wanted a tree in your living room—and, hey, who hasn't?—the next best thing is a natural-looking steel art replica tree. Shipped in color-coded sections for easy assembly, so you need not remove your home's roof to get your tree inside. At www.NatureMaker.com.

When winter arrives, what backyard is complete without its own outdoor sauna? Prices start at around $4,500.00. One maker is Callaway Woodworks at www.CallawayWoodworks.com.

And when summer rolls around, do not settle for any ordinary hammock. Heavens, what will the neighbors think? Artistically crafted hammock stands made with finely finished North Carolina cypress wood can be had for $595.00 to $795.00, quilted hammock fabrics for $125.00 to $249.00, matching pillows, $45.00 each. From www.Frontgate.com.

Visit www.LuxuryHousingTrends.com for more examples.

CHAPTER 25

Money Spent Dining Out

"The best way to have quiche for dinner is to make it up and put it in the oven to bake at about 325 degrees. Meanwhile, get out a large T-bone, grill it, and when it's done eat it. As for the quiche, continue to let it bake, but otherwise ignore it."

—COWBOY PHILOSOPHER TEXAS BIX BENDER,
DON'T SQUAT WITH YER SPURS ON

We love to eat. And we love to eat out. Restaurant sales now exceed $175 billion and have increased from 2004 to 2005, 2005 to 2006, and 2006 to 2007. Approximately 84% of Americans dine out at least once a month, 19% dine out six or more times a month, and 8% do it ten or more times per month. As you might imagine, frequent diners are more affluent and are more likely to patronize upscale restaurants more frequently. However, there has been an enormous boom for the midrange casual dining restaurants, notably major chains in that category, tied to the mass-affluent explosion. Chains benefiting most, based on sales per location and sales growth, include the

Cheesecake Factory,® P.F. Chang's China Bistro,® Olive Garden,® T.G.I. Friday's,® Outback Steakhouse,® Macaroni Grill,® Joe's Crab Shack,® Chili's,® and Red Robin Gourmet Burgers.®

My client Rory Fatt, CEO of Restaurant Marketing Systems and of Royalty Rewards,® companies working with more than 5,000 independent restaurants throughout the United States and Canada, says that "the number-one path to prosperity for an independent competing with the chains is frequent, even constant communication with its customers, so there's a relationship. Number two: creating entertaining and enjoyable experiences." The Best Independent Restaurant Owners' Association reports that its most successful members are increasingly target marketing affluent consumers. Even in the most mainstream of categories, pizza, the most interesting trend is gourmet, exemplified by my friend Diana Coutu's pizza business, growing by leaps and bounds, and selling at prices 200% to 500% higher than same-sized pizzas of major chains (www.DianasGourmetPizzeria.ca).

As a restaurant moves up, from anybody and everybody, to mass-affluent, to affluent clientele—targeted by its marketing and served by design of its product—price becomes less and less of a factor in customers' decisions about repeat and even frequent patronage. I listened during a staff meeting at an upscale restaurant as the manager explained, "*We* do not have specials. *Denny's*® has specials. *We* have chef's features." And that sums it up. While the lure of low price for a lot of bulk or price- or discount-driven specials is significantly important to the Denny's® customer and is of some importance to the Applebee's® or Outback Steakhouse® customer, it is of zero importance to the Fleming's® steakhouse customer.

The same applies to foods delivered to the home. If you compare Omaha Steak's® marketing to Allen Brothers'® marketing, you'll see that Omaha, catering to the mass-affluent, relies heavily on sales, special offers, and discounts, while Allen Brothers, selling to the more affluent, relies much less on price-related marketing.

While there appears to be fierce competition in the restaurant industry, it is more about each restaurant finding its market. Certainly the higher up the food chain one moves, pardon the pun, the easier it is to carve out and control a unique segment of the market. And the less competition there is.

Finally, there's a difference between a convenience restaurant and a destination restaurant. Fast-food, low-priced, and mid-priced restaurants marketing to mass-affluent and down tend to live or die by convenience to their customers. For fast-food outlets, location—even side of the street—traffic patterns, and population density are of enormous importance. This makes them vulnerable to shifts in such things, and, although you don't think of McDonald's® Burger King® Arby's® and so on failing, there are surprisingly large numbers of such stores that do close their doors every year, usually having to incur costs of relocation to follow the customers' movements. Better restaurants marketing to mass-affluent and up are only about 50% dependent on convenience and can successfully draw from a bigger radius around their location, as customers who like that particular restaurant will drive farther to patronize it. Upscale restaurants and upscale and unique restaurants are destinations, so convenience can be virtually nonexistent and they can still draw maximum crowds every night. Affluent customers are, according to the 2006 Food, Beverage and Hospitality Survey of

the Affluent, four times more likely than non-affluent consumers to drive farther than 40-minute round-trips to patronize
a restaurant of choice.

CHAPTER 26

■■■■■■■■■

Money Spent on Experiences

"Last week I spent $1,000.00 to fly out to California, $500.00 a night to stay at a resort to attend a $15,000.00 seminar titled 'Money Isn't Everything'."

—BOB ORBEN, TV COMEDY WRITER AND DIRECTOR OF WHITE HOUSE SPEECHWRITING DURING THE GERALD FORD ADMINISTRATION

I 'll borrow their ad copy:

Today, you rescued the plane, prevented a carjacking and shot your way out of a crowded subway station—and you never left our resort. Save the world by day. Relax with your favorite cocktail, vintage cigar, and fine cuisine at a true five-star mountain resort by night. A lifestyle typically reserved for secret agents and action heroes is now available to those who dare . . . Valhalla Shooting Club at Elk Mountain Resort. Ultra-realistic, theme-based, live-fire shooting scenarios put you in control of your destiny with pistol in hand. And when the shooting stops, our resort offers a full complement of activities and luxuries designed to satisfy you and your companion.

Aah, shaken, not stirred. As someone who played with a Man from U.N.C.L.E. attaché case in the backyard and grew up on Napoleon Solo, llya Kuryakin, James Bond, and the original Avengers, I find the Valhalla adventure appealing. It may or may not be your cup of tea, but some experience—some packaged grand experience or amazing adventure—would be. And there may very well be some such experience you can create within or as extension of your business with enormous appeal to some number of affluent individuals.

One of our long-time Glazer-Kennedy Insider's Circle™ Members running jewelry stores in small, Midwest communities once annually takes a dozen or so of his most affluent clients on a trip to the South African diamond mines, where they pick out their own diamonds firsthand to be placed in custom-crafted jewelry. They can also add on an African safari or cruise if they desire. He collects a sizeable "experience fee" for putting this trip together and escorting his group. The fees combined are nearly as much as one-fourth of the net profit from one of his stores for the entire year.

My long-time Platinum Member Ron LeGrand, the leading authority in America on independent, innovative real estate investing and "quick-turn real estate," has indulged a personal passion by buying an entire Alaskan fishing resort (which you can see at www.SalmonFallsResort.com). He has quickly transformed its marketing, to get away from selling room nights, meals, and boat rentals to fully packaged experiences as well as multi-year, pre-paid memberships.

Even the rather pedestrian cruise industry has grown up and gone affluent. Take the Four Seasons cruise ship. You do not just grab a cabin at a website, hop on board, and line up for the bon voyage buffet. Instead, you buy a time-share in it, for hundreds of thousands of dollars. The shares sold fast. Other condo cruise ships with penthouse cabins priced into the millions are at sea, with more under hurried construction. People purchasing these floating condos and time-shares aren't doing so purely to take cruises. They are buying into an elite gated community that floats, and they're purchasing a unique experience. One of these ultraluxury cruise ship residences, the *Magellan*, is described this way:

> **The facilities and services of the world's finest resorts are part of everyday life aboard *The Magellan*.** On-call housekeeping staff, a world-class spa, 24-hour concierge staff, indoor and outdoor pools, six restaurants, a 450-seat theater with Broadway quality entertainment, a casino worthy of Monte Carlo, and a 8,000 square foot greenhouse with onsite horticulturists are just a few of the conveniences that make living aboard *The Magellan* a unique experience.

Since when are a greenhouse with in-house horticulturist and six restaurants *conveniences*? Since now, for the ultra-affluent. Note this ad is not talking about taking a cruise. *Living aboard.*

Incidentally, time-shares, on dry land or afloat, are historically notoriously bad investments. Developers frequently flirt with fraud in overselling capacity, amenities deteriorate after units sell out, bankruptcies occur with regularity—even with this new type of high-end, luxury time-share. Overall, resale values rarely even match original purchase prices let alone yield gains. So, shouldn't ultra-affluent individuals know better? Only demonstrates that people are people.

My client Rob Minton, creator of the Income For Life real estate investing service offered in more than 100 cities, frequently urges people to "invest *to* demand." It's solid, sound advice, and not just for an investor choosing stocks, funds, or real estate, but also for an entrepreneur investing your time and energy as well as your money in developing products, services, and businesses and in acquiring customers. If you are following what most consider the smart money of late, you've seen it moving to companies, entrepreneurs, and projects creating and providing luxury experiences. As example, two of the world's richest men, Bill Gates and Prince Alwaleed bin Talal Alsaud, partnered in taking the Four Seasons hotel chain private—with its luxury time-share and condo properties and newest addition, cruise ships. Apparently they see big profit potential in this crown jewel company.

Turning to the mass-affluent, the company I admire most in the world, Disney,® continues to diversify, developing and offering new experiences for sale to its customers. Its wedding business, thriving and expanding. Its multi-generational family reunion business, thriving. Its experience resorts like the Animal Kingdom Lodge, booked solid at premium prices. The Fastpass® for many, but for some the $125.00-per-hour private guide with whom you bump all the lines, go backstage, take shortcuts. In the time-share category, the Disney® Vacation Club is rapidly expanding to meet demand. When I took one of my client groups to Disney World® on a research excursion, we had a private lunch with two Imagineers,® one of whom developed the group sales presentation used on board Disney® cruise ships to sell the club, who was thoroughly familiar with its growth. He predicted it would increase at least five-fold in less than three years, with new means of marketing and new luxury options. Since then, Disney® has opened the first of a number of planned stores in shopping malls exclusively devoted to selling the Vacation Club time-shares. The company has have also gone west, turning 2.5 acres adjacent to the Grand Californian Hotel and Spa® at Disneyland® into 50 Vacation Club villas.

In total, the Vacation Club time-share program is in its 15th year, has more than 350,000 owners, and simply can't add facilities fast enough to meet demand. Current expansion includes the new villas at Disneyland® in California and new Animal Kingdom Villas in Florida.

Time-shares aren't limited to something you stay and sleep in anymore either. Affluent customers are time-sharing collections of exotic automobiles and portfolios of expensive jewelry, and ultra-affluent clients are time-sharing a "family office," typically comprised of a CPA and life concierge on staff, supervising and coordinating all aspects of clients' lives, from paying bills to planning trips to finding someone to remodel the barn. Instead of owning only one or two exotic cars, you can buy into a time-share and drive dozens. Instead of owning only a few $50,000.00 to $500,000.00 pieces of stunning, one-of-a-kind jewelry, you can draw from a collection of hundreds and never be seen wearing the same piece twice. Instead of using your own Rolodex® to find pool cleaners, find home remodelers, organize trips, buy gifts, and check up on your money managers and investments yourself, you can share a dedicated management team with two or three other families.

Today, the affluent customer can get just about anything he can imagine—and will buy many things he didn't imagine on his own—in the experience category. Oh, if you feel like helicoptering into Valhalla as its next tuxedoed, pistol-wielding, martini-drinking, beautiful-woman-impressing secret agent, you may begin your adventure at www.ValhallaShootingClub.com.

MAKING OTHERS' MONEY DISAPPEAR, LEGALLY

Steve Cohen is a magician. A millionaire magician. As far as I can tell, his tricks are rather common and easily duplicated by other magicians. The trick he calls "instant ROI," the turning of $1.00 bills into $100.00 bills is clever use of a pre-packaged trick available in any magic shop. Yet Steve the Magician makes more than $1 million a year performing not on stage in Las Vegas but at private parties. How can that be? He sells himself exclusively to affluent clients, for their house parties and business events. He has, for example, performed at Martha Stewart's house (where he made a spool of thread levitate out of her meat loaf) and at Reebok® founder Paul Fireman's home.

He does have a nifty story: he was purportedly trained in the dark arts by a great uncle who studied under Houdini himself. But this is not really the magic behind his magical income.

Cohen charges from $10,000.00 to $25,000.00 per private performance. I checked around; most magicians charge those same numbers less a zero, down to a few hundred dollars. The fee differential has little to do with his magic and everything to do with his clientele. It all began in 2001, when he persuaded the Waldorf-Astoria® Hotel to give him a suite on Friday evenings, to perform close-up magic as a novelty for the hotel's guests and dinner guests. In short order, the affluent clientele frequenting the Waldorf began hiring him to perform at their private soirees. As soon as he had a few high-society clients and could drop their

MAKING OTHERS' MONEY DISAPPEAR,
LEGALLY, CONTINUED

names, he was able to levitate his fees from low to extremely high.

There's no magic here out of reach of any professional provider of just about any service, expertise, or, as in Cohen's case, entertainment. Another of my books in this No B.S. series, *NO B.S. WEALTH ATTRACTION FOR ENTREPRENEURS*, describes 26 Wealth Magnets. Cohen used Wealth Magnet 9: Be Somewhere. He strategically placed himself somewhere that clients with money to burn would experience him and could approach him directly. He organized his being discovered by affluent clients.

Source: Forbes magazine, October 10, 2005.

THE SECRET BEHIND THE SELLING OF EXPERIENCES

"Experiences provide greater happiness because relating to others one's experiences has **greater social value**. Social relationships can be enhanced by sharing stories of one's experiences, whereas the same cannot be said for stories about your material possessions. It's one thing to talk about your trip to Paris and quite another to talk about all the stuff you bought while you were there. Experiences are more likely to have a typical narrative structure with a beginning, middle, and end, both listeners and storytellers may enjoy conversing about experiences more than about possessions."

—From *Let Them Eat Cake: Marketing Luxury to the Masses as Well as the Classes*, by Pamela Danziger

■　■　■

"By moving the sale and delivery of your product or service as far away from a utilitarian transaction to a story-worthy experience as possible, you create much happier, more enthusiastic customers resistant to seduction by competitors and eager to tell others about you."

—Dan Kennedy

CHAPTER 27

Money Spent on Liberty

"There is only one success—to be able to spend your life in your own way."

—CHISTOPHER MORLEY, AMERICAN NOVELIST AND JOURNALIST

There are, I *think*, *three kinds of liberty*: day-*to*-day liberty, lifestyle liberty, and mental or emotional liberty. I'd like you to consider each one as something you may be able to deliver through your products, services, or business.

We'll begin with the day to day. The affluent are highly stressed. More than 75% of all affluent business owners and self-employed professionals work 60 to 70 hours a week. The average affluent household with children has each child involved in at least three to five separate, organized activities each week, requiring transportation, supervision, and parental involvement. Families are now spread out over the country, requiring more frequent travel and time away from home and business for personal reasons. Add to this the ever-rising intrusiveness and constant connectedness imposed by technology and the ever-increasing complexity of everyday life thanks to burgeoning choice in every product and service category. Also, the more affluent a person is, the more financial responsibilities, decisions, and seemingly endless paperwork flow he confronts. All added together, it equals high stress, low liberty. By "low liberty," I mean that this person feels as if he has no time for himself, feels as if constantly chasing and never catching, constantly at odds with himself and others, and always disappointing someone. I know these feelings well myself. You might think of us as *desperate* affluents.

On the rare occasions desperate affluents find someone of demonstrated, proven, reliable competence to whom they can transfer some responsibility, they will do so eagerly and pay generously for the relief. These desperate affluents often overpay people by normal or traditional standards but consider the liberty being purchased a bargain. I recently had a client tell me he paid his personal assistant $75,000.00 a year, a wage judged by his business partner, CPA, and others as $30,000.00 too much, but, because she can be counted on to anticipate his needs, think for herself, and relieve him of having to remember just about everything, he considers it a half-price bargain. Another desperate affluent businesswoman I know has a person who comes to her home twice a week and does the laundry, changes the bedding, goes to the grocer's and restocks the refrigerator, and takes and picks up clothes at the cleaners—for which she pays $500.00 a week. I imagine that works out to something like $50.00 an hour. Too much? Or bargain? What price the liberty to enjoy an evening out or to be able to come home and relax at end of a high-pressure day instead of having to wash clothes or finding nothing in the fridge suitable for a cobbled-together dinner and having to get back in the car and go out? What price liberty?

In his book *The Art of Selling to the Affluent*, Matt Oechsli writes, "When people are under a lot of stress, they look for relief. They initiate many major purchase decisions to reward themselves for their hard work and as a stress release. The last thing they want is a hassle." He goes further to give these seven drivers of significant buying decisions by the affluent (boldfacing of key words and phrases, mine):

1. They want to be **respected**, even honored, for the level of success they have achieved.
2. They are successful because of the professionalism and **competence** they apply to their work, and they expect no less from others.
3. They will react strongly to any attempts to deceive them, and when [they feel] that happens, they take their business elsewhere.
4. They define value **in their own terms.**
5. Instead of striving to keep up with the Joneses, they want to be **different** than the Joneses.
6. They experience enough tension and hassles in their daily work life—they want to be **free** from all that when dealing with people who would like to sell them something [and keep them as customers/clients/patients].
7. They can afford and are **willing to pay** for the best information, the best products, the highest level of **competence**, and the best professional service available.

Next, consider the magnification of this, to lifestyle. The affluent are on a search, a life and lifestyle quest.

They are on a quest for respect.

On a quest for competence.
A quest for integrity.
A quest for status and value meaningful to them.
A quest for relief from stress and difficulty and responsibility.
Most of all, a quest for competence.

They often arrange their lives and the locations in it in ways reflective of this quest. A very successful hedge fund manager (Roulac Global Places Fund) and long-time client of mine, Stephen Roulac, commented about me that I am obsessed with "time economics" and time preservation. Our Ohio home was chosen primarily for its 8-minute proximity to the racetrack where I race most of my horses. It is the best available that close to the track. There's an upscale community 20 minutes away I'd prefer living in, but it would mean 40 minutes of commuting on race days—unacceptable. This home is also exactly midway between the Cleveland and the Akron airports. And 15 minutes away from a nice hotel that ably hosts my coaching and client group meetings. Our other home, in Virginia, is 15 minutes from Dulles International Airport, but not in flight paths. A penthouse condo with amenities in its building, fine restaurants including Morton's® a brief walk away, a Barnes & Noble® less than a mile away. I find most affluents still active in businesses and careers try to similarly organize the locations of residences and offices for ease, convenience, and minimized stress in commuting and travel.

They delegate and transfer a lot of responsibility, even though, by nature and experience, they tend to be control freaks. The desperate need for relief from a myriad of overwhelming, stressful responsibilities supersedes their preference for hands-on control of everything. Consequently, many put some or all of their personal wealth under others' management. They hire personal chefs to choose and prepare the foods and meals they eat. They let a clothier choose their wardrobe. A personal shopper choose their gifts for others. On and on. In all these instances, they are not just attempting to buy a little time or convenience— they are seeking to buy lifestyle liberty. Not just a reality of minutes freed up or tasks done, but *a sense of* liberation from the mundane and time-consuming.

Which arrives at the third liberty they seek: mental and emotional liberty.

Napoleon Hill, legendary for his book *Think And Grow Rich*, wrote a lesser-known book as his last of many, titled *Grow Rich With Peace Of Mind*. That title has a double meaning: that the ultimate aspiration, achievement, and wealth was peace of mind and that you needed peace of mind to be truly rich. In that book, Hill told of finally having to disconnect all his phones, as his celebrity had put him under constant assault from all manner of people with requests for his time, money, and assistance. Donald Trump recently described his life as "one long telephone call." I am at the point Hill found himself, and need a number of barriers to restrict access to me in order to have any peace. You need to know that the affluent have enormous demands assailing them, and look, above all else, for breathing space. A multi-millionaire client recently told me of buying a very expensive "cabin" in a relatively remote area near Jackson Hole, Wyoming, a popular playground of the rich. He showed me a picture of the area around his place, just miles of snow-covered emptiness. He talked of going dogsledding. Mostly, he talked of enjoying the sense of distance and isolation from people and their demands on him.

Beyond this, the affluent are seeking liberty from critical judgment and guilt. This nation attacks its affluent relentlessly, in the media, in politics, in public and private discourse. The affluents' Spidey-sense detects envy, jealousy, resentment, and disapproval emanating from most of the people they interact with and from the public at large. One millionaire told me: "The more successful I get, the more I feel eyes in the dark hungrily watching me." Another said to me: "To my face, they are deferential. Behind my back, they are angry critics who believe themselves infinitely smarter and harder working and more deserving than I." Another described feeling as if the target painted on his chest got bigger and brighter with each passing year. In his outstanding book *Paranoia and Power*, Gene Landrum, the leading authority on the psychology of the rich and powerful, states: "Paranoia is rampant among super achievers." Further, attempts to influence the affluent with guilt for the admittedly growing gap between them and the have-nots is pervasive and unrelenting. It comes from close family members and distant relatives—as comedian and game show host Louie Anderson so painfully showed off in one of the most memorable Oprah shows ever and wrote about in his autobiography. It comes from the endless charities, causes, and others at their doorstep asking for or, in some cases, nearly demanding handouts. It comes from political demagogues, media, and even rich limousine liberals themselves, acting out of guilt. Behind closed doors, this is the frequently discussed, shared angst of the affluent.

How to Make Yourself Magnetic to the Affluent

If you truly understand this quest of the affluent, it's not difficult to see what is required of you to make yourself magnetic to them—and to their money.

Not necessarily in any priority order, there are three big things to do.

One, develop, display, and convey a profound position of expertise, good judgment, understanding, professionalism, and competence. Present yourself as the most trustworthy of advisors. The most trusted advisors relied on by the affluent automatically and certainly become very affluent themselves. Almost next to, or only a step behind, every person famous for wealth and power stands an almost equally wealthy—in some cases, wealthier—trusted advisor. Think George Ross to Donald Trump. A man whose name I can't recall and is rarely publicly uttered, who has basically run Warren Buffett's business and financial empire for decades. In politics, the Karl Roves and James Carvilles, and politicians' attorneys like William Bennett. There are kings and kingmakers. Millionaires and millionaire-makers.

Two, relieve your affluent clients of time, pressure, anxiety, stress, day-to-day hassle, tasks they'd rather not do or even think about or that should be below their own time's value. Create privilege and luxury-level convenience for them. Make standing in lines, filling out forms, mere mortals' normal burdens go away.

Three, give them acceptance, approval, and applause. They are extremely responsive to those who celebrate their success and respect it as earned. Become known as a supporter and advocate of achievement and affluence. Take philosophical positions that counter the constant criticism they receive from most other quarters.

We will flesh out specific strategies supportive of these three objectives in Book Three.

BOOK THREE

How Can I Get Them to Give
Me Their Money?

Reshaping Your Business, Products,
Services, Prices, Advertising, Marketing,
and Sales Practices: Specific Strategies for
Attracting the Affluent

CHAPTER 28

No Boundaries Anymore

"We're not in Kansas anymore."

—DOROTHY, IN *THE WIZARD OF OZ*

The number of high-net-worth individuals in the United States with assets of $1 million or more was up 8.3% from 2005 to 2007, topping 9.5 million such people, with spending power exceeding $37 trillion (up 11.5% for the same time period). Spending power increasing faster than the number of millionaires verifies the rich are getting richer, all the more reason to find ways to sell to them. But these are the U.S. statistics. We are no longer a leader in much. And we are no longer the leader in wealth creation. The affluent and ultra-affluent in other countries, combined, number roughly 8-to-1 those in the United States, and the fastest growth in new affluents is abroad.

There may or may not be a lot of affluent consumers right where you are. There is definitely an abundance, an oversupply, of them spread all over the United States as well as globally. The population of affluent consumers is explosively growing and large in number, but is still quite small as a percentage of the population, so it spreads thin over the whole country. For this reason, there is a lot more money to be made by marketing to all of them wherever they are rather than limiting yourself to the small number of them who may be within driving distance of where you are.

To make a lot more money, stop thinking locally and start thinking globally.

But why would somebody 1,000 miles away from you pay high prices for what you sell in Boise, Idaho, when there's some of the very same stuff within walking distance of his Boston townhouse? Or his *London* townhouse? The very asking of this question suggests you just haven't been paying attention.

Of course, there's no shortage of anything anywhere. Wherever you are, if you want to put together a Thanksgiving dinner, everything you need you can get right where you are. You need not import it from Dean & DeLuca.® If you have a craving for fudge brownies, there's a bakery close by, a grocery store nearby; you need not import them from Fairytale Brownies® in Phoenix. If you want to get flowers, there's a florist right down the block. No need to call 1-800-Flowers. If you want to invest in real estate, there are all sorts of it for sale where you live. No need to call my client, Darin Garman, in Cedar Rapids, Iowa, and buy an apartment building or shopping center there, sight unseen. But Dean & DeLuca is shipping turkey dinners and pies and caviar, Fairytale Brownies® is delivering boxes of brownies, Jim

McCann is taking an order for flowers to be delivered right down the street from you and your neighborhood florist, and people are calling Garman from Los Angeles, Miami, New York, Toronto, and Tokyo. Why?

Because any remaining boundaries are in your head and nowhere else.

My own consumer behavior strikes many as odd, but rarely strikes another really affluent person that way. I have two homes, one in Ohio and one near Washington, DC. My office is in Phoenix, but I never go there, and the Glazer-Kennedy publishing empire's offices are in Baltimore, and I hardly ever go there. My dentist is in Richmond, Virginia, hours away from the Washington, DC, home and a flight away from my Ohio home. My money manager for my retirement accounts is in Idaho, and I've yet to sit down with him face-to-face. My literary agent lives on a gentleman's farm in a tiny town, a long train ride from the hub of publishing activity, New York City, but it doesn't matter; I've had no need to see him face-to-face in years, even while having my last

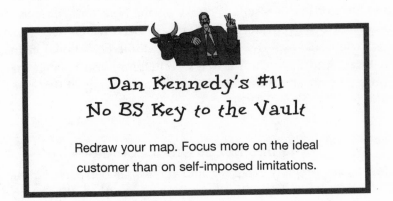

Dan Kennedy's #11
No BS Key to the Vault

Redraw your map. Focus more on the ideal customer than on self-imposed limitations.

five books published. My real estate investments are mostly in Iowa and surrounding areas, and I've never gone there or seen them. Our steaks come by FedEx® from Allen Brothers rather than from a local butcher or store. I buy most of my clothes, my nutritional products, and my gifts from catalogs. I recently got an $850.00 office chair—the Aeron chair, the best, most comfortable chair I have ever owned. I did not go to a store to get it. It was ordered for me from a website. I couldn't even tell you where its maker resides. I am unbound, as are the people who sell me things and provide professional services.

No matter your business, you must begin thinking unbound.

Open a regular airline magazine the next time you travel. You will see full-page ads inviting people to fly to a dentist in Texas, a cosmetic surgeon in Los Angeles, for carpel tunnel treatment in Kansas. Are there no dentists, cosmetic surgeons, or carpel tunnel doctors anywhere else in the country, so everyone must now trek cross-country for treatment? This isn't Mayo Clinic advertising, either (although it does, too). These are doctors in private practice. As far as I know, none of them has been on *Oprah* or had bestselling books on the *New York Times* list or otherwise achieved exceptional fame or been widely recognized for exceptional expertise. They just *decided* to be national instead of local. And if you think that's something, you need to page through the many different magazines aimed only at those of us who fly private!

The Internet as Great Liberator

Pick a category, any category, and traverse cyberspace. Nothing has dissolved geographic boundaries more than the internet.

And although it is still not favored by the affluent, they are steadily increasing embrace of it as means of investigating options, acquiring information, making buying decisions, and even getting deliverables, products, and services.

Somebody wants to buy a golf bag. Less than 20 years ago, his choices would be limited to whatever the pro shop at the club or a local sporting goods store might have, which would be limited by its space and funds. Now there are more stores. And golf bags are sold at Wal-Mart® and at Neiman-Marcus.® On the internet, there are thousands of stores selling golf bags. Some are giant sporting goods cyber malls, some devoted just to golf, some just for golfers who travel, some for just men, some for women, some for seniors, and some with golf-related goods only for the affluent. And many manufacturers sell direct from their websites, especially those with unusual or unusually expensive golf bags that stores might not care to stock. A company can now justify making and offering an extremely expensive, luxury version of its golf bags knowing it may sell only a few hundred all year long because there's no need to convince stores to stock them. Fashion designers can be in the golf bag business when, before, they couldn't. So, for example, one can buy a Louis Vuitton® Damier Geant Canvas Golf Bag built for travel for a mere $9,700.00. There are many things people can spend $10,000.00 on. A car or half a car. A number of mortgage payments. A year of their son's college education. Or this golf bag.

Dean & DeLuca® began in 1977 as a little gourmet grocery store, a single brick-and-mortar business, in SoHo, in New York City. Joel Dean and Giorgio DeLuca took trips around the world to find unusual, artisan foods, gradually discovering just how much price elasticity existed in their business, with the affluent customers attracted by their unique wares and store environment. In 1987, they moved from the little corner store to a 10,000-square-foot space. They now have two stores in New York, one in Charlotte, North Carolina, one in Washington, DC, one in California, and one in Leawood, Kansas, all affluent population centers. Their mail-order catalog, online catalog, and corporate gift businesses open up these brick-and-mortar walls to customers anywhere in the world . . . and make their shelf space unlimited, so they can offer $50.00 lobster frittatas, $36.00 bagel collections, the full line of very pricey Culinary Institute of America cookware, a $1,500.00 countertop coffeemaker, and the list goes on and on and on. I have used this company here and in Chapter 17 as a perfect example of the little business that could, one that starts out in a very traditional, local, confined way but morphs into multiple businesses under one umbrella (not roof) operating entirely free of geographic or physical boundaries in order to reach out to and serve its ideal customers wherever they can be found. Any business can follow this model. Focusing on affluent customers makes it easier to do so, as premium prices, exceptional margins, and above-par transaction sizes best support this sort of expansiveness. One of the keys to doing this successfully, in any product or business category is . . .

Selection. At the low end, the internet has democratized merchandising and purchasing. People who must or want to buy the cheapest option in a category or find the cheapest price for a particular item can search the world and all its vendors from the comfort of their recliner. But at the high end, the internet has made it possible for luxury merchants to create and offer premium, ultra-premium and ultra, ultra, ultra-premium versions of every imaginable product and service, even if only selling small numbers of them. And the unlimited-space aspect of the internet permits some merchants to offer the biggest and most varied selection of particular goods in their price ranges. Zappos.com, in the case history at the end of this chapter, is a good example. It is a *global* shoe store.

Whether you dispense investment or astrological advice, provide business consulting and coaching as I and many of my clients do, are an exotic dancer or a cosmetic dentist, have nutritional products, cosmetics, or golf bags to sell, bake brownies or knit quilts, there is absolutely no good reason anymore to think locally or accept any geographic or space boundaries—and every reason not to. Given that you are highly motivated to re-invent your business for successful marketing to the affluent, this is doubly true.

ZAPPOS.COM: A GLOBAL SHOE STORE

A very boyish-looking 33-year-old, Tony Hsieh, is ZAPPOS.COM's CEO, overseeing 1,300 employees, 350 of which are call center and "customer loyalty representative" staff; warehouse space in Kentucky near a FedEx hub (equal to 17 football fields); two outlet stores; and about 6 million customers he is determined to keep happy. His focus is NOT on advertising or marketing but instead on so consistently satisfying every customer that he keeps coming back for more and telling others. His expressed answer to how the business has grown so dramatically year to year is by taking money ordinarily consumed by advertising and investing it

---

ZAPPOS.COM, CONTINUED

in improving the "customer experience." Extra-mile services include free, next-day shipping for all orders received by 1 P.M. . . . something most mail-order and e-commerce companies charge extra for and do badly, often providing the overnight shipment three or four days after taking the order. Hsieh enunciates the reason for Zappos's "generosity" and insistence on TRUE next day brilliantly: **"We believe that the speed at which a customer receives a purchase plays a very important role in how that customer thinks about shopping with us in the future."** For years I have explained this to largely deaf ears—that time is different for buyer and seller. The buyer wants it the minute he orders it, so each day is a week, each week a month. The marketer is busy, has to make it or get it, and has two people out sick, so a week is a day, a month a week. This also illustrates my <u>"EVERYTHING IS MARKETING"</u> premise: in Hsieh's case, not selling anything not in stock in his warehouse, thus boosting inventory investment, providing FedEx delivery without added charge or markup, having more skilled phone operators, and so on is NOT *operations* (expense) but IS *marketing*. (Why can't more marketers get this point, that everything is marketing, everything matters, and may even have equal weighting?)

Every new ZAPPOS employee goes through THREE WEEKS of "customer loyalty training," combining company history, philosophy, and values with customer service tools, software, phone scripts, and interning in both the call center and the warehouse. Training does not stop there, either; it continues and is constant, with close supervision and oversight. This is another smart move

ZAPPOS.COM, CONTINUED

of ad dollars to customer experience: competent, knowledgeable employees.

<u>ZAPPOS'S online marketing is limited but effective</u>: an affiliate program with done-for-them options ranging from simple banner ads to full clones of the catalog, search engine marketing using generic terms (*high heels*) and brand names, a bimonthly e-newsletter to all customers plus different e-mails opted into by customers with different interests (list segmentation!!!), and a social networking and membership site where customers can talk with each other, like: "What shoes do you think I should wear to my sister's wedding? By the way, I hate my sister." Significantly, ZAPPOS does NOT rely much on coupons, promotions, or specials; **Hsieh does not want to train their customers to buy from the company based on price.** "If someone is buying just on price, then we really don't want them as a customer," he says. I preach this until I'm blue in the face. Easier than ever to do via the internet, yet nobody's willing to do it.

ZAPPOS is a great answer to the business owners who insist they are stuck in a boring or ordinary or commoditized business or beaten up by cheap-price providers. Not much is more commoditized and widely available everywhere than shoes. The <u>rare</u> commodities here are **vast selection** and extraordinary service. Zappos was created in 1999 by Nick Swinmurn, just a regular guy wandering around the mall looking for a pair of shoes—and getting tired feet doing it. Proof you do NOT need a revolutionary

ZAPPOS.COM, CONTINUED

new product or unique market space to succeed. This business model has legs elsewhere: marrying customers to you and thriving largely thanks to word of mouth by (1) creating vast selection in a particular category, (2) delivering extraordinary service including speed of fulfillment, and (3) communicating frequently and constantly with customers in a way that is welcomed and meaningful to them, including giving them control over the options and even an interactive relationship with all the other customers.

Source: Based in part on article in (November–December 2007), originally eM+C from *DM NEWS*, supplemented with online research.

CHAPTER 29

Recession-Proofing Your
Business

"Stock prices have reached what looks like a permanently high plateau."
—Noted economist Irving Fisher, in a speech made
nine days before the 1929 crash

What happens in bad economic times?
A more profound and dramatic version and acceleration of what has been happening over time anyway: the middle is shrinking, with two-thirds moving up, one-third moving down. This leaves you two merchant arenas. The bottom, where merchants wage price wars and consumers come, coupons in their sweaty palms, to scrounge for pennies. Using mass retail as example, this is where we find Wal-Mart,® its badly bruised and bleeding predecessor K-Mart,® its owned competitor Sam's Club,® its competitor Costco,® and, trying to stand just a few inches above this swamp, Target.® Toward the top, we find

Saks® and Neiman Marcus.® Above them, countless luxury goods retailers—for a good view, walk the Forum Shops in Las Vegas. At the bottom of the top, old-line department stores like Macy's.® In the middle, we find the most troubled and vulnerable merchants like JC Penney,® and Sears,® and the bleached bones of the gone and nearly forgotten, like Montgomery Wards? The middle is the worst place to be and doubly so in recession. Merchants in the middle find themselves unable to compete with the bottom on price or selection, or with the top on style, status, or service. They have no unique selling proposition to make to anyone. There's a reason to go to Wal-Mart®: *Low prices every day. Save money. Live better.* There's a reason to go to Neiman's: class. What is the reason to go to JC Penney®? The company itself doesn't know, and neither does anybody else. So people are exiting the middle and moving down or up or, sometimes, in both directions. In a recession, the middle's exits get more crowded.

I have lived through a *real* recession. A lot of my current clients and coaching members and a lot of the readers of this book have not. I know what it is like. You may not. I just about started out in business in the Jimmy Carter economy. Carter single-handedly did more economic damage at a faster pace than any President in history. In short order, he had us with a nasty trifecta ticket in hand: 18% inflation, 18% interest, and 18% unemployment. Plus gas lines. I can tell you from street experience, not ivory-covered-walls theory, that recession eats the middle.

At the bottom, buying drops by only 5% to 10%, because the poor spend 90% of their money on necessities. Necessities somehow get bought. That's why they got named: *necessities.* But the profit margin goes away, as merchants to the bottom battle over these consumers' shrunken spending power with price cutting as the only weapon. Big companies even sell products below cost just to keep factories, stores, and offices open, thus crushing small businesses who can't incur losses for months and months on end. In this kind of financial death spiral, you can still buy a birthday card for Uncle Mo over at the Wal-Mart® But Mary's greeting card and gift shop down the street in the strip center may be boarded up. It do get ugly at the bottom!

At the top, buying also drops by only 5% or 10% because the affluent spend a tiny percentage of their money on necessities. Inflation is least important to affluent consumers, so they continue to buy not just necessities but whatever the devil they want, regardless. But, good news for the merchants selling to them, they don't take away profit margin.

The poor use 80%, 90%, 100%, or—living off credit cards— 150% of their entire income to buy necessities and essential commodities: rent, heat, light, gas to commute to work, baby food and diapers, macaroni and cheese, and, now, cell phones and cable television. Inflation hits them hard. They have no space for it. Just 1% inflation has them reeling. The 18% inflation that occurred during the last major Democrat-induced recession during the Carter administration sends them into a tailspin. Inflation creep forces them to make tough choices, cut virtually all discretionary spending, postpone buying this or that, eat at home instead of going out.

I use about 2% of my earned income and 0% of my considerable investment income to buy necessities and essential commodities. Inflation of 1% isn't even noticed. Even a few years of Carteresque calamity, likely to be created should a Democrat reside at 1600 Pennsylvania Avenue and have the cooperation of a Congress controlled by his or her party, won't matter much to me and won't alter my behavior as a consumer much either.

Those in the middle are most affected by recession. They tend to be living at their means or above their means, yet spending only about 60% of their money on necessities. In recession, they stop spending the other 40%. They just cramp up. So merchants selling to them don't see a 5% or 10% drop; they get whacked with a 40% drop. Even price cutting doesn't help much. The middle dwellers could buy. They just won't.

So whom would you rather be depending on to support your business, as your customer? If you'd like to recession proof your business, by all means, trade up.

People have been mystified that the dramatic increases in oil prices haven't cooled off consumer spending. But the richest 1% of our population controls more wealth than the bottom 90%. The richest 20% account for more than 60% of consumption. Taking that into account, it's easy to see why the spending side of our economy has stayed so strong despite skyrocketed oil prices, war, housing slump, and so on. The spending is being done by consumers for whom such things don't matter much. As I was writing this book, we had an exceptionally bitter-cold month, and a neighbor mentioned to me that her utility bill had leapt from about $120.00 to $313.00 and she had to use a credit card to pay it. I hadn't noticed, but prompted by the conversation, I dug out my utility bill that I'd casually paid and found mine had also shot up to $300.00. That hadn't affected and wasn't going to affect my spending at all, because it didn't matter to me. But it wasn't going to affect her spending, either—she was barely scraping by anyway and wasn't buying much of anything but necessities. The big bump in our utility bills had zero impact on our contributions to the economy. While any increase in basic costs of living adversely affect her yet do not affect her spending, those same costs have no effect on me at all. Even a rise in the costs of living well might not . . .

Consider what's called the Cost of Living Extremely Well Index against the Consumer Price Index (source: Forbes.com), calculated by the federal government. In the year I wrote this book, the CPI suffered inflation of about 2%. The CPI is calculated on a "basket of goods" needed and regularly purchased by the average consumer. The Cost of Living Extremely Well Index is also calculated on a basket of goods, but these are goods regularly purchased only by the affluent. In the same time span, it was ravaged(!) by 6% inflation. That is 300% worse. And it mattered not.

Here are a few items on the affluent folks' shopping lists, and their price changes from 2006 to 2007:

Shopping List Item	2006 Price	2007 Price	Inflation % Change
Silverware—Lenox,® settings for 12 (real silverware)	$5,424.00	$6,960.00	+28%
Shoes—men's, custom-made black, dress, one pair	$4,128.00	$4,566.00	+11%
Wristwatch—Patek Philippe	$17,600.00	$19,200.00	+9%
Catered dinner for 40 from Ridgewells in Bethesda, Maryland	$7,469.00	$9,795.00	+31%
Motor yacht—Hatteras® 80 MY	$4,870,000.00	$5,118,000.00	+5%

During the same time period, sales of big yachts, custom-made shoes, designer-name wristwatches, and silverware all increased. All such businesses are doing very nicely despite this inflation. A few, very few categories showed price declines. The average price of a Thoroughbred yearling sold at auction dipped from $323,731.00 to $289,310.00, an 11% deflation. But most every luxury bought by the affluent incurred from 10% to 30% inflation.

Imagine what a 10%, 28%, or 31% inflation factor would do to the sales of most goods and services to average consumers. Most customers confronted with such shocking price leaps within 12 months would try very hard to clamp their wallets shut. Most businesses would be destroyed. Not those marketing to the affluent. Who can better get away with a sudden 31% increase to its prices: the Golden Corral® or Fleming's Steakhouse? Holiday Inn® or the Four Seasons?

This gives you the mandate.

Suppose we want to hurricane proof a home. We can reinforce its walls. We can buy pricey hurricane shutters for its windows. We can get a generator. We can do all those things and, still, if Mr. Windy can huff and puff and blow and blow, he can still knock our house down. Or we could move our house to a place never reached by hurricanes. Recession proofing a business does not require its physical relocation, although in some cases that might be a worthy idea to consider. Mostly, it means moving it to a different, more affluent group of customers.

HOW TO BOOST YOUR IMMUNE SYSTEM
AGAINST RECESSION

(The Wheels on the Luxury Cars Go 'Round and 'Round, 'Round and 'Round . . . even if the wheels come off the economy!)

Jim Ellis Automotive operates a number of auto dealerships in the Atlanta area, including Porsche,® Saab,® and Audi® luxury brands as well as Chevrolet,® Hyundai,® and Volkswagen® mainstream brands. "The luxury brands that we carry have done well through all the economic issues, housing fall, and rising fuel costs," Jimmy Ellis told a business reporter. Not stated but implied: nonluxury brands aren't as reliable as profit producers, in good times and bad.

Kevin Tynan, senior auto analyst for Argus Research, states that **the luxury segment of the auto market is more immune to economic downturns.** Even in a down economy, consumers keep buying luxury cars—so it's the luxury car dealerships that are expanding and making acquisitions. In 1985, luxury cars accounted for 7.1% of all U.S. car sales; today, they account for 11.6% (effectively, a whopping 50% increase), and some analysts predict that percentage to as much as double over the next 20 years. There's good reason for the optimism. According to the Ward Transportation Research Council, the prime age for buying a luxury automobile is 50 to 64, the fast-growing boomer population, which contains a high percentage of affluent consumers.

HOW TO BOOST YOUR IMMUNE SYSTEM
AGAINST RECESSION, CONTINUED

Of course, luxury cars also provide much higher profit margins than small and economy cars, so fewer transactions are required for each million dollars of profit.

Sources: Article from www.AtlantaBusinessChronicle.com, June 2007; Automotive Sales Institute.

CHAPTER 30

Affluent Consumer Entrapment

"Creativity is over-rated. Most business success comes from doing boring, diligent work. From developing a system that produces consistent results and sticking to it."

—RAY KROC

Y ou need a direct marketing system.

Here I lack space and time to belabor these points as I do in other works of mine, but here are two vital facts: One, all wealth derived from business is based on systems. Two, most businesses have some sort of operations system but lack the more valuable marketing system. To be successful attracting and marketing to the affluent, you will need to spend more per prospective customer, client, or patient (reasonable in light of their greater value), so you cannot afford to let any of them slip through your fingers. Further, they judge your competence and trustworthiness from the outset, so how organized you are in your marketing influences their willingness to do business with you. For these and other reasons, you need a direct-marketing system.

What is such a thing? As its name implies, it *directly* reaches out to, connects with, and brings the desired prospective customer, client, or patient to you.

All systems use bait to lure the desired creature into the trap. I'll switch to more elegant language in a few minutes, but for starters, tolerate my being deliberately coarse and simplistic with a basic example. Consider the company Fisher Investments. By my standards and my clients' standards, it has a primitive and simplistic system, but it will do as the basic example, and if you stop to think about it, you are probably aware of the company. It is a multi-product investment and money-under-management firm aiming at mass-affluent and affluent (but not ultra-affluent) investors. You've probably seen its 30-minute TV infomercials and TV commercials with the actor Hal Holbrook, magazine ads, *USA Today* ads, or *The Wall Street Journal* ads, or possibly received direct-mail solicitations. All that advertising does is offer bait to lure you into the trap. The bait is one or more free reports, like *The 9 Mistakes Affluent Investors Make*, a free audio CD, a free DVD, or a package of all that information. The titles and promises of what you will discover from these things are the real bait. You will discover lies your current broker, banker, financial planners are telling you, taxes you are paying unnecessarily, safe but high-yield investments you don't know about. You will get this from a highly credible and authoritative source. That's the bait. Whom is that bait for? Relatively new mass-affluents with little knowledge or confidence about investing. People aware they should be investing their money but who do not know what to do or whom to trust. Affluent people frustrated with stock market ups and downs or losses.

My comments mean no judgment, pro or con, about Fisher Investments as an investment firm. I have no firsthand knowledge and no opinion. I am only making observations in my area of expertise—marketing—and using Fisher's as example.

Fisher's bait lures those particular creatures into the trap. By design, there are a lot of creatures it does not lure.

The trap is a place where the creature's name, address, e-mail address, fax number, and phone number are captured and, of utmost importance, permission to use this information is secured. In case you haven't noticed, the government has been busy taking away your unfettered opportunity to communicate with people who might like to buy what you sell. The creation of the National Do Not Call Registry and related laws took away your opportunity to cold call or telephone canvass (unless, of course, you are a politician or a nonprofit; politicians are adept at exempting themselves from the onerous laws they impose on the rest of us). Changed laws governing broadcast faxing essentially took away a very effective and affordable means of direct marketing. The FTC is threatening a similar package of interference and restrictions for tracking and following up on visitors to websites, and several state governments are flirting with a do-not-mail list. It is my conviction these kinds of handcuffs will soon be added to our wrists. Not a question of if, but when, and how extreme in their stupidity.

You have to operate as if you needed express written permission from prospective customers, clients, or patients to communicate with them. This affects the construction of your trap. (If you go, for educational purposes, to www.DanKennedy.com and

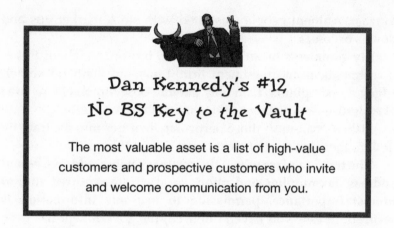

Dan Kennedy's #12
No BS Key to the Vault

The most valuable asset is a list of high-value
customers and prospective customers who invite
and welcome communication from you.

accept my Free Gift Offer, you will see certain language built into
your acceptance that gives Glazer-Kennedy Insider's Circle™ permission to communicate with you, which, by the way, we do not
abuse and you can withdraw at any time. You will also see that,
once you accept that gift, we go to considerable extremes during
our two-month honeymoon with you to cement a good, positive
relationship so that your permission becomes permanent.)

Additional information may also be asked for and captured
at a trap, such as age or occupation or income, so as to assign the
captured creature to a different subtrap, to be shown and fed
slightly different sales messages appropriate to him. From there,
a follow-up process begins. In Fisher's case, it is simplistic; the
package sent more an excuse for immediate and direct follow-up
by telephone agents than anything else. We can do better and be
more sophisticated, as I'll show you. Still, what Fisher does is
apparently effective and successful for that company.

The website is the ideal trap medium, as it allows us to automate this entire process, even to the point of the customer doing

his own data entry work for us. But a recorded message and voice mail, a call taken by a live human, a reply form or card returned by fax or mail can all serve as traps as well.

Before going further, there is one very important point to be made. Fisher Investments, targeting mass-affluent and affluent investors, in order to then offer professional money management services, does exactly the same thing as, for example, Tempur-Pedic® does to cast a much broader net and then sell mattresses, or the lowest of low-end "burial insurance for just 50 cents a day" companies advertising on TV do to target the very non-affluent and then sell a term insurance policy. Regardless of what they are selling or whom they are selling to, virtually all direct marketers do the same thing: they use bait to lure desired creatures into a trap. The only changes are to the bait. You need the right bait for the desired creature. There is no creature that can't be lured into a trap with the right bait. Let me say it again: There is NO creature that can't be lured into a trap. With the RIGHT bait.

Now we'll get more sophisticated, and use more elegant language, with which you may feel more comfortable!

Our direct-marketing system, just like the previous examples, will extend an invitation designed for a specific audience via a variety of means and media. You might use any or all of these to extend your invitation:

❖ Print advertising, in newspapers, magazines, newsletters, or other publications

❖ Banner advertising at others' websites

❖ Buying traffic for your website with Google™ AdWords® or other means

❖ Using publicity to get articles about you placed in different publications and places

❖ Direct mail to rented or compiled mailing lists

❖ E-mail to opt-in lists

❖ Radio or television advertising

And I could list a hundred more options.

Regardless of means or media, in every place, the same invitation is extended. It is kept simple and clean. It is NOT an attempt to sell your products or services at all. It is an invitation for the recipient to request and be provided something of relevance, interest, and value to him, free of charge. The more appealing and specifically relevant the item offered, the better the response. As an example, consider the ad for DentistryFor Diabetics® (in which I own an interest) appearing in magazines like *Reader's Digest* and *Diabetes Self-Management* and being mailed in some 150 areas throughout the United States by participating dentists in those areas to residents of certain age and other demographics. It is a classic lead-generation ad offering bait that should appeal to certain people being sought but not appeal to most. (Ad example shown in Figure 30.1 on page 254.)

This is Step 1, usually called LEAD GENERATON by direct marketers.

The individuals accepting your invitation arrive at your "place," and enter your foyer. And only the foyer. They are not permitted to roam the mansion as they please. The foyer is a nice place, be it website, recorded message, live human on the phone, or something like an exhibit booth at a consumer or business exposition or even your store, showroom, or office. But in many cases, it's a website or the handling of an incoming call. There, they sign the guest book. That means they provide the information you want, in exchange for receiving the appealing information or gifts you offered them in your invitation. Think of the foyer as nicely appointed, with the guest book on a big, gold podium, with a spotlight shining on it. But nothing else is there. It is premature to display product, describe services, talk price, or do anything else but get the guest book filled out.

At a website foyer, there may be what's called in internet lingo a *double-squeeze page*. It's actually two guest books. First, the person is asked only for his e-mail address, thus reducing the request to one item. In exchange, he may get an e-mail newsletter, e-book, or something else electronically delivered. When he provides his e-mail address, a door opens and a butler appears with yet a second guest book. In other words, a fresh landing page materializes, now asking for full physical address, possibly fax, possibly phone, and possibly additional questionnaire-type information. In exchange, the person will then be sent offline a package of information, materials, and gifts, likely including a book and/or an audio CD and/or a DVD. This strategy winds up creating two different lists for follow-up: (1) the timid and likely only curious or mildly interested people willing to provide only an e-mail address and (2) the more compliant, likely more interested, and likely better prospects willing to provide all their information. And depending on what information they provided, they may be further divided. We'll get there.

Now that they have signed the guest book or guest books, one of two things may occur immediately. One, they may be thanked, promised that the information they asked for will arrive in a few days, and politely ushered out. Or, two, they may be given the option of entering a very short corridor that provides access to only one or two rooms. Again, not free run of the whole mansion. There might be a nice little reading room, where they can read their e-book. Or a little theater where they can watch a short film, possibly of happy customers giving their testimonials. There is usually no direct, instant path into a showroom or sales-man's office where selling them is immediately attempted, although there are exceptions to this, including on the internet.

Step 2, then, is CAPTURE IN THE TRAP.

What I have described so far has many virtues. It alters your advertising from being product or service directed to being cus-tomer directed. It automates everything, so you or staff members are not engaged in unproductive, repetitive manual labor. It gives the prospect a nonthreatening, satisfying experience devoid of sales pressure. It provides you with a very valuable asset, a database of people who've stepped forward, raised their hands, and identified themselves as interested prospects. Finally, if you wish, it allows you to run smaller, simpler ads, keeping the front-end costs low and investing most of your resources only in interested prospects.

If this is new and unfamiliar to you, I can only urge you to stop and carefully re-read it, as there are ways it can go awry. And I encourage you to go to traps offered by sophisticated direct mar-keters and experience their entire systems for yourself. The best—and cheapest—way to learn this methodology is by playing prospect with companies doing lead-generation advertising.

Next, a series of proactive follow-up steps occur, from you, the marketer, to the prospective customer, client, patient, or investor.

We have prospects who have signed the guest book. We may treat them all the same and assign them all to the same Follow-Up Communications Program. Or we may divide them in some way, assigning different ones to different Follow-Up Communications Programs. Regardless, they will all get a series or sequence of multi-media follow-up communications, all designed to persuade them to take one next step. In rare cases, that step might be making a purchase. In many, it will be scheduling some sort of appointment; coming to your place of business or inviting you or your sales representative to their office or home; attending a seminar, webinar, or teleseminar; completing and returning an application. Whatever. Everything moves the prospects toward this one next step. Typically, there will be a deadline for taking that step, with rewards for doing so and penalties for not doing so. A sample series of follow-up contacts might look like this:

Day 1 after having signed guest book	Send requested book, brochure, and DVD. Send e-mail acknowledging request and telling them package is on its way.
Days 2–10	Daily e-mail, a lesson in a course on wise buying/investing/using the sort of thing being sold . . . tips plus reminder of offer.
Day 4	A letter with a booklet of customer testimonials . . . encouraging them to review everything sent.
Days 5, 7, 9	Three jumbo postcards, each focusing on a different benefit.
Day 10	"Only 5 days left" letter with encouragement to go to a website and view ten-minute special presentation.

Day 12, 13, 14	"Countdown to deadline" e-mails.
Day 15	Representative places outbound call.
Day 16	E-mail extending deadline and inviting then to 30-minute webinar and group question-and-answer session.
Day 19	"Last chance" letter with CD or DVD of the webinar.
Day 21	Representative calls again.
Day 25	"Offer withdrawn notice" letter.
Months 2–5	General e-mail newsletter, once a week.
Month 6	New series of letters or postcards extending original invitation and inviting them to re-raise hand and start process over with free information.

Step 3, then, is follow-up.

What I've just laid out is still somewhat simplistic, compared with the systems my businesses and many of my clients' businesses use. These systems may divide up the prospects to begin with and send different communications to 2, 4, or 20 groups. Those not responding to the entire system may be moved at its end to the start of another one, leading to the sale of a lower-priced or higher-priced or otherwise altered version of the product or service or an entirely different product or service.

The follow-up is where the giant opportunity is, because most businesses do little or no follow-up whatsoever. Response develops through follow-up. Whatever the response from a single attempt, it tends to as much as double with the second and third follow-up attempts, and double again with the fourth through whatever follow-up steps. So, if you got a 1% response from mailing out a package of information to a group of prospects, you would likely get another 1% or better from the second and third follow-up steps combined, and yet another 1% or better from the subsequent follow-up steps combined. If you begin with 1,000 prospects, that's 10 sales if you contact them only once or 30 or more with comprehensive follow-up. If you sell a $1,000.00 item, you're choosing between obtaining $10,000.00 or $30,000.00 or more from the same group of prospects.

When marketing to the affluent, this math changes, favoring follow-up even more. While many prospect groups' yield might be flat: 1%+1%+1%, an especially affluent prospect groups' yield might be tiered: .25%+2%+5%. My theory about this is that it takes more communication and more time to directly create trust with affluent customers. Because their value is greater, the added investment of more steps in follow-up is easily justifiable and usually a bigger economic win.

Once somebody understands the virtues of this kind of system, does he hurry to develop his and get it working for his business? Candidly, no.

Problems and Solutions

There are three chief reasons that, frankly, the vast majority of marketers shown this systematic-approach fail to develop it for their own businesses. My book *No B.S. DIRECT Marketing for NON-Direct Marketing Businesses* includes many inspiring and amazing case histories from people in a variety of non-direct-marketing businesses who have done the work necessary to transform their businesses this way, and I urge you to read it. And they are representative of experiences and results typical among all the Glazer-Kennedy Insider's Circle™ Members who follow this path. But I'll be the first to tell you, they are rare birds. Here's why.

Problem 1. It's work, to get it built, tested, and working for you successfully. Sadly and stupidly, most people would rather spend every day of their entire lives chopping wood manually with a dull axe, complaining all the while, than turn off the TV and put in a few extra hours a night for a few months building an axe-sharpening device or, better yet, an electric, power wood-cutting machine. When I do what I've done in this chapter, in much greater depth and detail, with clients in a room, one after the other excuses himself to go potty—and never returns. I'm now immune to the rejection. Matters not to me, I'm already rich.

Problem 2. It's complicated. Most people desperately want a magic pill, not a diet regimen incorporating food choices, portion control, nutritional supplementation, and exercise. That, incidentally, is why 99% of the fat folk stay fat. In business, it's the same thing. There's rarely a single, simple magic pill-like solution to any problem or exploitation of any opportunity. There's even virtue in possessing a complicated process, as most competitors will be too lazy and simple-minded to copy it, even if it is successful and shown to them.

Problem 3. Specific to marketing to the affluent—the higher up in affluence you go, the more protected are the prospects. Gatekeepers screen the communications you try to send to them. There are obstacles in your way. It is not necessarily easy to reach out to them and attract them. Also specific to the affluent—the higher up in affluence you go, the less responsive to advertising and more responsive to peer recommendations and referrals people are.

Now, for what it's worth, the solutions . . .

For Problem 1, work. What we are talking about here is nothing less than the transformation of your business from random acts of marketing that produce erratic and unpredictable results to a machine that runs dependably and efficiently, day in and day out, much of it automatically. Ownership of such a machine is a wonderful thing. But you can't expect to build such an enormously valuable thing for yourself with nominal effort or investment. You will need to, first, thoroughly understand it, and then experiment with specific application to your business.

For Problem 2, embrace the complexity! It's a source of power. But, to be fair, the actual mechanics of managing the prospects (databases) and the multi-step, multi-media follow-up with color-coded file folders and Post-It® notes or ordinary contact management software can be messy. There is one software system that has been built from the ground up to manage, automate, implement, and track exactly these kinds of marketing systems—and only one. It is called Infusion, and I urge you to investigate it. Free demonstrations are available (see Resource Box). In interest of full disclosure, I am a stockholder in and advisor to the company.

> ### Recommended Resource
>
> INFUSION SOFTWARE is the only all-in-one database,
> contact, customer relationship management program
> designed to support any business' implementation of
> a Kennedy-style direct marketing system. Information
> at: www.RenegadeMillionaireSoftware.com.

Problem 3 requires two things. One, appearing in the places where your affluent prospects pay the most attention. This will lead to different media choices than, say, your regular daily newspaper, mass-circulation magazines, or run-of-day TV or radio advertising. Two, direct mail to carefully selected lists (see Chapter 31), using more elaborate pieces and delivery means than ordinary mail. In business-to-business environments, you may need specific strategies for the professional gatekeepers. The good news is, there tends to be less clutter in their mailboxes, because the majority of marketers give up. You should not be deterred by this difficulty; it is in proportion to the value of the customer or client to be obtained. And make no mistake: the affluent customer or client can be drawn to the trap with clever direct marketing. The investment advisor currently managing my retirement funds started the process of securing me as a client with a direct-mail piece including a large roll of duct tape inside a plastic bag, delivered via Federal Express.

A maid service solicits homeowners in an exceptionally afflu-ent neighborhood by delivering DVD players preloaded with a

20-minute DVD of its clients' testimonials, filmed in the clients' luxury homes. It reported to me a 30% response rate from this campaign. This approach not only delivered media that could not easily be ignored or casually tossed in the trash but also addressed the fact that affluent customers rely more on referrals than on advertising, by delivering simulated referrals—clients like them, possibly known to them, speaking to them on the DVD from their own homes. Such social proof from true peers can successfully bridge the gap between advertising and the affluent client's preference for peer recommendations. This company has now moved this into a marketing system like I've described in this chapter, driving affluent homeowners into its website trap to request the DVD, or view it instantly there, and download free reports about care of antique furniture, stain removal from Oriental rugs, and similar topics.

If you are one of the rare birds who commits to development and implementation of this kind of direct-marketing system, you'll soon be sending me similar success reports.

FIGURE 30.1: Dentistry for Diabetes Ad

ADVERTISEMENT

..here's exciting new, important, FREE information:

It's Now Possible:
BETTER BLOOD SUGAR CONTROL, AUTOMATICALLY

- without drugs or more medication, *without* strict diets,
without exercise, without sacrifice!

A Free Information Kit is yours on request...and if you are diabetic or pre-diabetic, this is important medical news. You may have a Secret Enemy working inside your body every day accelerating your diabetes, making it worse, making your blood sugar levels impossible to control. You know the frustration of trying to eat right, exercise, even take your medication and still have out-of-control blood sugar levels! Well, the answer is not just upping the drug dosage. What you probably have NOT been told is: there is a "closed loop" between gum disease, undiagnosed low grade infections hidden deep inside gums, and dental health and the worsening OR AUTOMATIC IMPROVEMENT of blood sugar control. NEW BREAKTHROUGHS in dental care specifically designed for diabetics are now available. You need a dentist who pays special attention to people with diabetic problems, to assist them with periodontal care (gum disease treatment and control), low level oral infections, loose teeth or other problems. Our Nationwide Network of Certified DentistryForDiabetics^{SM} Dentists are ready to help you! And know this: whatever has kept you from getting the optimum, complete dental care you have needed in the past should not concern you now. Today's methods can be virtually pain-free; you can be assured of non-critical, respectful care in a relaxed environment; never any criticism for having put off treatment...and know that every dental problem has a solution. Whether you just need periodontal care designed to support better blood sugar control or implant dentistry, restorative dentistry or even a smile makeover, your local DentistryForDiabetics^{SM} Dentist can help.

First, though, let us rush **a complete FREE INFORMATION KIT** with a Special Report, *'How To Tame Diabetes And Its Side Effects'* and an Audio CD to you by mail, no cost, no obligation. To receive your **Free Information and get more details, go online to www.DentistryForDiabetics.com** or call 1-877-4DDSDIABETICS. (*If a loved one or friend is diabetic, please pass this along and encourage them to get this information.*)

FIGURE **30.2:** No B.S. Direct-Marketing System

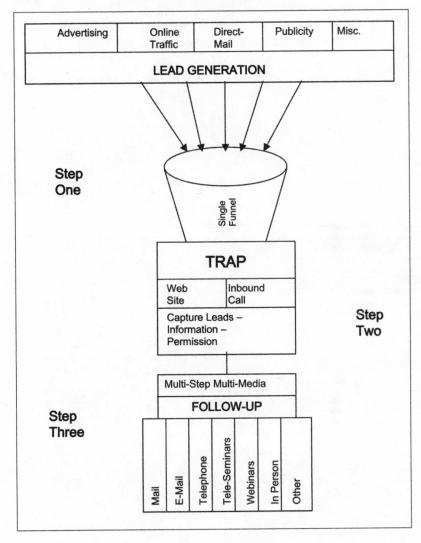

CHAPTER 31

We Know Where They Live

"If your ideal customer is a one-legged midget who bowls in a league on Tuesday nights, has one wife, two kids, three dogs, and a riding lawn mower, we can get you a list of them in your zip code. It won't be a very big list, but . . ."

—DAN KENNEDY, FROM HIS FAMOUS "MAGNETIC MARKETING" SPEECH

Twenty-two percent of U.S. households have more than 55% of all the earned income. Again: more than half of all the income is concentrated in only one of five households. Surely it must be easier to profit by marketing only to the one in five, while completely excluding and ignoring the four in five. Buying behavior supports such a notion. Based on data from the Mendelsohn Affluent Surveys, we know that the one-in-five group is roughly 200% more likely to own or lease three or more cars per household and 50% more likely to buy at least one new car this year; 200% more likely to own laptops and handhelds; 250% more likely to invest in real estate in addition to their own residences. They own 300% more life insurance. Over one-fourth of them own two residences, thus buying twice as much stuff. They outspend the four-in-five group in virtually every type of product category, except camping equipment.

Yet, as obvious as it is that selling to the top 22% while avoiding wasting even a penny or a minute on the remaining 78% has to be the winning strategy, few marketers act this way. Most invest in mass advertising that reaches five in five and hope to be noticed by the one in five. Hope may be a laudatory human emotion, but it is a very poor *strategy*. And an unnecessary one. We can do better.

A lot of people ask me about finding the affluent, as if they were all residing in secret, undisclosed locations. Actually, privacy in America and many other places in the world is dead. We not only know where they live but also know what they've been buying. Whether they've been naughty or nice.

For starters, there are people who have already gone to a great deal of trouble to spy on them, dig up data on them, monitor their buying behavior, and compile lists of them sorted by their interests and passions, by their level of affluence, by the frequency of their spending in a category, as well as by gender, age, ethnicity, marital status, home ownership, income, zip code, and a myriad of other divisions. In mailing list lingo, these are called *selects*. The world of mailing lists commercially available for rent is an amazing place, where you can pretty much find any kind of group of desired prospects, then drill down closer and closer to your ideal prospects within the group by these selects.

When you pass through the gateway to the mailing list world, you will discover that tens of thousands of mail-order, retail, service, credit card, publishing, and other companies have

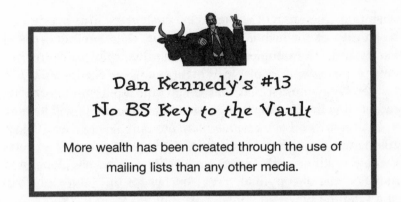

Dan Kennedy's #13
No BS Key to the Vault

More wealth has been created through the use of
mailing lists than any other media.

all their lists of past and present customers, cardholders, and subscribers as well as their prospects or inquiries available for rent. A dirty little secret is that many companies earn substantial sums this way, some eclipsing the net profits from their core businesses and a comparative few are in business solely to build and rent lists. These are called *response lists*, because people have responded to an ad or direct-mail solicitation or have otherwise asked that company for information or made one or more purchases. Another type of list is a *compiled* (nonresponse) list. These are even more widely available and generally less costly to rent. The people on these lists did not, in any way, volunteer to be on them. The list owner accesses one or more sources of public records and information and assembles the list for the express purpose of renting it. Both kinds of lists can be very useful. Both offer different kinds of selects.

For better understanding, we'll work our way through a few hypothetical examples.

Let's assume you own a very upscale French restaurant with a good wine cellar, snooty waiters, and high prices—and you wish to go in search of affluent new customers. This happens to be an easy one, which is why I picked it. There are hundreds of list choices. For example, there is a compiled list of yacht and private plane owners, available by state or county. There are 213,090 prospects on the list. On that list, within a 45-minute driving radius of your restaurant in Beachwood, Ohio, there will be only a small number. Let's assume there are only 200 of them. Those 200 names may be very valuable. We know to create and send them a mailing with planes and boats on the envelope, and maybe a line of copy like "Free Voucher for the Adventure Trip of a Lifetime Enclosed." Inside, we can tell them we know they appreciate the finer things in life, appreciate new experiences, and often fly their own plane or sail their own yacht in search of them. But did they know they could take a trip to one of the finest restaurants in all of France, only a short drive from their own home?

There is also a list available of people in any zip codes of your choice, arranged by birthday. As far as we know, everybody has one, once a year. So, in every month, there are quite a few people in reach of your restaurant having a birthday, and most people go out to dinner to celebrate. You can select from that list only married people, or people who own homes in pricey neighborhoods, or people with certain incomes. A colleague of mine operates a company that does these "Happy Birthday" mailings for restaurants and consistently gets tremendous response and very good return on investment.

But we could get very sophisticated and merge or purge. That means taking only the names appearing on two or more lists. The duplicates. The yacht and plane owners' list giving us only 200 names in our area might thin out to only 10 to 20 birthday names

Recommended Resource

For birthday, new mover, and other precision-targeted direct-mail campaigns for your business, contact Dean Killingbeck at New Customers Now, Fax 517-546-2815, Phone 517-548-5522.

in any given month. But they are the quadruple-perfect prospects. So instead of sending them a birthday card or letter and a coupon for a free birthday dinner, we might send them a beautifully wrapped gift box, a copy of our menu, and a fancy certificate on parchment paper. Doing this, we would spend a lot more per prospect, but we would be spending all our money on ideal prospects.

Let's try another one. You own an upscale but not ultra pricey women's fashion store featuring one-of-a-kind and unusual items. There's a response list available of Peruvian Connection® catalog buyers. The catalog sells knit and woven sweaters and other clothes made from luxury fibers native to the Andes. The women buyers range in age from 35 to 55. Their average household income tops $100,000.00. They're perfect for the clothing store but may also be good for a spa, medical-spa, even a cosmetic surgeon or dentist, a gift shop, or even the French restaurant. We won't know unless we test.

Here is the point: if you can describe your ideal affluent customers—whether ultra-affluent, affluent, mass-affluent, young, old, male, female, and so on—you can go into the inventory of

available lists and find them, already rounded up for you. In all cases, you can get their physical addresses. In many cases, you can also get their telephone numbers, fax numbers if they are business owners or professionals, and e-mail addresses.

The obvious question is: Why not skip all this and just mail everybody in rich zip codes? In some cases, that will produce satisfactory results. But it deprives you of several key ingredients of optimum direct-marketing success, notably precision matching of prospects with offers. Getting down to a smaller number of carefully chosen high-probability prospects allows you to invest your money more wisely, market more efficiently, and craft and present a story about your business as well as an offer that is seen as specifically relevant to the recipient. If you are seeking appointments with affluent investors, you could just mail the rich zip codes. But if mailing the *Investors Business Daily* subscribers in those same zip codes, you know you are hitting active stock market investors, and you can tailor your message to them—"Disappointed with Your Results in the Stock Market? What If . . . ."

The mechanics of finding, choosing, and renting these lists are not usually one-stop shopping easy or simple. I'm afraid this is going to get a little technical. Here's how it works:

You can find a broker active in the list categories of interest to you and rely on that one broker to find and recommend all the response lists you test and use. For example, in the health buyers category, a number of my clients rely on a brokerage called Macromark. However, most such brokers are not eager—some are even unwilling—to do much work on behalf of small-list users. Most lists have 5,000-name minimums, which I'll discuss in a few minutes, but beyond that, most brokers want clients renting hundreds of thousands of names per month or quarter. A single dentist just trying to rent names from response lists for his local office would not be welcomed. That's why, as example, in the DentistryForDiabetics® business I helped develop and advise, lists are obtained each month for the entire group of more than 100 dental offices spread out throughout the United States, then parceled out for each dentist's use. So, you may or may not be able to go the broker-working-for-you route, depending on the size and nature of your business. Darin Garman, who sells investments in heartland of America apartment buildings and commercial properties to individual investors residing all over the United States, Canada, and several foreign countries, can. Another commercial real estate broker in Iowa dealing only with local sellers and buyers can't. (Which is why the information in Chapter 28, "No Boundaries Anymore," is so important, regardless of your butcher, baker, or candlestick maker status.)

Most small-business owners will wind up basically being their own list finder and then dealing with a number of different brokers or list managers. All the information needed for this exercise can be sourced at www.SRDS.com.

Getting compiled lists is easier. Major compilers like InfoUSA offer lists by business category, by occupation at home addresses, by income of household, and by countless other basic demographic divisions and identifiers. For example, if you want a list of married homeowners with children living at home, household income between $75,000.00 and $125,000.00, in suburban but not urban or rural zip codes, it's easy to get from a compiler of publicly available data, like InfoUSA. If you want those same demographics but only people who are known to go camping and buy camping, hunting, and fishing products, a compiler such as InfoUSA may or may not be able to produce that list from its databases; in all likelihood, you'll be going into SRDS to look for response lists of catalog buyers. However, you could get a list of RV owners matching these demographics from a compiler.

How Much Do We Know?

We know just about everything! One way or another, from one or multiple databases, it is possible for all marketers national in scope and for many only local in reach to obtain and develop a hit list of ideal prospects.

Here are some categories of Leading-Edge Boomers, born between 1946 and 1955, that have been identified and organized into databases by the research company Mature Data Profiles™:

SEGMENT	GEOGRAPHY	PROFILE
Gold 'n' Gray	Suburban	Exclusive suburbs. Married, kids in college, many still working part-time, consulting. Buy: luxury travel, portfolio management. Retirement nest egg investors.
Credit Commandos	Suburban	Slightly above-average income and heavy credit card users. Empty nesters. Making up for lost time by buying on time.

SEGMENT	GEOGRAPHY	PROFILE
Settled Suburbanites	Suburban	Incomes and home values above average, empty nesters happy to stay where they are—they have the longest average length of residency. Heavy mail-order buyers.
Urban Mix	Urban	Apartment and condo dwellers. Many single. Professionals. Above-average education.
Trailing Boomers, born 1956–1964		
Metro Influentials	Suburban	Highest income and home value, into stocks and other investments, luxury travel, fine wines. Are about living out their dreams.
And Seniors, born 1945 or earlier		
Rich Retirees	Urban (Concentrated in Northeast cities.)	Well-educated, well-off. Small households. Eclectic interests indulged, from cooking to theater to travel. Big mail-order buyers, not surfing internet.
Boomerang Bohemians	Suburban	Free-wheeling RVers, travel, bounce between homes and kids' homes. Use e-mail, shop online.

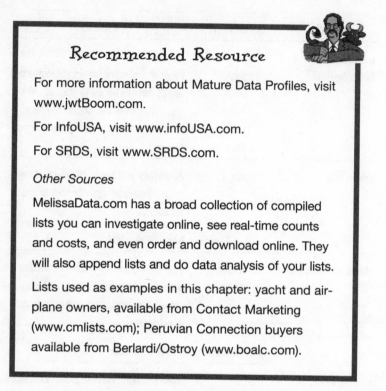

Recommended Resource

For more information about Mature Data Profiles, visit www.jwtBoom.com.

For InfoUSA, visit www.infoUSA.com.

For SRDS, visit www.SRDS.com.

Other Sources

MelissaData.com has a broad collection of compiled lists you can investigate online, see real-time counts and costs, and even order and download online. They will also append lists and do data analysis of your lists.

Lists used as examples in this chapter: yacht and airplane owners, available from Contact Marketing (www.cmlists.com); Peruvian Connection buyers available from Berlardi/Ostroy (www.boalc.com).

I've listed only 7 of 34 breakout categories encompassing 130 million names, addresses, and so on, which can also be pulled apart by exact age, gender, geography, mail-order response, marital status, net worth, occupation, even whether they wear corrective lenses! A list compiled from this data could also be over-layered against a specific company's list of subscribers or buyers. In short, you can drill down with incredible specificity, to identify and reach out only to people perfectly, precisely, and multi data-point matched with your current customer, ideal customer, or product or service offer. And you should.

Think of the power of combining precision-targeted lists of affluent buyers ideally matched with your business with a marketing system as described in the previous chapter!

A SAMPLE AFFLUENT LIST—AND WHAT WE KNOW ABOUT IT

Magellan's is a leading catalog and mail-order company selling travel-related products, including luggage, in-flight comfort products, health and safety items, books and DVDs, dual-time wristwatches, men's and women's apparel, and items specifically for globe-trotters, like adaptor plugs and translators. The company's catalogs can be seen and obtained at www.Magellans.com.

Their customers are mass-affluent and affluent, with an average household income of $75,000.00. Average age 55-plus, 59% female. If renting its lists, you can select by age brackets, gender, and geography as well as purchase activity. For example, as of this writing, there were 265,600 customers who had purchased at least once within the past 12 months; broken out, 51,000 of those had purchased apparel.

Direct-marketing companies that repeatedly rent and mail to segments of this list include obvious ones, like Omaha Steaks,® Orvis,® Grand European Tours,® and *Condé Nast Traveller*, as well as less obvious ones, like *The Wall Street Journal* and AARP. These users suggest that any marketer of the obvious—travel, gourmet foods, wine—as well as marketers of financial publications, financial services, investments, and anything related to upscale retirement living could potentially use this list. Had I such a business or a client in such a business, I would definitely investigate further.

Sources: www.CatalogSuccess.com/infocenter and www.BelardiOstroyALC.com.

WHERE THE MILLIONAIRE HOUSEHOLDS ARE POPPING UP

Here are projected growth rates for the number of new, additional millionaire households for 2008–2012:

Atlanta	68%	Los Angeles	54%
Dallas	68%	Tampa	54%
Houston	67%	Boston	54%
Sacramento	64%	Indianapolis	53%
Denver	64%	San Francisco	52%
Washington, DC	63%	Chicago	51%
Orlando	62%	Miami/Ft. Lauderdale	51%
Phoenix	62%	New York City	51%
Portland	59%	Philadelphia	50%
Minneapolis	58%	St. Louis	49%
San Diego	57%	Detroit	47%
Baltimore	56%	Cleveland	44%
Seattle	55%		

Here's an important point: *even in Cleveland*, currently ranked as "THE poorest big city in America," the number of millionaire households will likely increase by nearly half over the next 48 months. Significant mass-affluent and millionaire growth can be found in every part of the country, even in market areas viewed as generally depressed.

Based on information from *Merrill-Lynch Worldwide Wealth Report*, U.S. Census data, and economic projections from Affluent City Trends. Millionaire households defined as having net worth in excess of $1 million not including or in addition to, equity in primary residence.

WEALTHIEST CORE AREAS

If you're going hunting for deer, you might want to know about the woods with the densest deer population, the most number of deer per square foot. Here are the densest areas of millionaire populations:

Rank		# Households with at Least $1 Million of Investable Assets	% of Households
1	Los Alamos, NM	1,516	19.25%
2	Bridgeport, CT (including Stamford-Norwalk)	45,034	13.54%
3	Washington, DC-area (including nearby MD, northern VA, and WV communities)	264,452	13.03%
4	Naples, FL, W. Marco Island	17,149	12.62%
5	San Jose/Santa Clara, CA	74,789	12.61%
6	Oxnard/Thousand Oaks, CA	32,396	12.35%
7	Torrington, CT	9.202	12.14%
8	Trenton, NJ	16,190	12.11%
9	Juneau, AK	1,413	11.91%
10	Gardnerville Ranchos, NV	2,319	11.73%

11–25: Napa, CA; San Francisco, CA; Easton, MD; Santa Cruz, CA; Hartford, CT; Barnstable Town, MA; Boulder, CO; Santa Rosa, CA; Truckee-Grass Valley, CA; Hilton Head Island, SC; Vallejo-Fairfield, CA; Lexington Park, MD; Boston, MA; Honolulu, HI; Minneapolis, MN.

Source: *Investment News Databook 2007*, www.InvestmentNews.com.

WHERE SHOULD YOU DRILL FOR OIL?

Years ago, I got to know a "professional psychic" I met at the bar, after his show in the lounge at the Playboy Club in Phoenix, Arizona. He had a home worth more than a million dollars perched high on Camelback Mountain, drove a Rolls-Royce, and seemed wealthier than might be expected for an entertainer working such small venues. He told me he used his performances only to "drill for oil." By that he meant making himself visible and approachable to a few wealthy patrons who chose to employ him privately for advice on a variety of matters, at substantial fees. He said he named his approach "drilling for oil" in honor of one of his first patrons, a very rich Texas widow who had inherited her late husband's oil business. She hired the psychic to walk her vast oil fields and choose the next five places to drill new wells and paid him an ongoing royalty on the production of any successful wells. He bore none of the costs of the dry holes. And, as he said, "how psychic must you be to pick one winner out of five—in an oil field!"

CHAPTER 32

You Need to Choose Your
Words Carefully

*"Some things a king never has to say: 'Can I play too?' . . . 'Hey guys,
wait for me.' . . . 'I never seem to get laid.'"*

—GEORGE CARLIN

I n marketing or selling to the affluent, language matters
more than in most other selling situations.

The affluent tend to be better educated, with better
vocabularies than the general public. Beyond that, they are more
language sensitive. By that I mean they are consciously and
unconsciously judging the people speaking to them or the media
communications directed at them for appropriateness. *Is this a
person of my station?* is the question.

Sydney Barrows, who offers a terrific telecoaching program
for business owners and doctors in all kinds of professional practices on SalesDesign,® is exceptionally intuitive and skilled at

Recommended Resource

SALES LANGUAGE is critical. Mark Twain said the difference between any word and just the right word is the difference between lightning bugs and lightning. You can fine-tune your own sales language, develop ultra-effective scripts, and convert ordinary selling into performance art—all dealt with in-depth, in Sydney Barrows' short-term telecoaching program. Information at: www.SydneyBarrows.com.

script that communicates class and secures trust. In her first business, she discovered that asking, "And how will you want to take care of this?" rather than "How would you like to pay for this?" made a measurable difference in selling to an affluent clientele. Most businesses have opportunities to substantially increase sales purely through choosing and using more sophisticated, better-crafted language—when answering the phone and greeting customers, clients, or patients, during the actual sales presentation, and in advertising and marketing materials.

By far, one of the most interesting uses and values of precisely chosen language is what I call *romancing the stone*, giving rather ordinary products the kind of elite cachet that creates differentiation, competitive edge and support for premium pricing out of thin air.

I would like you to read three different product descriptions from a J. Peterman catalog and see what common strategies—

and odd strategies—are in play. We'll discuss them after you read them.

Sample 1

Gatsby was amazing. He even managed to see to it that the book about him was regarded as a novel, fiction, as though he didn't exist. Even Fitzgerald, by the time he was through writing it, believed he'd made the whole thing up. There were those who knew the truth all along, of course; knew everything except where all that money came from. (Even by today's standards, when millions mean nothing, only billions matter, Gatsby was incomprehensibly rich.) Gatsby walked into rooms wearing a shirt with no collar. Even a little thing like that made people talk. And probably will still make them talk. The Gatsby shirt, of course, has no collar. Only a simple collar band. The placket is simpler also: narrower. (Gatsby had them made in France, originally.) The cotton we have used in our uncompromising replica of Gatsby's shirt is so luminous, in and of itself, that even a person who notices nothing will notice something. Gatsby, of course, could afford stacks of these shirts; rooms of them. Never mind. All that matters is that you have one, just one. A piece of how things were.

Sample 2

Fame isn't gradual; one moment you're comfortably obscure; the next you can't buy a cantaloupe without navigating through a thicket of fans and well-wishers. Without consulting you, people will choose a photograph; it will appear in all the documentaries, all the newspaper articles, all the books written by or about you. It will become more than you. Forever. Churchill understood. He decided what he wanted that image to portray ten years before that famous "spontaneous" photo was snapped. What image do you want to leave for posterity? The Irish Tweed Vest . . . .

Sample 3

New York Subway strike of the late '70s. Bank presidents start wearing sneakers to work. JFK goes hatless at his inauguration. Good-bye, hats. Steve McQueen, Sean Connery, Bill Holden discard ties in favor of turtlenecks. Some of it is progress. Now, marooned for a week in Paris or Osaka, this turtleneck sweater will keep you or me well dressed. Relaxed, but just a little dressy. (Both at the same time.) 55% silk, 45% cashmere. Pretty seductive stuff. Warm, but not heavy, not bulky. Beautifully detailed and finished. Sleek 7" high ribbed turtleneck. Set in sleeves. Good with blazers, old tweedy jackets, slacks, jeans. People expect to see a Walther PPK strapped over it, so you don't even need to bother.

The Gatsby shirt sells for $89.00. There are 104 words before the product is referred to! This violates every known rule of mail-order catalog or direct-response copywriting. One of the reasons for such a violation—nearly universal throughout every Peterman catalog—is the *who* he is selling to: affluent consumers with above-average educations, who wish to perceive themselves as sophisticates, as well as, of course, to a great degree, his own "Peterman cultists," as explained in his own words at the end of this chapter (see pages 283–301). What is even more important to see here is what he is actually selling—and it is not a shirt. Here is that same block of copy again, with boldfaced type underlined to make what is really being sold leap out at you, rather than gently permeate the subconscious, as was intended by delivering it wrapped in the story.

Gatsby was amazing. He even managed to see to it that the book about him was regarded as a novel, fiction, as though he didn't exist. Even Fitzgerald, by the time he was through writing it, believed he'd made the whole thing up. There were those who knew the truth all along, of course; knew everything except where all that money came from. (Even by today's standards, when millions mean nothing, only billions matter, Gatsby was incomprehensibly rich.) Gatsby walked into rooms wearing a shirt with no collar. Even a little thing like that **made people talk.** And probably **will still make them talk**. The Gatsby shirt, of course, has no collar. Only a simple collar band. The placket is simpler also: narrower. (Gatsby had them made in France, originally.) The cotton we have used in our uncompromising replica of Gatsby's shirt is so luminous, in and of itself, that **even a person who notices nothing will notice something.** Gatsby, of course, could afford stacks of these shirts; rooms of them. Never mind. All that matters is that you have one, just one. A piece of how things were.

An aspiration is being sold here, not a product. The overall aspiration is to be like Gatsby. To be different, iconic, and interesting, even a bit mysterious. The more specific aspiration is to be noticed and talked about. And in case you hadn't noticed, affluent people like being noticed, and most go about that deliberately, whether very consciously or unconsciously.

This copy also uses language that would usually be dumbed down for advertising purposes. These high-brow words are strategically chosen and used to convey a sense of superiority onto the buyer. By involvement in dialogue at this level, the reader is being recognized as a more sophisticated, intellectual individual. To say it in a very unclassy way, its meaning is: *You're a classy fellow and we know it, and this is for the classes, not the masses. They won't even appreciate its description.* With that in mind, I've bold-faced and underlined some key words:

Gatsby was amazing. He even managed to see to it that the book about him was regarded as a novel, fiction, as though he didn't exist. Even Fitzgerald, by the time he was through writing it, believed he'd made the whole thing up. There were those who knew the truth all along, of course; knew everything except where all that money came from. (Even by today's standards, when millions mean nothing, only billions matter, Gatsby was **incomprehensibly** rich.) Gatsby walked into rooms wearing a shirt with no collar. Even a little thing like that made people talk. And probably will still make them talk. The Gatsby shirt, of course, has no collar. Only a simple collar band. The placket is simpler also: narrower. (Gatsby had them made in **France**, originally.) The cotton we have used in our **uncompromising** replica of Gatsby's shirt is so **luminous**, in and of itself, that even a person who notices nothing will notice something. Gatsby, of course, could afford stacks of these shirts; rooms of them. Never mind. All that matters is that you have one, just one. A piece of how things were.

Finally, the end—**all that matters is that you have one, just one**—defies selling logic. The first impulse of most marketers is to encourage buying one of each of the four available colors, probably with a buy three, get one free offer. I confess it instantly occurred to me when I read the catalog page. Instead, this line dares to discourage buying more than one. In doing so, an air of exclusivity is conferred on the product, as might ordinarily be attached to a unique piece of jewelry, a classic car, or some collectible.

Sample 2 sells a rather odd tweed vest for $199.00. Or does it? The entire scenario described here speaks to two aspirations of the affluent: importance and legacy. The thought of having fans and well-wishers and photos snapped of you is a very appealing fantasy for a great many people. I know it for fact; I have that experience; and I am constantly asked what it is like. Further, the idea of being the author of a book has strong importance and legacy appeal. In fact, my Platinum Members Bill and Steve Harrison, who conduct the *Publicity Summit,* publish *Book Marketing Update,* and provide a range of services to authors, very effectively use a story about people coming in large numbers from far away to a person's funeral because they were influenced by his book. Again, as a much-published author, I can assure you, every successful person believes he has a profoundly interesting and important story to tell, a book within. All this to sell a vest! This *is* how your thinking about whatever you sell and do must change if you are to be effective with affluent clientele and rise to the top price or fee levels in your business category.

As an aside, this copy reveals something about the age of the Peterman customers. The references to documentaries and to Churchill will be meaningful to those 50 and over, most meaningful to those 60 and over, and pretty much a disconnect for anyone under 40. For those in the last category, documentaries or news reels were shown in the movie theaters before every movie throughout the World War II era, and were very popular in early television. Winston Churchill is, of course, famous, but you probably don't know about the photo referred to unless you are of a certain age.

Sample 3 sells a turtleneck sweater for $250.00, or $185.00 on sale. We can certainly find nice turtleneck sweaters for half that price in many stores and catalogs. But we can't find *copy* like this anywhere else!

First, there is aspirational identification. Here I've bold-faced and underlined the key references:

New York Subway strike of the late '70s. Bank presidents start wearing sneakers to work. **JFK** goes hatless at his inauguration. Good-bye, hats. **Steve McQueen, Sean Connery, Bill Holden** discard ties in favor of turtlenecks. Some of it is progress. Now, marooned for a week in Paris or Osaka, this turtleneck sweater will keep you or me well dressed. Relaxed, but just a little dressy. (Both at the same time.) 55% silk, 45% cashmere. Pretty seductive stuff. Warm, but not heavy, not bulky. Beautifully detailed and finished. Sleek 7" high ribbed turtleneck. Set in sleeves. Good with blazers, old tweedy jackets, slacks, jeans. People expect to see a **Walther PPK** strapped over it, so you don't even need to bother.

As noted earlier, you need to be of a certain age. If you are, not only are the five iconic figures (the 5th is James Bond—not named, but we know his gun of choice) familiar to you, but they instantly conjure mental pictures, maybe even mental movies. They are the men women swooned over but men admired, not resented. Countless products and services are bought by consumers because of the "I Want to Be Like ____" factor, and even the most affluent consumers respond to such appeals.

This copy also puts us into mental movies:

New York Subway strike of the late '70s. Bank presidents start wearing sneakers to work. JFK goes hatless at his inauguration. Good-bye, hats. Steve McQueen, Sean Connery, Bill Holden discard ties in favor of turtlenecks. Some of it is progress. Now, **marooned for a week in Paris** or Osaka, this turtleneck sweater will keep you or me well dressed. Relaxed, but just a little dressy. (Both at the same time.) 55% silk, 45% cashmere. Pretty **seductive** stuff. Warm, but not heavy, not bulky. Beautifully detailed and finished. Sleek 7" high ribbed turtleneck. Set in sleeves. Good with blazers, old tweedy jackets, slacks, jeans. **People expect to see a Walther PPK strapped over it, so you don't even need to bother.**

The reader can visualize himself in his turtleneck, at a Paris café . . . then catching the attention of a beautiful and mysterious woman. As a stand-in for James Bond, a dashing, romantic, fascinating figure. And who *doesn't* want *that*?

The temptation will be to presume none of this applies to you, because you do not sell shirts and sweaters; you are a dentist or financial planner or you own a landscaping company or even manufacture safety devices sold to and installed in food-processing plants. Resist this temptation! Commitment to talking about what you do or sell in factual, logical, straightforward, and thus dull and uninteresting language leaves you vulnerable to commoditization and price-based competition and bars you from ever becoming a subject of fascination among a target audience of affluent clients. Being boring and ordinary is choice, not something forced on you by your particular business.

This also goes far beyond your advertising. As a professional direct-response copywriter routinely commanding project fees for ads, direct-mail campaigns, websites, and the like upwards of $100,000.00 plus royalties, I have enormous appreciation and admiration for copy like the Peterman catalog examples dissected here. I spend many hours of every week surrounded by thesauruses, swipe files, even novels, agonizing in search of precisely the perfect word or phrase or story to get a persuasive point across in print. But to narrow this to print misses a greater opportunity and a more critical need.

Out of the Mouths of . . .

This approach does NOT apply just to words put into print. It applies equally to what you and your salespeople say verbally. Here, frankly, a toxic waste dump of sloppiness has occurred in most businesses. What comes out of the mouths of most people about their products and services is, bluntly, trash and slop. It is thoughtless. Uncrafted. Inconsistent. When captured via recording and transcribed and reviewed in print, it is humiliating. The affluent consumer is as repulsed by this as if the sales professional reeked of garlic, alcohol, sweat, and uncontrolled gas.

I am consistently appalled at what I hear professionals, business owners, and sales professionals saying.

This gets to a philosophical decision. I and the aforementioned Sydney Barrows share a view of selling as performance art. As such it is to be planned, scripted, physically choreographed, rehearsed, and ultimately performed. Most sales professionals unfortunately view the presentation as something that they should just be able to *do*.

This also gets to sales management and management decisions, if you employ salespeople or nonsalespeople who still have sales job functions, such as front-desk staff in a professional office. The question is whether you are going to tolerate sloppy, inconsistent, ineffective communication or you are going to design the most effective language and choreography possible and insist on its implementation. To help you make this important decision correctly, and act on it successfully, I suggest reading my book *No B.S. Guide to Ruthless Management of People and Profits*.

THE CATALOG THAT STARTED A CULT
by John Peterman

"Two eggs over easy, crisp bacon, hold the grits." Sarah, my usual waitress at the Saratoga, knew my breakfast order by heart. This morning, though, in November 1990, she brought something extra on the tray: a newspaper with an article circled.

"Special of the day, John," she said.

I took a closer look. It was a piece by Tom Peters, the best-known business thinker of our time, writing on a subject close to me:

I wish the J. Peterman Co. of Lexington, Ky., would win the 1991 Malcolm Baldrige National Quality Award. Their Winter 1990 catalog, "Owner's Manual No. 8," just arrived; as usual, I dropped what I was doing and sat down to read it.

No photos, just hand-drawn illustrations. And wonderful, whimsical text . . . . The J. Peterman catalog is fun. The products and presentation are "world-class quality" writ large. A few thousand more J. Petermans and we could kiss our economic woes goodbye.

I didn't need sugar in my coffee after that.

A fairly steady rain of other articles soon began to appear, like one by Holly Brubach, in *The New York Times Sunday Magazine*, that made me check my hat size:

THE CATALOG THAT STARTED A CULT, CONTINUED

The stuff of J. Peterman's catalogue copy—the acute powers of observation, the delight in the smallest details of everyday life and the urge to record them—is the stuff of literature and it sets J. Peterman apart from his fellow mail-order entrepreneurs: he is a merchant poet.

The fact is, I never had myself confused with the charming fellow that people sensed was there, just out of reach, behind the words on our catalog pages; he was the product of more than one mind. But my memories and convictions went into him. I was delighted, once, to come across a certain small detail of life from long ago—a pair of fawn-colored leather spats. I had no intention of reproducing the spats for sale; instead, we ran a drawing of them with copy entitled "Circa 1906," to express something of what I felt the company stood for:

They are old. They are useless. But they are beautiful.

I bought them at a vintage clothing sale—not to sell, but as a reminder of how well stuff used to be made: pearl buttons 1/8" thick, leather seams with 14 stitches per inch.

They also remind me of more recent things, which (amazingly) we've given up with hardly a murmur of protest.

Peaches worth eating and doctors who make house-calls. Real starch in shirt collars. Bakelite. Books sewn in signatures. Strike-anywhere matches. Soapbox orators. Car engines you can tune yourself. Meaningful S.A.T. scores. Lüchow's, foghorns, taffeta dresses, and sparklers on July 4th.

THE CATALOG THAT STARTED A CULT, CONTINUED

Isn't it time to take some kind of stand here?

I'm saving all I can. I hope you are too.

I guess that is as close to poetry as you'll find in a mail-order catalog.

■ ■ ■

A recent friend of mine told me that years ago, late at night on Nantucket, she and her housemates used to sit in their waterfront rental, listening to the waves break on Tom Nevers beach, drinking Barolo, and reading from the Owner's Manual. "Steff was getting married that summer," she said. "I needed a dress to wear to the wedding, and she needed something to wear to a cocktail party in her honor. We started reading our catalogs out loud as we were looking through them, and soon, the others were in on the act. We'd start with the copy that was there, then make up our own finishes. Or we'd 'introduce' one product to another—'The tall, thin, brooding man in the J. Peterman Shirt meets the woman wearing the Flip-Up Sunglasses at Café de Flore, 1 A.M. sharp; secret documents are exchanged.'

"Knowing about the catalog was sort of an inside thing," she said. "It was like being a member of a club, and you felt more a part of it with each issue."

People loved to read the Owner's Manual even if they never actually bought anything. When we'd take them off the mailing list, eventually, they'd write letters pleading with us to put them back

THE CATALOG THAT STARTED A CULT, CONTINUED

on again. Some customers confided that they bought an item once a year or so to make sure that they didn't miss a mailing. Fortunately, others bought a lot more.

(As the catalogs kept coming out, getting thicker and thicker, direct-marketing experts became converts, too; they called us "the anti-catalog," and meant it as a compliment.)

Many people related to the catalog in a very personal way, almost as if it were a letter written by a good friend who can take you out of yourself, out of your routine—or remind you of who you really are. We told stories, gave candid opinions and confidential advice. We often spoke in an intimate one-on-one way, as in this copy for our Women's Tuxedo Shirt:

> *The question, really, is how did you get by this long without it? No wonder you've been a little sulky; I know I'm not the only one who's noticed it.*

In return, readers weren't shy about letting us know when we pleased or displeased them. We once took a matching tweed jacket and pants that had a wonderful, gentleman-in-the-country quality and named them the "E. Digby Baltzell Memorial Tweeds," in tribute to the dapper sociologist who wrote The Protestant Establishment and invented the acronym "WASP":

> *"You must meet the WASP man," hostesses would say. A dashing figure at the Germantown Cricket Club, around the*

THE CATALOG THAT STARTED A CULT, CONTINUED

quad at Penn. Invariably wore candy-striped shirt and bow ties with his tweeds, although he'd defend, in principle, your right to do otherwise.

A former student wrote in, outraged: how dare we exploit the great man for our tawdry commercial purposes? But Mrs. Baltzell wrote to us, too. She thoroughly enjoyed the copy. The suit was just like the ones her late husband favored. There was going to be a symposium in his honor, and all his old colleagues would be wearing the Memorial Tweeds.

The Owner's Manual was filled with references to Alexander the Great, the Russian Navy, Kanchanaburi, Tolstoi and Vita Sackville-West, Ludwig Wittgenstein and chaos theory, Georgia O'Keeffe, "Bear" Bryant, Gable and Harlow, and Wendy Hiller, some of them pretty obscure. "Thanks for bringing back memories of my rum-running days," someone would tell us. Or, "Where can I get that P.D. Ouspensky book you referred to?" When we made errors, occasionally, vigilant readers were quick to respond. "Churchill was elected in April, but he didn't move to 10 Downing until October." "You can't 'clubhaul a ketch.'"

Several times, scrupulous college professors wrote in for an OK to use our material in their literature classes. Well, why not? We offered everything from fresh aphorisms ("A shirt is the pedestal upon which a human face stands to present its case") to whole novels condensed into a few paragraphs, like this copy for our WWII Canadian Air Force Duffelbag:

THE CATALOG THAT STARTED A CULT, CONTINUED

A farmer's son, growing up in Alberta, Canada, sees a lot of sky.

It sets him dreaming.

At 16 he's flying a crop duster.

At 23 he's an RCAF volunteer in the Battle of Britain. Bader's 242 Squadron. A Hawker Hurricane of his own.

Scrambling twice a day to intercept German ME 109s soon convinces him that he is not, in fact, immortal. But there are compensations.

At the pub in Duxford, the wings on his uniform have a persuasive effect on the local solicitor's daughter. (Other envious soldiers are now referring to fighter pilots as "The Brylcreem Boys.")

No question of marriage. Not until he's demobbed. And that will happen in '43, thanks to fragments of a 7.92mm slug encountered over France.

He will limp a bit walking down the aisle.

She will think he never looked more handsome.

It wasn't only the writing that was admired. Collectors asked (and still do) to buy Bob Hagel's artwork. People who know about these things say Hagel has a line that can't be confused with that of any other artist; it gets to the essence of things in an energetic, unhesitating way that's never merely pretty to look at.

THE CATALOG THAT STARTED A CULT, CONTINUED

Some customers even wanted to collect me. I received quite a few mash notes from ladies all over the world inviting me to dinner, if ever I were in their neighborhood. One California woman applied for a position with the company as a massage therapist; she enclosed a nude photo of herself leaning against a fine specimen of an elm tree.

Little did she know that Audrey, my wife, was in charge of the mailroom, and opened all my mail before I got it.

■ ■ ■

The rapport that customers had with the company showed in another remarkable way: they often turned to us as a kind of Society for Historic Preservation, sending in things they were afraid might disappear from the face of the Earth unless we reproduced them—an authentic old Norfolk jacket, a 1928 Air Corps briefcase, a great-great grandmother's blouse.

Our earliest "customer-sourced" item was The Counterfeit Mailbag. A retired mailman from Houston sent us the mailbag that had served him for 30 years, thick leather with a large rounded flap in front, a style discontinued by the cost accountants. Some details were missing, so I got another from a former letter carrier in Lexington and found a manufacturer; the bag went on to become as much a perennial as the J. Peterman Shirt:

THE CATALOG THAT STARTED A CULT, CONTINUED

The secret thoughts of an entire nation were carried in leather bags exactly like this one . . . I borrowed an original from a friend, a retired mailman who, like thousands before him, was kind enough to test it out, for years, on the tree-lined streets of small towns everywhere. Before you were born.

A few years later, we had a surge in consignments of WWII military uniforms and equipment, like Army shirts with buttoning neck flaps to protect against possible mustard-gas attacks; we put together a collection and ran a piece entitled "We Were Soldiers Once, and Young":

I think the 50th Anniversary of D-Day sparked it.

Veterans around the country got up from the 6:30 news to rummage through closets and battered trunks, emerging with wonderful WWII gear, a lot of which they forwarded to us: "Can you do something with this?"

Here are three of the items. Faithful reproductions of shirts in which they trained, fought, grumbled, flirted with Red Cross doughnut girls, and when you come down to it, saved the world.

That one didn't produce any big sellers, but I felt I owed it to Uncle Joe.

■ ■ ■

THE CATALOG THAT STARTED A CULT, CONTINUED

The J. Peterman Company was looking good from the outside during the early 1990s, and it looked good to us on the inside, too. Revenues grew from $19.8 million in 1990 to $45 million in 1992. Profitability was up. We moved to bigger offices in an industrial park on Palumbo Drive. They were palatial compared with Midland Avenue; there was even a tree in front.

It felt like the sky was the limit.

We had done a lot of in-house training up until that point—my assistant Paula Collins, for example, developed into one of the best merchants in the business. I kept that policy, but I also realized that we had to have seasoned, professional help with our increasingly complex finances and our growing need for new products. In April 1990 I hired John Rice as our CFO and head of operations, and in October I brought Tom Holzfeind on board as our first vice president of merchandising.

John was at Haband, the mail-order giant run by Duke Habernickel, "The Prince of Polyester," which sells a million pairs of pants a month. He hadn't been looking for a job. I won him over because we were a more exciting place to be, and, on a pragmatic level, we were offering options. He had always wanted to work someplace where he could be more than just an employee, he told me. John hit the ground running, spending his first two weeks at Commercialware, our software provider in Boston, nailing down our new fulfillment system. We were soon taking orders, shipping product, and getting paid like clockwork.

THE CATALOG THAT STARTED A CULT, CONTINUED

Tom came from the ritzier Horchow catalog operation, where he worked directly with the legendary Roger Horchow as head of merchandising; he now runs the Smithsonian Catalogue. Tom grasped the Peterman concept right away. His taste was impeccable. He knew what it takes to put a catalog together. He'd developed good agent contacts on his travels overseas. And he was secure in himself, with none of the confrontational attitude that is all too common in the world of retail, merchandising, and catalogs. That made him an excellent teacher who played a major role in developing our merchants.

On the creative side of the business, Don seemed reluctant to share responsibility for writing the catalog—he could create a perfect world there, where he had absolute control—but he was having a tough time turning out dozens of new pieces for each edition by himself. He tried a number of big-name copywriters, without much success, before enlisting Bill McCullam, who became the senior writer for the company until we closed our doors. Bill had been a creative director on BMW and Waterford Crystal, among other upscale advertising accounts, and had started in direct marketing; some of his direct-response print ads and TV commercials had run profitably for over ten years. Later, he was joined by a select group of other writers including Amy Bloom, author of the novel *Love Invents Us* and a National Book Award finalist.

■ ■ ■

THE CATALOG THAT STARTED A CULT, CONTINUED

One day in 1992, I realized as I was walking through the halls that I didn't recognize all my employees anymore. I was hiring managers and interviewing prospective merchants, but there were a lot more souls coming on board than that—John Rice was hiring, Audrey (reporting to John) was bringing in customer-service reps, the warehouse manager was staffing up, etc.

I didn't like not knowing the people who were working for me, and, more important, I didn't like them not having a firsthand sense of who I was. So I started to hold regular Friday breakfasts, a practice that lasted until 1997. My assistant would pick eight employees from around the company at random, all levels, all departments. We'd meet in my office and sit around my old Philippine mahogany poker table for a get-acquainted meal and conversation. This was not a bagels-and-orange-juice buffet. Waiters served scrambled eggs and Potatoes O'Brien and fresh fruit on real china. We used a House-of-Commons coffeepot and silverware. I'd ask questions to get to know everyone, and they'd ask questions, too—hesitantly, at first, but as the event became an established fixture, more freely. We'd cover a topic, from kids and restaurants to what we were selling, how the business was doing, what their ambitions were. We eventually held lunches, as well, because having to show up at 7:30 A.M. could put a strain on commuters.

Morale was excellent in the early 1990s. Turnover was very low. We were goal-oriented, not method-bound. People had freedom

THE CATALOG THAT STARTED A CULT, CONTINUED

to solve problems the way they thought best. They could work their way up to responsible positions at a much earlier age than elsewhere, and legitimately feel identified with the company's success. There were lots of celebrations, too, brought off with skill by Audrey—company picnics, Christmas dances, Halloween costume parties. I've heard rumors of a photograph showing me in a Roman toga, with a tilted laurel wreath on my head, standing next to John Rice decked out as Dame Edna, but no blackmail demands have been made yet.

One other thing: we trusted each other. Employees were often surprised at that, having come from companies where regimentation was the rule. I recall Robert Bolson, who'd been a dispatcher at the Lexington Police Department. He started as our head nighttime service rep when we were still on Midland Avenue and stayed with us until the end, ultimately becoming a writer. When Audrey gave him the keys to lock up on his first night, he looked at her in astonishment and smiled. "I'm going to like it here," he said.

■ ■ ■

The catalog seemed to have an insatiable appetite for new products now. Tom, Paula, Don, and I were frequenting antique shows, small clothing shops from SoHo to Ghirardelli Square, and beginning to travel to Europe. We only wanted things that were unique or hard to find elsewhere.

THE CATALOG THAT STARTED A CULT, CONTINUED

We were way ahead of the curve on many items, and I'd say we launched the curve in some cases, like the collarless shirt and other period clothing. During Operation Desert Storm, we were the only place where civilians could obtain the same high-tech sunglasses issued to Stealth-bomber pilots in the Persian Gulf. We were also the first catalog to carry those chunky, comfortable walking shoes made by a certain French company called Mephisto. We bought our Mephistos from the person in charge of their U.S. distribution; it was one of the few times we purchased from a sales rep—they usually want to sell to as many outlets as they can, which guarantees the item won't be special—but the Mephisto man was just starting to figure out the territory, and his product really was wonderful:

> *Weeding my way through the jungle of "biomechanically perfect" and "orthopedically engineered" and "air-injected" running-jumping-springing-catapulting shoes out there, I believe I have found the ultimate walking shoe. (Walking, after all, is what most of us do most of the time.)*

I met Martin Micheali, the owner of Mephisto, on my first European buying trip. Don and I took the train from Paris to Sarrebourg, where the Mephisto factory is. The Sarrebourg station has a large cobblestone square in front, and cars have to park on the other side. Only one car was there, with a gent I assumed to be Martin standing next to it. As we walked across the cobble-stones to join him, he seemed to be appraising my gait. He held

THE CATALOG THAT STARTED A CULT, CONTINUED

out his hand; "Peterman?" "Yes," I replied. "Hmm, I thought you'd be taller."

On the London leg of that first trip we stayed at Blakes Hotel, which became my standard for hotels and for customer service in general. Blakes is a small place in South Kensington, set in a row of 19th-century townhouses, and identified by a discreet brass wall plaque; it's favored by film and music types who value their privacy. I went up the front steps, through the large doors, across an intimate lobby that glowed like an Old Master painting (mirrors, dark burnished leather, mellow wood, baskets of oranges). "Ah, Mr. Peterman, we've been expecting you; you're checked in." No questions, no forms to fill out; I presented my credit card at the reception desk and that was it. From then on the entire staff did everything they could to make us feel like personal guests.

We spent a week "working" London, from Savile Row to Portobello Road to Jermyn Street, discovering hunting coats and Victorian carpet bags and a glorious bone-handled badger shaving brush which we sold with copy that captured the feeling of our expeditions:

Jermyn St., and nearby Old Bond St., are exactly what you (if you were an Englishman) might dream about if you unexpectedly found yourself pinned beneath an avalanche of boulders at the bottom of the Min Gorge in China.

Waiting to be rescued, your mind might turn to the cool hushed perfection of all the tiny elegant shops along certain London streets, shops where clerks read your mind,

THE CATALOG THAT STARTED A CULT, CONTINUED

anticipate your wishes, bringing forth soothing potions, perfectly fitted shoes, impeccable linen suits, cartridge belts, shooting gloves, rare oriental carpets, cucumber sandwiches, leather-bound first editions, coin-silver snuff boxes . . .

Dreaming of these things, no doubt, has kept many an Englishman sane.

We did most of our getting about in those black London taxis built roomy enough to accommodate a gent in a top hat. The drivers always knew exactly where we were going; to qualify for a license, they spend at least two years traveling around the city on motorbikes acquiring "The Knowledge"—memorizing over 16,000 streets, landmarks, stores, restaurants, and other destinations in a 113-square-mile area. (Curious fact: The part of the human brain dedicated to spatial relationships grows significantly larger in London cabbies.) In the evenings we'd stroll the hushed back alleys of Kensington; if there'd been no cars, we could have been in 1900 or even 1850—but there were cars. Classic Bentleys, Jaguars, an occasional Vauxhall, even a 1920 Pierce-Arrow parked casually, its owner unafraid of crime.

All that magnificent machinery set me thinking. We were planning to visit Chartwell, Churchill's home; why hire a car with a driver, when we might rent something special on our own? So I told the desk clerk at Blakes that we'd like a Morgan roadster for a few days. "We'll get right on that, Mr. Peterman." Within two hours, the phone rang in my room. "Mr. Peterman, we've had the staff

THE CATALOG THAT STARTED A CULT, CONTINUED

check every Morgan dealer and car-rental agency in London and we're unable to find a Morgan. The manager's brother owns a Morgan, though, and the manager is contacting him to see if it's available now."

As it turned out, the chap was out of the country. We never did get the car. But the effort that went into trying to fulfill my request was remarkable. Most hotels would have made a few calls and abandoned the search. Not Blakes.

■ ■ ■

The Owner's Manual had a simple guarantee printed on the inside cover: "Absolute Satisfaction. Period." My Blakes' experience made me determined to live up to that guarantee. One time, Audrey marched into my office with a small army of customer-service reps, holding a pair of boots at arm's length. A customer had worn them out doing farm work, and he felt they should have lasted longer. He'd mailed them back to us for replacement, still covered with cow manure. The reps looked at me imploringly. These were dress boots, not intended for heavy-duty use. The man had gotten his money's worth. They were only defending the company's best interests.

It was a Big Moment. "We either have absolute satisfaction or we don't," I said. "Ninety-nine-point-nine percent of our customers are honest. This man probably does feel the boots didn't hold up. If we send him another pair, he'll tell his friends about our great

THE CATALOG THAT STARTED A CULT, CONTINUED

service. They'll become customers, too. That's the kind of company we want to be. That's the kind we're going to be."

We sent him new boots for free.

■ ■ ■

People who achieve fame are usually brighter and more adventurous than average, whatever their public image. So I wasn't surprised when the catalog became an "inside thing" early on with celebrities—Nicole Kidman, Clint Eastwood, Tom Brokaw, Paul Newman and Joanne Woodward, Kim Basinger, Tom Hanks, Mia Farrow, Bill Murray, Angela Lansbury, and Sidney Pollack, among others. Once, as I was walking through our customer-service area with a venture capitalist, we happened to overhear a conversation. The VC's eyes widened. "Is that *the* Frank Sinatra on the phone?" he asked. I looked at the service rep's computer screen. "Well, his middle name *is* Albert."

We had a rule that any customer who wanted to talk to me should be put right through if I were available. I took an order that way from Kelly McGillis, who bought fireman's coats for herself and Jodie Foster. I felt shy about asking her bust size; being an actress, she wasn't a bit shy at all. I ended up as a sort of personal shopper for quite a few well-known people. One was Bill Simon, former secretary of the treasury. I used to spend time on the phone with him each November as he planned his holiday shopping. He liked to get my take on what different products

THE CATALOG THAT STARTED A CULT, CONTINUED

were really like, whom they might suit, should he get this or that to furnish the house on his ranch? He didn't place orders with me; his secretary would call one of our service reps later. One time, though, he did ask me if he could get a discount on a big order. "Bill," I said, "when you were secretary of the treasury, did I get a discount?"

■ ■ ■

Oprah Winfrey was one of our major fans, and when her producer called and asked if I would be on a show about catalog shopping, I didn't see how I could turn down such an excellent customer's request.

The drill was much as it had been when I was a plant doctor on Good Morning America. They sent me the airplane ticket, I flew to Chicago, was met by a limousine, taken to a good hotel, then whisked to Oprah's studio early next morning. They put me to work in the makeup room this time—I'd been asked to bring lots of possible items for models to wear, and I made up outfits on the spot to suit their looks. There was a fellow in charge of wardrobe who had his own ideas on how to dress the models, but because we were presenting Peterman, and I was Peterman, they ended up dressed the way I wanted.

I met Oprah when I joined her onstage. The program was in progress; they were at a commercial break. I walked on, shook her hand, and said, "I'm John Peterman." She smiled warmly.

THE CATALOG THAT STARTED A CULT, CONTINUED

"No, you're J. Peterman . . . 'J.' is more mysterious." She turned to face the audience and the camera light blinked on.

Mostly, I just sat back and enjoyed the show. Oprah was a dynamo of enthusiasm. She swept here and there, picking up item after item, holding them out, putting them on, saying how the Owner's Manual was her favorite catalog, how she loved the copy, loved this dress, loved that coat, owned three of those shirts. She tried on several hats, turning around, asking the audience, "Isn't this great?" She put on the Shepheard's Hotel bathrobe and confided that it was the softest, most luscious robe and that she wore hers every morning.

The show ran just after Thanksgiving, and at the end of my segment they flashed our 800 number on the screen. Our incoming lines started to sizzle. The show aired first on the East Coast, and the volume of calls mounted in waves as it went on in successive time zones. Everyone in the company was manning the phones, scribbling orders on scraps of paper because our computer system was overtaxed. We managed to take about 25,000 calls in an atmosphere of pandemonium . . . then sudden silence.

Hurricane Oprah had crashed the Lexington, Kentucky, phone system.

Chapter from the book *Peterman Rides Again: Adventures Continue with the Real J. Peterman through Life and the Catalog Business* by John Peterman. Chapter and Peterman catalog copy in preceding chapter used with permission from John Peterman.

CHAPTER 33

The Language of Membership

"You're so vain, you probably think this song is about you."

FROM THE SONG "YOU'RE SO VAIN," BY CARLY SIMON (1972)

I learned a long time ago that subscriptions lack the cachet of membership, and when I began simply calling a subscription to my original marketing newsletter a membership in my inner circle, we saw an increase in response to solicitations and were able to inch up the price. Over time, it has morphed and evolved into a *real* membership, with an entire portfolio of benefits with my newsletter as its centerpiece. Today's Glazer-Kennedy Insider's Circle™ Members have access to a vast collection of online resources and online communities, two major conventions each year, boutique seminars, teleseminars, and webinars, local chapters meeting regularly in more than 100 cities, several different levels of coaching, mastermind, and peer advisory groups, at annual fees ranging from under $1,000.00 to as much as $35,000.00. Free test-drive memberships are available to this book's readers—refer to page 429.

I take a backseat, though, to the powerful copy written about membership in the Sovereign Society, which I've reprinted at the end of this chapter (page 307). This membership is, fundamentally, a subscription to financial and investment newsletters. But it feels like something of much greater significance, elite status, and value, thanks to this copy. I urge you to examine it very carefully and thoroughly. To point out just a few nuances you might overlook, the very first paragraph describes a philosophical position, and the second states "those who join *The Sovereign Society* tend to share this view." The fourth paragraph describes a "typical" member in a very aspirational way; the reader would certainly like to be like that typical member. He identifies with the description more as a desire, I can assure you, than as a reality. This type of paragraph has its roots in Hugh Hefner's "What Sort of a Man Reads Playboy?" ad series.

This language of membership is not limited to the sale of newsletter subscriptions. Actually, it doesn't matter whether you are converting pizza shop customers to members of a gourmet pizza aficionados' society, as does my friend and brilliant marketer Diana Coutu of Diana's Gourmet Pizza, or selling membership in a vacation residences club to the ultra-affluent with an initiation fee of $235,000.00. Shortly before finally exiting the retail menswear business he'd grown up in, Bill Glazer, CEO of Glazer-Kennedy Insider's Circle,™ ran an experiment at his suburban mall store and proved he could sell memberships to customers, entitling them to cost-plus pricing representing substantial across-the-board discounts and other benefits. Would people pay a membership fee to be permitted to buy clothes in a store? Yes. In just 37 weeks, he generated more than $183,425.00 in membership revenues!

The growing popularity of concierge medical practices, closed to the public, serving only a limited number of affluent patients paying annual access fees, is a prime example of American Express's famous (and trademarked) "Membership Has Its Privileges"® idea applied to a business where, initially, it was met with almost universal skepticism. The fact is (emphasis on *fact*) that affluent clients want privilege, and they want to be served in an environment where they have access that others do not.

The language of membership, then, needs to focus on two things in order to be persuasive: (1) aspirational identification and (2) elite and exclusive access and privilege.

For the first, the intangible membership has to feel like a tangible, physical place, and the place to be for your client—as he is and as he aspires to be. For 29 years, I was a member of the National Speakers Association, a trade association for professional speakers. At least 70% of its members would not meet any rational definition of *professional*. Speaking is not their profession. They do not earn a full-time living from it. Many of its members are there because they aspire to be professional speakers. It is perceived as the place to be, the thing to belong to, to validate that aspiration. In fact, to many, belonging *is* being. This is true of a great many associations, clubs, country clubs, charitable activities. People belong to them or participate in them because they believe it is the place to be or the thing to belong to, to be the person they want to be, to have the status and importance they aspire to. As an eclectic reference, there is a *Family Guy* episode in which little Stewie dresses up in baggy pants and goes to high school, determined to show that he can "outcool the cool." He finds two great-looking girls and two guys in a cluster and asks them if they are the cool kids. When they acknowledge they are and demand to know who he is, he begins his rap. Shortly, one of the girls says, "If he says one more cool thing, he's in." The simple words "he's in" have great significance. Everybody is trying to be "in"—with what they perceive to be the right people, in the right place. If you can make your membership sound and feel like the place and the group that your clients should aspire to be like and be in, you've created a very valuable marketing asset.

For the second, the most perverse aspect of human nature is wanting what we do not and cannot have. An extension of this found in all strivers, mass-affluent and affluent alike, is that they want what others do not and cannot have. When I moved to Phoenix in 1978, a very popular nightclub with long lines at its front door most nights sold a membership card entitling you to stand in the shorter line at the back door, the one with the black velvet rope instead of the yellow one, with the bouncer in suit and tie instead of slacks and polo shirt. It also sold a much pricier membership, and only sold 100 of them, that entitled you to bypass that line at any time and be seated in a raised room with glass dividers, looking out and down on the other customers. The memberships had visible, tangible privileges. Many businesses have comparable opportunities. Those that don't, that deal with their customers only via long distances, need to creatively invent the same feelings for their customers. For example, in website-based businesses, this is achieved with the password-protected area—only members of a certain level or status can enter it, but everybody can bump up against its front door and see or understand a little bit of what's on the other side. This is the equivalent of the two doors, two lines.

As you can see, both of these aspects of membership can be facilitated physically. But the language used to describe the membership and its members is even more important than the physical distinctions. And remember, there are code words meaningful to the affluent to incorporate in that language.

THE SOVEREIGN SOCIETY

In 1998, a small group of internationally recognized experts in business, economics, investments and law founded *The Sovereign Society*. We chose this name intentionally because we believe every individual has the right to unfettered freedom and protected prosperity.

Those who join *The Sovereign Society* tend to share this view, and seek to live as "sovereign individuals." They opt to build their financial house not in a single country determined by the accident of birth, but across the spectrum of nations, holding their assets and even their citizenships in the countries and legal structures that offer the greatest freedom . . . and protection.

Today, based on these founding principles, we help over 16,000 members in countries around the world locate the most innovative, legitimate, and lucrative opportunities worldwide to protect their wealth and grow their assets.

THE SOVEREIGN SOCIETY, CONTINUED

A typical member of *The Sovereign Society* may have bank accounts in Switzerland, Austria, or Denmark, own European stocks in a trust set up in Bermuda, incorporate a business in the Isle of Man, buy insurance through a company domiciled in the British Virgin Islands, retire in Panama, and hold passports from two or even more countries. Their assets are secured and out-of-reach from would-be suitors. Their portfolio grows at a nice clip because they are not limited by national borders and have access to a wider pool of opportunities than the average investor.

More important, these members have received guidance from some of the most experienced and respected legal and financial experts in offshore asset protection and investments—so they know the choices they make are 100% legal and are designed for safety, privacy and the prudent growth of their wealth.

I'm glad you've joined us, and I look forward to showing how you can take advantage of the many benefits of membership—and enjoy the freedom of total wealth for yourself. Use this guide as your ticket to a whole new world. After all, we exist for the sole purpose of providing you with the access, legitimate information, expertise, connections and opportunities you need to live the kind of life you want. The more sovereign, the better.

Welcome aboard . . .
Erika I. Nolan
Executive Director
The Sovereign Society
www.SovereignSociety.com

CHAPTER 34

You Need to Get Client Referrals on Purpose, Not by Accident

A famous story: A down-on-his-luck stockbroker came to Baron Rothschild to ask for a loan. The baron refused to lend him money but offered to do something more useful; he took the broker to the London Stock Exchange and walked alongside him from one end of the trading floor to another.

For people like me, in the marketing business, this is a very unwelcome fact: the higher up the financial food chain you go, the less likely you are to obtain a customer, client, or patient "cold" through advertising, direct mail, or other proactive outreach. Warren Buffett does not look in the Yellow Pages for a chiropractor, nor will he be motivated by a chiropractor's TV infomercial. If he has back pain, he'll call his billionaire buddies for a recommendation.

Greg Furman, Chairman of the Luxury Marketing Council in the hospitality industry, has called it "a nuclear arms race" to woo the affluent clients who travel frequently for business and pleasure, and describes the best weaponry as "bragging rights experiences." In this category, a Silicon Valley golf resort dispatches massage therapists to the links to deliver a quick rub to that sore shoulder or achy back between greens. Hilton's super upscale Conrad Hotel offers a "pillow menu" and individual concierges. At St. Regis, your personal butler carries his PDA with him at all times, so you can e-mail him your requests, never spending a minute on hold listening to John Tesh music.

You probably don't operate a hotel or a resort, but you can learn a lot from the most upscale of them. The best have committed clientele, unwilling to stay elsewhere unless absolutely unavoidable, and urging their peers and friends to follow their lead.

Most businesses settle for whatever word-of-mouth advertising or specific referrals they get by accident, but in marketing to the affluent, it is more vital to get them and each referral is more valuable, so specific, strategic investment of time and money is warranted. There are three main strategies:

1. creating experiences customers are motivated, preferably compelled, to tell others about—that is, being the basis for storytelling
2. recognizing and rewarding those who refer
3. tracking, measuring, and managing referrals

The second and third aren't very useful without the first. A lot of what has already been advocated in this book—from taking the time to understand the psychological and emotional drivers of affluents' buying behavior and enthusiasm for what they buy and whom they buy from to crafting the most appropriate sales language and choreographing your sales process—all combines into the Total Experience as felt by the customer. That total experience determines a customer's willingness to refer when asked as well as the likelihood of him spontaneously recommending you to others of his own initiative.

An important thing to understand is that satisfaction is *not* sufficient. There are many businesses I buy things from and do business with, with which I am sufficiently satisfied to continue as a customer. Wal-Mart,® my dry cleaners, the local car wash, the local jewelry store, and my CPA firm all come to mind. But I have zero motivation to tell others about these businesses, let alone passionately urge others to use them. On the other hand, I have actively referred people to my dentist; my private air charter company; a cartoonist I use in business, Vince Palko, who did the cartoons in *No B.S. Guide to Ruthless Management of People and Profits*; a first-rate upscale restaurant, Blue Canyon; and the best hotel to hold meetings at, period, the Hilton Garden Inn in Twinsburg, Ohio. Why do I champion these businesses but not the others? Because they do more than satisfy. They meet a higher standard. The secret to referral stimulus is the difference between

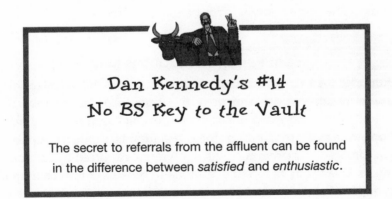

Dan Kennedy's #14
No BS Key to the Vault

The secret to referrals from the affluent can be found in the difference between *satisfied* and *enthusiastic*.

312,   NO B.S. Marketing to the Affluent

satisfaction and enthusiasm, produced either by merely meeting expectations or by exceeding them.

Getting recommendations and referrals from your clients is about turning them into storytellers about their experiences with you. Nobody gathers a crowd around at a cocktail party to tell them, "My dry cleaner gets my clothes clean, folds them, and puts them on hangers." It's just not much of a story.

Here's why this is particularly important in working with affluent clientele: Surveys show that the affluent are 30% less likely than the general public to return or exchange unsatisfactory merchandise, seek out management to lodge complaints, or otherwise make their disappointments known. Their time is too valuable to spend on such activities. They simply go elsewhere. If the experience you are delivering is unsatisfactory or merely ordinary, you can't rely on your affluent customers to do your work for you and alert you to your mediocrity. You have to determine it, based on poor referral statistics or other statistical measurements and observation. Affluent consumers are, however, more demanding, even though they may keep their disappointments to themselves and go searching elsewhere for better experiences.

Peer Recommendations Rule

Abundant survey and statistical data supports the premise that, the more affluent the consumer, the more likely he is to rely, in whole or part, on word-of-mouth information and recommendations from peers in selecting stores, restaurants, products, services, and professional providers. If his interest is captured by advertising or direct solicitation, the millionaire consumer is at least four times (400%) more likely to ask around among his peers about

CHAPTER 34 / YOU NEED TO GET CLIENT REFERRALS ON PURPOSE, NOT BY ACCIDENT

the company than is a consumer of average means. To give you a personal example, there is a heavily advertised, expensive product of such high interest to me that I have answered the ads and requested the offered DVD and information three times over a couple years' time, but am only, finally, nearly persuaded to purchase it by a report from a peer who bought one. On the other hand, I have very, very, very bad things to say about a company selling a heavily advertised, expensive, high-tech bed. Three different peers of mine have been on the verge of buying it and mentioned it to me; all three reversed their decisions—one canceled his order via cell phone on the spot—based on my negative comments.

With the affluent, word of mouth is far more critical. And far more valuable. And must be earned through complex creation and delivery of exceptional experiences that serve as basis for positive, interesting storytelling.

I would add that having a marketing system such as I described in Chapter 30 in place is extremely helpful in capitalizing on word-of-mouth advertising. When people recommend your business to others, and they call for information or, more likely, go to your website, if you have a good trap in place, they won't get away.

With that in place, you *will* get referrals. When you do, Strategy 2 (recognition and reward) should occur. I cannot tell you the number of times I've heard the same unhappy story—"I sent my friend/client/neighbor to x and never got so much as a thank-you note." Each person telling me that story is expressing deep resentment of not being shown deserved respect and appreciation, and reinforcing his determination never to recommend that business to anyone else. I don't think most businesspeople understand just how much it irritates people to deserve appreciation but not get it. This is multiplied with the affluent, who feel privileged to begin with and take the absence of appropriate response as a slap in the face. When they do you a favor, such as referring a customer, they are waiting for an appropriate acknowledgment. Checking their mail. And—pure and simple—*pissed off* when nothing arrives.

The good news is that recognition and rewards motivate more of the same behavior. I guess we can all be Pavlov's dogs. The best way to turn a first-time or occasional referrer into a frequent one is: recognition. And, the more affluent the customer, the more personal the recognition should be. He does not need a Starbucks® gift card that you buy a dozen at a time to reward referring customers. If it must be a generic gift, then it needs to be a high-end gift the recipient will genuinely appreciate, accompanied by a personal, preferably handwritten thank-you note. In the generic category, I've often used Omaha Steaks® or Allen Brothers® steaks delivered to the recipient's door. But, ideally, you find and obtain something of specific relevance to the individual and his business, family, pets, or personal interests.

Finally, Strategy 3 is holding yourself, your staff, and even your clients accountable for referral activity. This means measuring effectiveness every way you can, beginning with overall stats. I often ask a dentist or chiropractor to tell me how many referrals he's received per active patient this year to date vs. last year to the same month—and he has no idea. You can't manage what you don't measure. Depending on the nature of your business, you may be able to measure one staff person's efficacy at securing referrals against anothers. You can certainly track referral numbers, frequency, and consistency for each customer,

---

client, or patient. The courageous marketer will single out the clients referring below par and engage them in frank discussion about it. The point is that referral productivity is something to be proactively managed, not passively accepted, whatever it is.

THE HAPPIEST GROCERY STORE ON EARTH

In one of the cities in which I have a home, in northern Virginia near Washington, DC, you'll find a chain of grocery stores named Wegmans.® But calling their 100,000- to 150,000-square foot places grocery stores or supermarkets is misleading. They have created Destination Shopping Supermarkets that people drive way out of their way, right past more convenient supermarkets, to get to and from, incurring round-trips of one to two hours, to patronize. Once there, shoppers routinely spend hours on the premises. For some it is a new weekend diversion, supplanting hours at the mall. *USA Today* has called Wegmans and other chains emulating it "grocery Disneylands" for good reason. Walt Disney's number-one marketing principle—"Do what you do so well and so uniquely that people can't wait to tell others about you"—is alive and well in aisle 6.

At Wegmans you can find 500 different kinds of cheese. Fresh French bread flown in daily from a bakery in Paris. Honest. Amazing food selection.

At Wegmans you may encounter cooking demonstrations, wine tastings and wine selection classes (which sell out, 60 people

---

THE HAPPIEST GROCERY STORE ON EARTH, CONTINUED

paying $29.00 each), celebrity chefs autographing books, bag-pipes on St. Patrick's Day, Santa Claus at Christmas. And knowl-edgeable, courteous, helpful employees. To ensure they are knowledgeable, for example, Wegmans runs its own Cheese University to educate its employees. The store has its own execu-tive chef. And a white-tablecloth café with haute cuisine. And free child care, so harried moms can enjoy lunch and leisurely shop-ping together.

Wegmans is not alone in creating a unique and varied experi-ence rather than just a place to get groceries. The pioneer in this was Stew Leonard's in Connecticut, written about in Tom Peters's classic management book of the '80s, *In Search of Excellence*. The president of Whole Foods® has borrowed Starbucks'® definition of itself as a *third place* outside work and home for people to meet, hang out, eat, shop, and share an experience. Andrew Seth, co-author of *Supermarket Wars*, says these kinds of super-experience stores are "making shopping aspirational and pleasurable."

The payoff is zealotry. Raving-fan mass-affluent and affluent cus-tomers spreading the gospel of a new, different, enjoyable kind of grocery shopping experience that replaces a chore with a pleas-ant and interesting outing. Wegmans's customers famously brag to others that they shop there, urge their friends to do so, drag them there with them. **Which gets to the pregnant question for you: How can you transform the experience people have in**

THE HAPPIEST GROCERY STORE ON EARTH, CONTINUED

doing business with you into such an unexpected and fascinating and entertaining pleasure that they will drive past a dozen competitors and go out of their way to come to you . . . . ignore direct-mail from anybody else in your category . . . cheerfully pay premium prices or not even think about price at all . . . and above all else, become committed, enthusiastic zealots evangelizing on your behalf, even forcibly dragging customers to you?

Based on April 17, 2006, article in *USA Today*, article in *No B.S. Marketing to the Affluent Letter*, and personal experience of the author.

CHAPTER 35

Banish the Ordinary

"If I've learned one thing about the rich, it's that they have a very low threshold for even the mildest discomfort."

—DONALD TRUMP

T he highest-grossing independent restaurant in the United States, as I write this, was Tao in Las Vegas. In its first full year, 2006, it raked in $55.2 million, a full $16 million more than number two, the venerable Tavern on the Green in New York. From zero to number one in just 12 months. Here are the facts 'n' figures: 60,000 square feet, average check of $70.00, 50% from booze, open 24/7, and here's what's most important—multiple experiences under one roof. Its brain, Richard Wolfe, says that the "multiple-experience strategy" gives Tao "a big competitive advantage . . . . You never want to leave our premises to go somewhere else to do something different."

This is the Disney® premise. Tao features its restaurant, a lounge, a dance club, and a beach club with $1,000.00 cabanas, complete with plasma TVs and X-box® consoles. A reserved table near the dance floor on weekends carries a $5,000.00 minimum.

Wolfe says the restaurant sells "stratification" with a price level for everyone, from a few-hundred-dollar dinner tab to the $1,000.00 cabana rental to $5,000 bottles of wine and table minimums.

Tao offers a model for all sorts of businesses seeking to appeal to the mass-affluent, affluent, and ultra-affluent: stratification + multiple experiences.

With stratification, you give customers tiered and price-differentiated choices, so that they have a sense of control—and never have to simply choose from yes or no and never have to feel excluded. Mercedes® has stratification, from about $30,000.00 to $150,000.00 and up. Ritz-Carlton® has it, with room size and suite choices. No choice should be bland or bare-bones, but each next-higher price choice should offer more appealing products, services, privileges.

With multiple experiences, you give customers, clients, or patients more reasons to choose your business over other options. In fact, the ideal is the development of a category of one. There may be other businesses that provide comparable parts of your whole but no competitor matching the whole.

Disney's® spectacular Animal Kingdom Lodge, connected to its Animal Kingdom theme park, in Orlando, achieves both. In stratification, it offers several different-sized rooms and suites at different prices as well as concierge floors with premium-priced rooms; only guests staying on these floors may take the private behind-the-scenes Dawn Safari and have access to the lounge, with comfortable furnishings, continental breakfast, afternoon snack, evening desserts, and beverages all day long. The experiences available include the better-than-a-zoo, private habitat only at the lodge plus the park, itself offering multiple experiences, from rides and attractions to a zoo to live shows, like *Lion King*. At the lodge, organized play activities and storytelling for the kids. So, there are other zoos. There are other amusement parks. There are other shows. There are other resort hotels. There are other safaris. In Orlando and elsewhere. But there is no comparable combination of all those things.

My friend Diana Coutu of Diana's Gourmet Pizzeria,® mentioned in an earlier chapter, is "Where to go to for Gourmet" take-out. There are specialty pizzas and create-your-own pizzas, but you can also purchase take-and-bake versions of any pizza to bake fresh yourself at home. You can buy dough balls of the whole wheat, Moosehead® beer, or other crusts or entire pizza kits, to have the experience of making your own pizza (nearly) from scratch—a great family activity. You can stock up on fresh-frozen versions of the restaurant's pizzas to have ready at a moment's notice. Different choices, different experiences. Prices for large pizzas range from as little as $13.99 to as much as $31.99. It hopefully won't surprise you that the majority of customers buy more than one way from Diana's—a customer picking up a pizza baked and ready to take home and eat also picks up a frozen pie to stick in the home freezer. Not only is this store's average transaction significantly higher than any other pizza shop, but its yearly customer value is much higher. The customers skew mass-affluent, and the main store is, incidentally, not in Beverly Hills 90210—it's in Winnipeg, Canada. (See it at www.DianasGourmetPizzeria.ca, call 877-489-9587 for recorded message, and, if interested in franchise availability, enter 7777 when calling that number.)

If you can create multiple experiences and stratification in the pizza business, you can do it in any business.

Banish the ordinary!

A VISIT TO MATTERHORN NURSERY, WHERE THE ORDINARY HAS BEEN BANISHED
by Pamela Danziger

Matterhorn Nursery Inc. is a 38-acre preserve located off Palisades Parkway in Rockland County, New York, that combines exquisite display gardens with a retail center called Matterhorn Gardener's Village, where the aspiring gardener can buy plants, tools, and equipment to re-create Matterhorn's garden lushness. As the entrepreneurial founder of Matterhorn, Matt Horn has won more awards than you can shake a garden hoe at, like the 2003 "Garden Center Innovator of the Year" award from *Garden Center Merchandising and Management* magazine; the 2004 "Retail Sales" Award and "Landscape Design Program Honor Award" from Perennial Plant Association; and the New York State Nurseryman's Association "Environmental Beautification Grand Prize Award."

If you wander into Matterhorn Nursery expecting to find just another garden center, you're in for a surprise. With over 20 separate stores making up Matterhorn Gardener's Village laid out along pathways and around ponds, the nursery is designed to give visitors a refuge from hectic day-to-day life. Horn's business formula is down-to-earth simplicity itself yet innovation in today's business world of spreadsheets, financial plans, and balance

A VISIT TO MATTERHORN NURSERY, CONTINUED

sheets. "What makes our nursery so different is that we are different," Horn explains. "It is easy for everybody to be the same, like Home Depot,® Wal-Mart,® K-mart.® We look for more eclectic and odd things that people might enjoy. We are really giving people ideas, which a lot of other places don't."

Providing a wonderful experience together with gardening knowledge and enlightenment is the motivation behind the display gardens at Matterhorn, a fee-based attraction where visitors can see an exclusive David Austin rose garden and a Japanese garden along with other gardens devoted to ferns, hostas, and ornamental grasses, as well as Matt's Folly, where Horn gives his creativity wing. "Even in the greatest gardens I've seen, in all honesty they are very simple gardens. They are immaculately done, creating an ambience and outdoor living areas that people can live in and enjoy. But they are simple," Horn explains.

With a passion for growing things in all aspects of his business, Horn has figured out the secret of getting people to pay $2.00 for a petunia, when they can get a four-pack for 50 cents at Wal-Mart®; and that means delivering an outstanding quality experience. "The word quality is so overused, but quality is definitely the keyword of what sells. When you see our petunias growing in the right soil and then take them home and find out how very successful they are in your garden, people are willing to pay more for quality," Horn says.

Regarding luxury in the garden, for Horn it's not about spending lots of money or being the most expensive thing. He says, "Just

A VISIT TO MATTERHORN NURSERY, CONTINUED

because you have money doesn't mean you have taste. Everyone has luxury in them. It's how you get it out of them. Luxury doesn't need to be expensive."

With his business about evenly divided between garden retailing and landscape design and services, Horn's clientele is composed of affluent luxury consumers. For the future, Horn sees developments in indoor gardening and greenhouses, as well as in tropical plants introduced as "temporary perennials." "People are going out and paying $150.00 to $200.00 for a palm tree, putting it in for the summer, and then throwing it out at the end of the year. Someone coined the term *temperennials*, which are temporary perennials. But you see people who put in tropicals and perennials that are hardy in the South but who don't have the luxury dollars to just throw them away at the end of the season, so they bring them inside over the wintertime. In the future, you are going to see an evolution of more people having greenhouses on their property and more sunrooms."

For Matt Horn and his like-minded customers, the reward of gardening goes beyond just having a beautiful landscape to look at. It is really about the experience of getting your hands dirty to make something beautiful grow. Horn says, "The real reward for me is keeping a garden. Once a garden is created, it takes lots of work to maintain the garden to the expected values of the customer. To me, that is the real experience."

Reprinted with permission from *Let Them Eat Cake: Marketing Luxury to the Masses as Well As the Classes* by Pamela N. Danziger.

CHAPTER 36

How to Create Unique Value from Thin Air

"On the surface, Nordstrom is a department store much like other department stores . . . . If you can buy the same article of clothing at another store, and one store is not farther from your home than the other, and the pricing is competitive but not demonstrably better, what brings a shopper into Nordstrom and not another store just as easy to patronize? Am I crazy, or is it the pianist?"

—Michael Levine, *Broken Windows, Broken Business: How The Smallest Remedies Reap The Biggest Rewards*

A t its heart and soul, my kind of marketing is modern alchemy. In medieval times there were purportedly alchemists who could turn ordinary metals into gold. There was also a young woman able to spin hair into gold on a spinning wheel, so I guess we shouldn't take the idea of alchemist wizards too seriously. But you can actually spin thin air into gold, by creating unique values that appeal to the affluent and support premium pricing for goods and services.

Illustrate Your Process

I invented this strategy for myself in 1979, so it is at least 29 years young. An example that I created for one of the most successful

Recommended Resource

You can hear one of the interviews that Glazer-Kennedy Insider's Circle™ Members get every month, this one about Naming Your Process, with Bill Glazer and James Phelps, free at www.NoBSBooks.com, in the section of the site devoted to this book. And you can get a FREE TRIAL GOLD MEMBERSHIP at www.DanKennedy.com. See page 429 for more information.

and celebrated real estate agents in all of North America, Craig Proctor, appears in Figure 36.1. As you can see in his example, when you Illustrate Your Process, you take everything you do in delivering your services or products and break it up into individual, named steps. Some are things everybody in your type of business does, but that doesn't matter. Others may be things you do so routinely you give them no thought and assign them no value, yet they have value to your clients. Some may actually be unique. By putting them in chronological sequence, in an illustrated diagram, you convey a high level of expertise, competence, and reliability and make it easy for the buyer to SEE the value you deliver. In my book, an Illustrated Process is worth 1,000 words—and millions of dollars.

Elevate Your Status

In Figure 36.2, you'll find the Hierarchy Pyramid of Income and Power. The higher up the pyramid you go, the more status you

FIGURE 36.1: Craig Proctor Ad

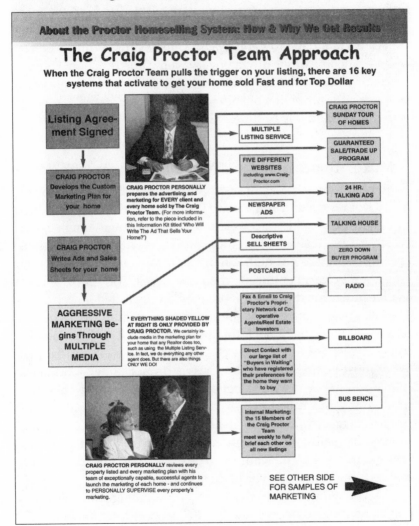

have, thus the more attractive you are to affluent clients, the higher compensation they feel you are entitled to, and the more likely they are to brag to others about being your client. Status is especially magnetic to people who value status. While a person of lesser income or wealth may very well value function, convenience, or price above the status of the provider of the goods or services, the affluent consumer often places status higher in importance than any of those other attractors.

Make Your Clients Qualify to Do Business with You

For many years, I have put prospective clients through a process, a series of hoops they must jump through before being permitted to do business with me. It irritates, offends, and repels some, which is fine. It screens out those who cannot follow directions, are impatient, are not highly motivated to secure my assistance, and cannot clearly enunciate their objectives. The specifics don't matter much for this discussion; they are included in my books *No B.S. Time Management for Entrepreneurs* and *No B.S. Sales Success.* Suffice to say, here, that my intent has long been not just to get clients but to get good clients, and I have criteria for that. What most people in most businesses do not understand about this is epic. They devoutly believe they cannot use strategies of limited and controlled access and of qualifying clients in their unique business, and they fear it will cost them clients and money. In reality, in virtually every setting, it has the reverse effect; it makes people want to do business with you all the more and reduces or erases their price or fee resistance.

Maybe you've seen the television commercials that eBay began running sometime late in 2007. In one, humans line up at

FIGURE 36.2: Hierarchy Pyramid of Income and Power

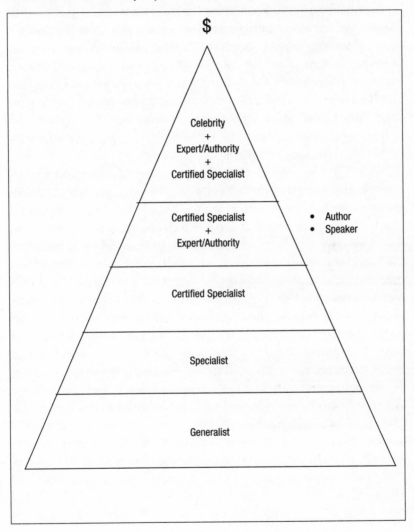

the starting line on a dog track and race each other to get their hands on some item. In another, they are on a scavenger hunt in the woods. In every commercial, the person who gets the desired item is leaping about, holding it aloft, as if having won an Olympic medal. The tag line is: "Shop Victoriously!" That is exactly the sense you want your customers to have when they are able to secure a telephone or personal appointment with you, then are able to gain acceptance as your customer, client, or patient—you want them to feel that they have pursued and successfully, victoriously achieved something.

When I was considering the purchase of a vacation time-share membership designed only for the affluent, with a minimum initiation fee of more than $200,000.00, plus substantial yearly dues, plus use and service fees for each property, I was sent a lengthy and detailed application to complete and return so the company could "determine my suitability as a member." If I passed, I and my wife would be assigned a telephone appointment with a club executive—my wife's attendance was required—for him to "further assess the appropriateness of our membership" and answer any questions. Ultimately, a personal meeting might be required. This is the obvious inverse of the way time-shares are normally sold to the masses: *C'mon down for a free dinner or free weekend, get a free alarm clock or TV, and sit through a sales pitch.* You have undoubtedly been exposed to that approach. The approach used by the club I was considering may be foreign to you. Know that it is not foreign at all to the affluent. In fact, having to qualify to buy in this way adds value to what is being sold. Not having to qualify raises suspicion about value with the affluent.

IF BUYING OR SELLING A LUXURY HOME, SURELY YOU DON'T WANT AN ORDINARY REAL ESTATE AGENT, NOW DO YOU?

There sure are a lot of real estate agents. A bazillion, at last count. But only a small number of members of The Institute for Luxury Home Marketing, "the premier independent authority educating and certifying real estate professionals in the art of handling exceptional properties." The Institute advertises itself thusly to real estate agents, as a source of specialized training and "certification," to elevate the member-agent's status. To the consumer, the Institute promotes its purpose as "helping buyers and sellers of high-end homes find quality real estate professionals who have been uniquely trained to handle upper-class properties."

To be clear, this is a clever business—the word *institute* self-proclamation. It is the brainchild of a speaker working the real estate market, Laurie Moore-Moore. To elevate her status, she chose the specialty of teaching strategies for listing and selling luxury homes and wrote and self-published a book, *Rich Buyer, Rich Seller: The Real Estate Agent's Guide to Marketing Luxury Homes*. Her self-created Institute now bestows her self-created certifications on agents: CLHMS, standing for Certified Luxury Home Marketing Specialist, and CLHMS-MG, standing for the previous plus Million Dollar Guild. These certifications are awarded to Institute member-agents (i.e., her paying clients) who have met certain qualifications (notably including having paid certain fees for her ascending levels of training). In short, they are paid-for credentials, and Moore-Moore is in the business of selling

IF BUYING OR SELLING A LUXURY HOME, CONTINUED

them. Now, don't misunderstand my comments; I am not being critical of this. In fact, a number of my clients have businesses that are even more sophisticated than this, but include the selling of their own certifications and credentials. If curious about such businesses, visit www.info-marketing.org. I do not mean to criticize the business model or suggest any judgment, good, bad, or indifferent, on the training the real estate agents buy and get in this case. I only want to point out that the consumer is intended to view it in a certain way, different from its reality. And further, and more importantly, to point out that anybody, including you, can go into a room on a Saturday morning, create your own Institute, decide on the impressive-sounding, status-elevating credentials it will bestow on you and possibly others, design the logo, the certificates, and the website, and be back out of the room in time for afternoon tea 'n' cookies. You need no permission or authorization from anybody else.

CHAPTER 37

Every Marketer to the Affluent
Should Be in
the Information Business

"We all like to buy something from an expert—somebody we like, respect and trust. The buyer thinks—'I don't understand any of this technical stuff, but hey, if he understands it, the product must be super!' "

—JOSEPH SUGARMAN, DIRECT-MARKETING GENIUS BEHIND MANY SUCCESSES, INCLUDING BLU-BLOCKERS,® AND AUTHOR OF *ADVERTISING SECRETS OF THE WRITTEN WORD*

The more affluent the customer and the more significant the purchase or its price, the more likely perceived expert status will play into the decision. As the stakes rise, the affluent consumer looks for a bona fide expert for assistance. This may mean the cleaning of Oriental rugs or leather upholstery or the management of a windfall of several million dollars obtained from the sale of a business. By positioning and presenting yourself as an expert in your field, you gain competitive differentiation and advantage, create support for charging premium prices and fees, make yourself more attractive to the affluent customer and lay the groundwork for media acceptance and publicity. It is, in short, well worth doing!

There are several intertwined paths to expert status. All but one are open to anyone, anywhere, at any time. The one that is not is academic qualification and bestowed or earned credentials. Fortunately, these are of the least importance in influencing customers and clients. So if it is too late for you to pursue your MBA from Stanford or you chafe at the patience, hoop jumping, butt kissing, and other silliness required to get some association, committee, or made-up body of authority to confer upon you a certification, relax. The other paths have more power and are immediately accessible.

For nine consecutive years, I was a featured speaker on the number-one public seminar tour in America, sharing the platform with former U.S. Presidents, Lady Margaret Thatcher, Mikhail Gorbachev, and countless business leaders, and, more importantly, for about 20 years I made more money per year as a professional speaker than 99.9% of my peers in the profession's association. I never obtained one of its several professional designations, got none of its alphabet soup letters to place after my name. Lacking these "credentials" had zero effect. For nearly 30 years I've been a highly paid advisor to brand-name corporations and their CEOs as well as entrepreneurs the world over, and, in the most recent tax year concluded, paid taxes on more than $2 million in personal income from my consulting activities. I have a high school education. I never served any sort of formal or informal apprenticeship in my field of advertising. I belong to no consultants association, have no professional certifications or credentials. If I should need an MBA for some odd reason, there are thousands of people with MBAs who can be rented quite inexpensively. My clientele has never once cared about or questioned any of this. The world has accepted me—and will accept you—based on my self-developed presentation. Period. Should you wish to be embraced as an expert or even as *the Expert* in your field, be it dog whispering or interior decorating or travel to Morocco or investing in municipal bonds, in your community, nationally, or globally, there is one simple thing far, far, far more important than any sort of credentials you may or may not have: decision.

The affluent, incidentally, are even more likely to accept you as you present and credential yourself than other socio-economic groups, because so many of them have achieved their status through self-determination rather than academic or other qualification, certification, or appointment. They got there more by guile and grit than gift or credentials. There is a never-acknowledged secret handshake, an understanding between all us emperors with no clothes. As disturbing as all this is to people who have painstakingly piled up degrees and framed diplomas and alphabet soup designations after their names yet make far less money than we do, often while working for us, it is reality.

So, to the three paths to expert status:

Path 1: Publication
Path 2: Promotion
Path 3: Publicity

Path 1: Get Published or Publish Yourself

You can take a traditional path, by becoming a "real" author and having a book published by a "real" publisher. For purposes of promoting yourself as an expert to a selected affluent group, there's little advantage to that over self-publishing. The faster path is publishing your own books, white papers, and newsletters. The principle at play is: If it looks like a duck, walks like a duck, quacks like a duck, it'll be accepted as a duck. If your self-published book looks like a bookstore book, it'll be just as useful to you as one published by a real New York publisher. People attach a lot of mystery to all of this it doesn't deserve. Printing is printing.

As an author of 11 books published by real publishing houses plus countless books and other information products and newsletters of my own, I can assure you that you are automatically granted a certain amount of expert status purely and solely as a result of having authored a book. As the classic advertising maxim goes, perception is reality, and people's perception of authors is favorable. I believe, at barest minimum, you need a book you've authored and a newsletter you publish consistently, preferably monthly, that presents you as a knowledgeable expert.

Path 2: Promote Yourself as Author and Expert

Now you have something to promote other than your products and services, for instant elevation from merchant to expert, which also provides natural competitive differentiation. Over the years, I've switched many clients from promoting their businesses to promoting books about their expertise. And, while your affluent prospect might throw out your junk mail about real estate investing unread, he may not be so quick to discard his monthly copy of the *Bay Area Investors' Real Estate Trends Letter.*

Path 3: Publicity

Being the author-expert is the door key to the media. Your local newspaper may not be eager to give free advertising to your nursery, but it may be eager to write a feature story about the local author of *101 Secrets of Green Thumb Gardening: How Anyone Can Amaze Their Friends and Neighbors with a Beautiful Backyard.* Your local talk radio host may not be eager to give you free advertising for your financial planning practice, but he may welcome you as a guest to discuss your book *10 Dumb Mistakes Very Smart People Make about Money.*

You may even find, as you employ these strategies for promotion of your business, that you'd be interested in making a second business out of it. Countless numbers of my clients and Glazer-Kennedy Insider's Circle™ Members have found their way to multi-million-dollar business opportunities as well as interesting and fun activities, prestige and prominence, and personal growth along this evolutionary path. This is such a common occurrence in our world that we host an annual conference, the Info-Summit,™ just for information marketers. If this interests you, I recommend another book from this publisher, *The Official Get Rich Guide to Information Marketing: Build a Million Dollar Business within 12 Months,* to which I contributed. You can also get more insight into this field at www.info-marketing.org.

IS AN EXPERT AN EXPERT IF NO ONE KNOWS?

Here is a phone conversation recounted by Dr. Thomas Stanley, one of the foremost authorities on millionaires and author of the bestselling book *The Millionaire Next Door*:

> DR. STANLEY: Who is your main adviser?
>
> DECAMILLIONAIRE: A securities broker in California.
>
> DR. STANLEY: But didn't you tell me you're a resident of New York? Did you once live in California?
>
> DECAMILLIONAIRE: "I'm a New York native—never lived in California.
>
> DR. STANLEY: Then tell me how you became a client of a stockbroker in California.
>
> DECAMILLIONAIRE: I read his articles on investment strategy. I called him on the phone. He is quite famous.

Once we know where the fish are and who they are, we can make ourselves more attractive to them. How can we condition them to recognize us and to develop favorable images of us? The top producers in the insurance industry as well as related areas are often endorsed by the business media within their market territory. These top producers write articles about the insurance and financial problems of their target market. They appear on television programs that feature business topics and experts. They conduct seminars that attract not only prospective customers but also key

IS AN EXPERT AN EXPERT?, CONTINUED

influencers such as accountants and other trusted advisers. You too must develop an appreciation for the benefits of being perceived primarily as an expert rather than as purely a marketer (of insurance). Publicizing your expertise via highly credible channels of communication will enable you to reap handsome rewards.

The person that most people, including me, consider the best professional fisherman on Lake Lanier, one of Georgia's most popular lakes, is Bill Vanderford. When I think of fishing on Lake Lanier and catching the big fish, I think about Mr. Vanderford's guide service. He is considered the top expert . . . . In addition, no one knows more about how to market his services than Bill.

Bill teaches a continuing education course at a local college on how to fish Lake Lanier. When the Atlanta or Georgia media want to do a story on Georgia fishing, they interview Bill. Bill is the author of *Everything You Ever Wanted To Know About Fishing Lake Lanier*.

What Bill has done is to stake out his claim to the Lake Lanier market.

Prospects are likely to feel more confident about hiring a fishing guide who has written a book on fishing. This is especially important if the prospect is an executive who hopes to entertain clients.

Abridged from a chapter in *Marketing to the Affluent* by Dr. Thomas Stanley.

CHAPTER 38

Who Can Have the
Highest Price?

*"If you can actually count your money,
you are not really a rich man."*

—J. Paul Getty

In November 2007, a New York restaurant, Serendipity 3, set a Guinness World Record for the highest price for a dessert: $25,000.00. Partnering with luxury jeweler Euphoria, the restaurant rolled out its Frozen Haute Chocolate Sundae, a blend of 28 different cocoas, infused with 5 grams of edible 23-karat gold flakes, served in a goblet lined with edible gold, topped with whipped cream, and accompanied by a side of La Madeline au Truffe from Knipschildt Chocolatier (which sells by itself for $2,600.00 a pound). It is eaten with a gold spoon decorated with white and chocolate-covered diamonds, which can be taken home. It comes with a souvenir 18-karat gold bracelet with white diamonds, at the goblet's base. This same restaurant has, for over a year, had a $1,000.00 ice-cream sundae on its regular menu—and it sells briskly to rock stars, socialites, and executives alike. No to-go cup available.

At the coffee shop in the Times Square Westin,® you can pay $1,000.00 for a bagel. One bagel. Topped with white truffle cream cheese, Riesling jelly with golden leaves. The $9.00 charge for a side order of two strips of bacon, a bargain by comparison.

What madness this be?

There is method in the madness.

This is but one example of restaurateurs in many cities trumping each other with outrageously priced, luxury meals, snacks, desserts, and drinks rolled out at a dizzying pace in recent years. It is a trend. Possibly inspired by the long-standing Neiman Marcus® holiday catalog's offering of one-of-a-kind items and experiences priced into the tens and hundreds of thousands of dollars, in recent years, many other catalogers, fashion, furniture, jewelry, and even eyeglass companies, and restaurants have been playing the "Who can create the highest-priced item?" game. You might want to stop laughing or shaking your head in disbelief and instead ponder application to your business.

First and foremost, these marketers are smartly using price as path to publicity. That means free advertising. Local and national print and broadcast media consistently respond favorably to this Barnumism. From the *New York Times* and *Town & Country* to the *Today Show* the outrageously priced luxury items make news and are shown off. Such publicity has both immediate and lasting value.

Second, it can also create buzz among the affluent customers you seek. It makes for great cocktail conversations. Some people quickly go out of their way to have these experiences or buy these odd items, in order to own the story of doing so. In telling the story of eating the $25,000.00 sundae and showing off the souvenir bracelet, such a patron also tells 10 or 50 ideal customers about the restaurant, the menu, the chef. When arriving at the golf tournament carrying the $9,700.00 golf bag, he will tell the admirers about the website with the amazing array of unusual items for golfers.

Third, it can make your other high prices seem reasonable.

If the restaurateur never actually sold a single $25,000.00 sundae, all the effort of creating it would still be worthwhile.

But these things *do* sell. A few $1,000.00 bagels equal the profit from a few thousand $1.00 bagels. In marketing, in general, I teach this as the *slack-adjuster strategy*. It came to my attention from the automobile business, and it is slang car guys will recognize. It means having something you can sell occasionally that has so much margin and delivers such a big pile of profit that it makes up for selling large numbers of low-priced, skinny-margin items. In the coffeehouse, it might be the $1,500.00 home coffee machine displayed and sold only a few dozen times a year. Or the $15,000.00 gold-plated one sold once all year. In the chiropractic office with $45.00 treatments, it may be the $3,000.00 massage recliner on which $1,500.00 is made. In the hardware store, it might be the $15,000.00 custom-built and installed grilling station.

A client of mine in a dermatology practice sells a $100,000.00 Lifetime VIP Membership, entitling that patient to unlimited access to any and all procedures, services, and products desired. He sells four or five of these every year. Most of the buyers will never come close to using even half of this value. He can absorb that delivery over time into his overhead, so he can extract these slack-adjuster monies from his practice and put 100% of them into pension fund and other investments, second or third home, or lifestyle. Continually showing membership as available helps support his other fees and prices.

A famous financial advisor promotes "the million-dollar gift," a million-dollar life insurance policy packaged elegantly, with gilt-edged and calligraphed certificate in leather presentation box—perfect as a graduation, wedding anniversary, or birthday gift. I have no idea how many he sells to clients who might otherwise not buy another million dollars' worth of coverage. Some, I'm sure. But it also serves to initiate conversations about insurance that would otherwise not occur, leading, I'm certain, to the sale of a lot of life insurance. It's a very safe bet that the recipients of these gifts tell family and friends about it and that the buyers of these gifts brag to others about it, giving the broker considerable word-of-mouth promotion. He has brilliantly turned an intangible into a tangible, changed the conversation about his product and service, and pre-established a high price.

CHAPTER 39

Price, Profits, and Power

"One of the most fundamental principles of human nature is that people want something that everyone else wants or no one else has."

—GEORGE H. ROSS, EXECUTIVE BUSINESS, LEGAL,

AND NEGOTIATIONS ADVISOR TO DONALD TRUMP

Would you like to know your personal weakness, which will sabotage your success in making maximum profits from marketing to the affluent?

If you are inclined to consider price in making a purchase, you have an Achilles' heel. It will be difficult for you to embrace the *principle* that price does not matter. Yet immense power is there for the taking, for the marketer who takes a new view of price.

If we are not selling to poor people, then price has power over buying decisions only when it is presented naked, out of context. In *The Paradox of Choice*, Barry Schwartz uses this example:

How do you determine how much to spend on a suit? One way is to compare the price of one suit to another, which means using the other items as anchors. In a store that displays suits costing over $1,500.00, an $800.00 pinstripe may seem like a good buy. But in a store in which most of the suits cost less than $500.00, that same $800.00 suit might seem like an extravagance. So which is it, a good buy or self-indulgence? Unless you are on a strict budget, there are no absolutes.

That is the essence of price: there are no absolutes.

Schwartz has perfectly described the need for context, in this case comparison in order to determine whether a stated price is outrageous, reasonable, or a bargain. The providing of similar anchors as he described is the most common and least sophisticated approach, very frequently used by retailers and catalogers. In selling pricier goods or services to affluent con-sumers, you'll often be better served with dissimilar anchors, engineering what I call *apples-to-oranges* comparisons. For example, in selling a seminar on case presentation (selling) to cosmetic dentists for $15,000.00, I would not use other seminar or conference fees or typical costs for continuing education credits as the anchor. I would use their own average case size. Given that their average cosmetic case may be $30,000.00, the seminar fee is recovered by only one-half of one case you wouldn't secure without the information and strategies taught at the seminar. On the face of it, $15,000.00 to attend a seminar sounds pretty darned stiff. And there are lots and lots of seminars sold in the dental profession for one-tenth that fee. To sell the $15,000.00 fee, I must use one or more anchors that make it seem reasonable or a bargain and not, in any way, encourage apples-to-apples comparison.

Dan Kennedy's #15
No BS Key to the Vault

Any price can be made a bargain.

The price of anything, by itself, will almost always be too high. The price put in proper context and compared with the right anchors can always be made a bargain.

Because most business owners are not target marketing to the affluent, and are approaching price through their own biases and fears, and are presenting it badly, without best context, most are grossly underpricing. It is very common for business owners I influence to be able to raise prices by 25% to 250% with no loss of customers, reduction in conversions of leads to buyers, or other negative ramifications—although, if you run numbers, you can come out way ahead when losing some customers or sales while commanding significantly higher prices for those you keep. Assume you sell an item for $500.00 and presently sell 1,000 of them a year, creating $500,000.00 of gross income. If you raise the price to $697.00, you can lose up to 20% of your business, sell only 800 units, and wind up with $557,600.00. A 10% increase in sales with a 20% loss of volume. Would you lose 20% of those sales? Almost certainly not. Most people are shocked to discover they have untapped space to raise prices or fees with little or no loss of volume. In some cases, sales increase, as the higher prices actually attract more customers.

Stop Striving for Lower Prices

In the next two chapters, I'll give you some quick price-increase strategies. Here, let's talk about why you should strive to charge the highest prices you can—probably a concept contrary to everything you've ever been taught or advised.

If you can't bring the absolute lowest prices forward and guarantee that, then having the almost-lowest prices is no competitive or marketing advantage. What can you honestly say? C'mon down, we have the third- or fourth- or maybe fifth-lowest prices? Furthermore, lowest price is a totally unsustainable advantage. And only poor people have their *choices* controlled by price—and we're not looking for poor customers. So, if you aren't going to have the cheapest price, and the next cheapest offers no legitimate advantage, you might as well stop worrying about where you are on some competitive price ladder altogether. Concentrate instead on making sales in a competitive vacuum using the marketing system described in this book and on creating and delivering extraordinary experiences that make price a nonissue.

Which brings me to one of the best reasons to sell at higher prices: You can then afford to create and deliver much better experiences. You can overstaff rather than understaff and pay above-par wages and incentives to attract superior people and make great demands of them, instead of paying below-par wages, forcing employment of inferior people from whom you can demand little. You can make your sales and buying environment more pleasing or elegant or impressive—a Disney® hotel rather than a Motel 6.® You can improve your after-sale service. You can do much, much, much more to *wow!* your customer before, during, and after the sale. And still make more profit per sale.

But here's an even better reason: you can afford to spend a lot more to get your customers than anyone else competing with you for their attention can or will spend. This is where you gain enormous power. It's a very misunderstood power source. Most business owners try to spend as little as they must to acquire a customer, but I coach my clients to spend as much as possible, to put themselves in the position of being able to outspend everyone else, to spend a multiple of what everybody else will spend to get a customer. While the other carpet cleaners hang fliers on doorknobs, we will send out DVD players with preloaded DVDs via Federal Express. While other financial advisors send out ordinary letters easily trashed by gatekeepers, we will send what I

Dan Kennedy's #16
No BS Key to the Vault

Put the power of transaction size to work,
to your advantage.

call a *shock 'n' awe package* with a 300-page book of testimonials, two audio CDs, a DVD, and a beautiful brochure, all packed inside a briefcase, delivered by a messenger. While others do little or no follow-up, we'll do endless multi-step, multi-media follow-up. How can we do these things without spending ourselves broke? By targeting more valuable customers and by raising our prices to provide all the extra marketing dollars.

One of the secrets I present in my Renegade Millionaire System (www.RenegadeMillionaire.com) is the power of transaction size. To acquire a million dollars with $10,000.00 units of sale requires only 100 customers—fewer if they buy more than one unit. To get to the million with $1,000.00 transactions requires 1,000 customers. Contrary to common belief, it is a lot easier to find 100 people each willing and able to pay $10,000.00 for something than it is to find 1,000 people each willing to pay $1,000.00. There are a number of reasons that this is true. For one thing, there are fewer marketers hunting for the 100 who'll pay $10,000.00 than there are fighting over the 1,000 who'll pay $1,000.00. Another, when making a $10,000.00 sale, you can invest more in making it than when making the $1,000.00 sale.

Consider a client of mine I convinced to sell a particular service for $5,000.00, which he initially believed should have been priced below $2,000.00, probably at $1,500.00. From 500 qualified prospects, he sold 100 at $5,000.00, for a total of $500,000.00. But to produce the same $500,000.00 with a $1,500.00 price, he'd have needed 333 sales from the 500 prospects. That high of a response percentage is a much bigger impossibility than the $5,000.00 price. The 100 buyers out of 500 represented a 20% conversion rate, but the 333 would have been a whopping 66% conversion rate. Would 233 more have bought at the lower price? No. In fact, most attempts to buy volume by discounting fail, especially when targeting affluent customers. In many situations including this one, the person who wanted this service wanted it, pure and simple, basically at any price. The person who did not want it didn't want it, and couldn't be made to want what he didn't want just by offering it to him at a cheaper price. In selling to the affluent, it's always more about desire than price. Every one of the 500 on this list could easily pay the $5,000.00 price *if he wanted* the service.

This is a truth of price that's very difficult for many marketers to accept, especially if they personally are restricted by price or are not of the same or a higher level of affluence than the people they're selling to.

Consider this example. At different times during an evening, two affluent executives on business trips, sitting alone in their luxury hotel bar, having a nightcap, are each approached discreetly by a professional lady of the evening, offering private entertainment for $1,000.00. One accepts. The other, committed to his marital vows, declines. If she offered to reduce her fee, would she sway the second man? No. His refusal had nothing to do with price.

When a marketer or seller erroneously decides he has a price problem and drops his price but does not buy more conversions by doing so, transaction size is his enemy. If the aforementioned lady's success rate was 50% consistently, so that out of 100 men approached, she would encounter 50 who refused her because of firm commitment to their marital vows (or any other reason but price) and 50 who accepted her offer, and she reduced her fee to $750.00 in hope of getting a higher percentage of those approached to say yes, she'd only succeed at a 25% pay cut. Nothing more.

Now let's take another look at how the power of transaction size works to someone's advantage. Assume a restaurant has 30 tables, 120 seats, and can turn them 3 times on a Saturday night, thus serving 360 meals, ringing up 360 units of sale. If its menu prices now yield an average of $50.00 per person, that's $18,000.00. But if the menu prices were upped to yield $70.00 per person, the same $18,000.00 could be achieved at only 71% capacity (257 units). However, if it lost only 10% of its business because of the higher prices and stayed at 90% capacity, it would make $22,680.00 on Saturday night. A pay raise of $4,680.00 times 50 Saturdays = $234,000.00 more for the year. Is there any other way to boost this little restaurant's revenues by $234,000.00? Probably not.

Transaction size can work for or against you, as you choose. Nothing can confer more power upon you than getting it to work for you, to maximum advantage.

HOW MANY STEPS MUST YOU TAKE TO GET TO EACH MILLION DOLLARS?

$1,000,000.00	1 Step
$100,000.00	10 Steps
$10,000.00	100 Steps
$1,000.00	1,000 Steps
$100.00	10,000 Steps
$10.00	100,000 Steps

Why not take bigger steps and get there faster?

"PRICE MAY BE IN THE EYE OF THE BEHOLDER, BUT IT IS IN THE CONTROL OF THE PROVIDER"

A Doctor's Prescription for Successfully Obtaining Prices or Fees Higher than Competitors' or Your Industry Norms

KENNEDY: *I want to talk with you about price—about setting fees, raising fees, and what you've discovered, even what has surprised you about fees.*

DR. BARRY LYCKA: I grew up in a working-class family, with the penny saved, penny earned philosophy. I never got anything without earning it. I often thought—well, I, personally, would not pay what my patients do for cosmetic surgery! That kept me from raising my fees for years. Interestingly, when I finally began raising my fees to reflect my expertise, I became more desirable—not less— to patients. And, about ten years ago, I began specifically working on appealing to more affluent patients and found fees a nonissue. So, to give you some frame of reference: for procedures most doctors in my area might charge $6,000.00 to $8,000.00 to perform, my fees are $10,000.00 to $12,000.00. Despite the impression you get from the media, invasive cosmetic surgery procedures are actually decreasing; 2006 saw a 9% decrease against 2005, but I've had year-to-year practice growth every year. As a result, my 2007 revenues were $2.9 million, and that's with me taking 12 weeks off for vacations, and taking time away from practice for my writing, lecturing, and coaching other cosmetic surgeons throughout North America. My practice, incidentally, is in Edmonton, in Canada—not exactly the glamour capitol of the

"PRICE MAY BE IN THE EYE OF THE BEHOLDER,"
CONTINUED

world nor an exceptionally affluent area. I might add that it is my ability to attract affluent patients and obtain top fees that affords me the luxury of earning more while working less, continually investing in the latest technology and other practice improvements, and delivering the very best patient experience.

KENNEDY: *What do you think supports your above-par fees and year-to-year growth?*

LYCKA: There are many factors, but three of the biggest that you discuss frequently and have included in this book play a major role. One is the concept of no boundaries. While my practice as well as my med-spa are dominant in my local market, I have also cracked the code for attracting affluent patients from far outside my local area. In fact, I have patients coming to me from as far away as Greece, Saudi Arabia, Thailand, and Australia. Second, I understand I'm not in the "sucking fat" or "makeover" business, that I'm in the self-esteem and life improvement business. Third is expert status. I make certain I am frequently interviewed on radio and television and written about in newspapers; locally I create events that are covered by the media such as black-tie events at my spa or charity golf tournaments; and I publish a considerable amount of information for my patients. Prospective patients receive what you call a shock-and-awe package with a book I've written, a DVD, an audio CD, and a collection of information—not just an ordinary brochure. I would also mention that I continually

"PRICE MAY BE IN THE EYE OF THE BEHOLDER,"
CONTINUED

invest in my own education—advertising, marketing, sales, and business, not just clinical—and in improvements in my businesses. As you know, I have been in Glazer-Kennedy Insider's Circle™ coaching groups for years and travel and take time away from practice for those meetings. I've brought Sydney Barrows to my spa twice to do on-site analysis, consulting, and training. I am never in the leave-well-enough-alone mode. I also take a balanced approach toward the clinical and the business aspects of practice. Many doctors let themselves dislike or neglect the marketing, or try delegating it entirely away—mistakes.

KENNEDY: *What do you now know about price that others don't?*

LYCKA: It's entirely elastic. It can be 100% determined by the provider, not the buyer. It can be set in what you call a self-created competitive vacuum. Further, by strategically seeking affluent consumers, you have even greater freedom with price. Of course, you have to do everything there is to do to support your position. In my case, I have to be consistent. An upscale reception room, upscale reception staff, even the quality of the sound system playing the proper music in my office is a consideration. State-of-the-art techniques and technology are also important to my patients. We utilize computer imaging, so the patient can see their future face. Our body sculpting is done with the most technologically advanced procedures. Consistency with your positioning is very important.

"PRICE MAY BE IN THE EYE OF THE BEHOLDER,"
CONTINUED

BARRY LYCKA, MD, FRCP, has a thriving cosmetic dermatology practice and a med-spa. He is the author of a number of books for consumers and for professional peers and is a frequent lecturer at medical conferences. His marketing-to-the-affluent systems are now provided with personal coaching to one doctor per defined market area, and most doctors he works with have added upwards of $1 million to $2 million per year to their practice revenues. Doctors can access information about Dr. Lycka's programs at www.CosmeticSxProfits.com or fax an inquiry to (780) 425-1217.

CHAPTER 40

How to Raise Prices without Raising Prices

"If you can think of only one answer to a question, and you are paid above the laborers' lowest wage, you are grossly over-paid, and whoever is responsible for authorizing such largesse should be found out and fired. Or shot."

—CHARLES F. KETTERING, INDUSTRIALIST

In their book Mass Affluence, Paul Nunes and Brian Johnson lay out three strategies their research revealed as viable for helping all marketers capitalize on the newly expanded profit opportunities available with the moneyed masses, paraphrased:

1. Give customers the chance to spend more. Offer new premium versions, adding on product upgrades and differentiated service levels to existing offerings.

2. Honor customers with the recognition they desire. Create status levels that reward willing-to-spend customers.

3. Offer the right price to each customer.

They have it exactly right. In fact, the first of their strategies is one that I have routinely and frequently used for my own products, services, and business as well as hundreds of clients. Whenever you are unwilling to outright raise prices for particular goods or services, at least create premium or deluxe versions of the same goods or services offered optionally, at a premium price. In almost every case, if a premium version of a product or service is available, no less than 5% to 20% of the existent or traditional customers will opt for it. Since the profit margin built into the premium version is usually substantially greater than in the basic, 5% picking the premium can actually create a 50% or 100% increase in profits from the same number of units of sale.

A common place you see this is at hotels, with the concierge floor. Typically, the rooms may or may not be slightly larger or better appointed, but still, they all have a bed and a bath and require the same linens, towels, maid service, and electricity; key access in the elevator (added cost: zero); a lounge with continental breakfast and evening snacks (cost: but a few dollars per guest); and two newspapers outside your door. The price differential may be from 20% to 50% of the basic room. But the added cost may be 2% to 5%. That differential item, the upgrade, carries a much higher markup than does the basic room. Same goes with the leather-bound edition vs. the hardbound edition, express delivery vs. ordinary delivery, even supersizing the burger and fries.

Sometimes this strategy leads to truly remarkable profit improvement. Recently, I had a client, marketing via a website, who was offering a basic product for $49.00. He also, at my suggestion, began offering a second, related product for $49.00 as an immediate upsell. In his industry, under normal circumstances, about 20% of the customers would buy that upsell. In this case, 80% were taking it. Based on that, he bundled the two together as a $98.00 product and created a new, different, additional upsell priced at $49.00. Conversions of website visitors to buyers was not suppressed at all. Before, the average transaction, with 80% taking the $49.00 upsell, was $88.20. Now the average jumped to $98.00. But then 60% took the new upsell. That brought the average transaction all the way from $88.20 up to $127.40. Per 100 sales, that's $3,920.00 more. For him, for the year, this produced $94,080.00 of added revenue.

The second strategy presents yet another way to ease into higher prices: differential pricing. An attorney in one of my coaching groups was at capacity. He had the busiest and most successful practice of his kind in his city, with clients literally standing in line and waiting for his time, yet he was deathly afraid of simply raising his fees. At my urging, he hired an associate, but instead of setting the associate's fees lower than his, he set the fee for cases handled by his associate at his present fee and began asking 50% more for cases handled by the associate but personally supervised by him, and 100% more for cases he handled personally. This presented each client with three different status levels for fundamentally the same service. As you can guess, he stayed nearly as busy but was also able to fill his associate's calendar. This same strategy has been employed by cosmetic dentists, chiropractors, CPAs, and hairstylists whom I know personally.

Affluent clients are considerably more likely to respond positively to differential pricing than others, especially if it is linked to differential status. For several years, I attended an annual investment and financial conference catering to affluent entrepreneurs.

Regular registration was priced at about $500.00. A limited number of people were *permitted* to purchase VIP registrations entitling them to preferred seating, luncheons with the speakers, an extra hour of time in the exhibition hall, and a nice blazer with the conference logo, identifying its wearer to all as a VIP for $995.00. An even more limited number were permitted to purchase Eagle VIP registrations entitling them to all VIP privileges, a different jacket, plus a cocktail reception, a backstage pass to the speakers' lounge, and a postconference series of private investment briefings for $1,995.00.

CHAPTER 41

Price Strategies

"Don't assume that logical pricing is smart pricing."
—HARRY BECKWITH, *SELLING THE INVISIBLE*

I have an entire entire full-day seminar on price strategies and I discuss them in great detail in other works of mine, and they can't be done justice here in a single chapter. But in limited time, I can give you a few examples of price strategies that illustrate how much opportunity there is just in re-arranging price and presentation of price.

The Secret of Selling Big-Ticket Items

The Orvis® catalog features outdoor and casual apparel, winter coats and hats and gloves and even pairs of socks, luggage, and

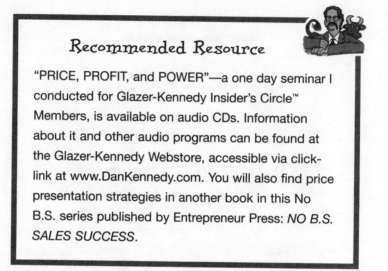

Recommended Resource

"PRICE, PROFIT, and POWER"—a one day seminar I conducted for Glazer-Kennedy Insider's Circle™ Members, is available on audio CDs. Information about it and other audio programs can be found at the Glazer-Kennedy Webstore, accessible via click-link at www.DanKennedy.com. You will also find price presentation strategies in another book in this No B.S. series published by Entrepreneur Press: *NO B.S. SALES SUCCESS*.

a wide variety of things hunters, fishermen, hikers, and outdoorsmen need and want. You might order a $20.00 pair of socks, a $50.00 Coleman® lantern, and a $60.00 plaid wool shirt. You can also order a $366,000.00 fly-fishing cruise for you and 27 friends from a full-page ad in that same catalog.

Yes, I said: $366,000.00.

You'll find the copy from the catalog page at the end of this chapter (page 368). And you can explore all the trips the company offers at www.Orvis.com/travel.

This reveals a very important secret about selling to the affluent: just because your store or shop or restaurant, your catalog or website, or your professional practice or service business routinely sells relatively low-priced goods and services does not mean it cannot also successfully sell very, very high-priced goods and services. In fact, it probably should. This is a secret that just might re-pay your little investment in this book 10,000 times over. Or more. By itself.

The Slack Adjuster

One $366,000.00 cruise sold makes up for small profits from a boatload of pairs of socks. That's the principle of the Slack Adjuster, a slang term from the used-car business.

Several years back, a member of one of my coaching programs owned two small-town, independent, old-fashioned hardware stores. In both towns, Wal-Mart,® Home Depot,® Lowes,® and Sears.® A lot of his customers came there to buy odd nuts and bolts and screws and hinges and small tools that the big chains didn't stock. But that created a whole lot of $5.00 and $10.00 transactions. At my urging, he installed a selection of very high-priced, high-end massage chairs, and, in season, a tent with displays of the priciest, most extraordinary backyard barbeque grill and cooking stations, one with its own 42-inch plasma TV. On a chair, the average profit was about $900.00. On a backyard grilling station, about the same, right around $1,000.00. On the top-line, most elaborate one, built into the backyard in a brick wall with fireplace, TV, and bar, about $4,000.00. In the smaller of the two stores, where the net profit for the prior year had been just shy of $120,000.00, he sold a chair a month (adding $10,800.00 net for the year), 12 grilling stations ($12,000.00), and two "big mommas" ($8,000.00) . . . boosting net profits by $30,800.00 or 25%. Sure, he might use up the available customers in that small town for such things, but having learned the strategy, he has numerous other options—such as game room and home bar setups, wine cellars and coolers, closet- and garage-organizing systems. He can keep rotating different slack adjusters in and out of his stores, leveraging his real asset: the customers coming in to buy $5.00 worth of screws.

Ascension

Creating an ascension ladder for customers or, better, customers converted to members is a great way to improve averaged transaction size and overall customer value. If you take me up on my free gift offer on page 429, become a Glazer-Kennedy Insider's Circle™ Gold-Level Member, like it, and stay, you will see our ascension ladder, giving members additional goods, services, and benefits organized so that they move from Gold to Gold+ to Gold+/Luxury to Gold+/Peak Performers, and a limited number into our international coaching groups. Our entire model has been copied and used in a wide variety of businesses, like restaurants, health clubs, and real estate brokerages working with investors. In most cases, this is hooked to monthly continuity, meaning the customer's credit card on file is automatically charged a pre-agreed amount on the first of every month for the products, services, and privileges provided during that month. The marketer is getting paid in advance, has a reliable income, and locks in greater usage by the customer than would occur from à la carte buying. It's worth noting that affluent customers are pre-conditioned to want to be in the most elite group, at the highest level, and will often ascend quickly, in big leaps.

The 20% Factor

The least scary way to raise prices is, as I discussed previously in this book, creating an optional, premium version of the same product(s) or service(s) you sell now, offered at a higher price, as an A-or-B choice (in place of a yes-or-no choice). If the premium proposition makes sense and has appeal, almost all marketers discover no less than 5% to, more commonly, 20% of their customers, clients, or patients opting for the higher-priced choice.

Upsells

This is a strategy you are certainly familiar with, as it's used on you often—yet so many business owners fail to institutionalize it in their own businesses. The rule is: for every purchase, made any way—in person, by phone, online—there should be an immediately offered upsell. At the movie theater counter, it's "Get a giant tub of popcorn instead of medium for just 50 cents more—and get free refills" and "Would you like a box of candy or a drink with that?" It translates anywhere. At my favorite upscale restaurant, the servers almost always present a featured steak of the evening, then explain that you can have it or any steak on the menu Oscar style with lump crabmeat or create a surf-and-turf meal, adding three jumbo shrimp or three jumbo sea scallops. You can replace the regular Yukon Gold mashed potatoes with lobster mashed potatoes. Each for a slight upcharge, of course. It's their elegant version of "WouldjaliketoSuperSizethat, bub?"

If the upsell offer(s) make sense and are appealing and are presented well according to a good script, no less than 5% to, more commonly, 20% will say yes.

This 5% to 20% factor is critically important to exploit. The *net* profit from the premium versions and upsells can equal or surpass the *net* profit from the core goods and services in most businesses.

Charge for What Was Free

A lot of business owners and professionals give away or include one or more things that can be separated and separately charged for, creating a de facto price increase.

Here's an interesting example: Two professionals—the specifics of their businesses don't matter—compete for the very same prospects in the same town, using the same media and the same mailing lists. They are both commission compensated for the work they do with a client once they get him, and the average client is worth $2,000.00 in first-year commissions. Each of these professionals has office overhead, client service costs, and kids and dogs to feed, so they are each willing to spend no more than half that, $1,000.00, in costs of getting new clients—on advertising, mailings, hosting seminars and dinner meetings, and so forth. One changes his game and begins charging new clients a $395.00 one-time client activation and membership fee. He can now spend 40% more to get each client: $1,395.00. Do you think his difficulty of getting clients leaps by 40%? Not at all. Both secure their clients, ultimately, in one-on-one, face-to-face meetings. The new fee is invisible until the moment of decision, to be a client or not be a client. This is an actual situation, and it made absolutely zero difference in the number of prospects met with who converted to clients. None. But it translated to my guy being able to spend $34,000.00 to promote one of his events in his market vs. his competitor's spending $20,000.00.

A growing trend in working with affluent clientele is charging for access. In health care, concierge medicine is controversial but very successful. Essentially, a doctor closes his practice to the public, limits the number of patients who can be members, gives them more time, attention, ready access, assistance and advocacy if they are hospitalized, and other benefits, and charges them a yearly fee just to belong, plus all normal and customary charges for needed services. A doctor taking just 100 patients at a $10,000.00 yearly fee banks $1 million before swabbing the first throat or tapping the first knee. The idea is spreading to diverse businesses—from the obvious, like CPA or investment advisory practices, to the surprising, like dog grooming.

GIVE THE ULTIMATE FLY-FISHING GIFT TO YOURSELF AND 27 OF YOUR CLOSEST FRIENDS.

We have picked the very best week to fish the remote coast of Patagonia and reserved it for you and 27 friends, to make for the single best angling gift and adventure of a lifetime. February 28–March 7, 2009, your angler's trip of a lifetime will be realized. Your accommodations for the week will be aboard the new luxurious *MV Atmosphere*, a 150-foot yacht specially designed for fly fishing and natural history cruises. The ship will tour some of the most remote and mountainous coastline on earth, and is outfitted with 14 private luxury cabins, a helicopter, jet boats and a 30-foot Zodiac with two 250 HP motors to give you access to the most remote estuaries and backcountry fishing in Patagonia. At the disposal of all 28 lucky travelers are nine fishing guides, two naturalists who are experts on the region's wildlife and history, a gourmet chef, sommelier, and, of course, a masseuse to work out the sore muscles from those long days of catching wild trout that few, if any, anglers have ever fished. Return at the end of each exhilarating day to exquisite food and comfort. This is one trip only for one select and lucky group of anglers and non-anglers alike. A gift of a lifetime. $366,000.00.

DELUXE EDITIONS LEAD TO SUPER SALES

What leaps price barriers in a single bound? Gets to millions in revenue faster than a speeding bullet?

Several years ago, a senior vice president at Marvel® Comics was brainstorming with colleagues, in search of an idea for a new product to tie in with the release of the *Fantastic Four*® movie. The result was *The Fantastic Four*® *Omnibus, Volume 1*, the polar opposite of a comic book—you know, that colorful magazine on tissue-thin paper you used to buy for a dime, then a quarter, today maybe a buck. A disposable commodity. The Omnibus is a giant, hardbound coffee-table book that weighs more than 5 pounds, contains 848 pages, and went to market priced at one penny less than $100.00. It contained reprints of the first 30 comic books in the Fantastic Four® series.

A hundred dollars is pricey for <u>any</u> book, let alone a comic book.

The entire edition sold out in just a few weeks. Its success has spawned what the industry calls a "coffee-tableization" of comic books, with Marvel® churning out more than a dozen other giant omnibus collections of its super-heroes' past comics, and other publishers following suit. While sales of single-copy comic books are in decline, thanks to distribution problems, the internet, and other factors, the nostalgia of boomers is fueling this renaissance in high-end, pricey collection editions. An executive at the largest distributor of English language comics in the world says: "It [this trend] reflects the demographics of the consumer, who is both

DELUXE EDITIONS LEAD TO SUPER SALES, CONTINUED

older and more affluent. They can afford to buy the complete Fantastic Four or Frank Miller's library for $100.00 or so a piece."

Paul Levitz, the President at DC™ Comics (Superman®; Batman®), said, "We love our passionate readers who spend from $1,000.00 to $1,500.00 a year on comics, but there are a lot more people who are willing to pay $300.00 or $400.00 a year on luxury editions." This is always a surprise to marketers, although often true; there are actually more available customers for luxury versions of a product than there are for its basic versions.

This successful invention of an entirely new business within the comics business embodies many marketing-to-the-affluent lessons, notably demonstrating that the affluent market's very existence makes possible and should govern the creation of deluxe and premium versions of products.

Sources: NewYorkTimes.com, "Media and Advertising," December 3, 2007; *Publishers Weekly*, various issues.

CHAPTER 42

The Trouble with Having
Money

"The gratification of wealth is not found in mere possession or in lavish expenditure, but in its wise application."

—Miguel de Cervantes, Spanish novelist

Poor people have limited choices. If they live in a depressed inner city and are dependent on public transportation, they may have a choice of but one neighborhood grocery store and, ironically, pay higher prices than a mass-affluent mom in suburbia with three large supermarkets kitty-corner from each other, competing for her business. Poor people's choices of clothes and colleges and everything else from A to Z are similarly limited by their severely restricted spending power and lack of discretionary income and by the shortage of merchants and service providers eager to bring products and services to them, for obvious reasons. Lack of choice rules their lives.

As you move from impoverished or low-income consumers to middle-income, then to mass-affluent, to affluent, and to ultra-affluent, choice expands exponentially.

To get from Cleveland to Los Angeles, the poorest traveler may still have no choice but Greyhound or Amtrak® and will have no choice but to travel on its schedule, likely having but one route. This traveler will stop wherever the vehicle stops for however long it stops. To make that same trip with an eye on economy, a middle-income earner may find a number of low-fare choices on airlines like Southwest,® may very well have choices of times of day to depart, even of routes and cities he'll stop in. The mass-affluent has the entire airline industry's offerings to choose from. If he wishes, he can even plug in a layover in Las Vegas going or coming back or both. Or he can pick a nonstop on Continental, and he can fly first class, get breakfast, and watch a movie. If he chooses not to be bothered with anything but a small carry-on, he can send everything else he needs to his hotel the day before via Federal Express. The affluent traveler has even more choices, as he may opt for private aviation, and charter a plane or buy flight hours in bulk as I do.

These travel choices are all beneficial for each person more affluent than the other. But having the most choice is not such a clear-cut advantage. In fact, the dizzying array of choices confronting affluent consumers can be a source of confusion, worry, family disputes, time consumption, paralysis, and stress no one but somebody with access to the same choices can fully understand. It's easy to laugh that off and have no empathy or sympathy for the person bothered with too many choices because he has too much money, but as a marketer to the affluent, you'll need to take this seriously.

A book published in 2004, *The Paradox of Choice*, is now a bit dated in its statistics but still well worth reading for its conceptual accuracy. Summarized, it makes the case that, at some point, too many choices translate to less power, freedom, and happiness than do fewer choices or even too few choices. My take on the author, Barry Schwartz, a Professor of social theory and social action, is that he is a liberal with a personal bias against free enterprise and capitalism, wealth, and certainly against conspicuous consumption, so you have to take that into consideration, just as you ought consider my own bias for unfettered capitalism, unlimited wealth, and doing whatever you damn well feel like doing with whatever wealth you produce, with zero social obligation or guilt. Despite his bias, however, I rank his book as a must-read for understanding the trouble people with money confront when spending it: far too many competing and confusing choices. Your greatest, most golden opportunity lies in solving this conundrum for them by successfully positioning yourself as the only choice in the category of product or service they seek to buy something in.

First, a bit more about the problem. People of modest means have fairly limited choices for saving and investing. They may only have or feel willing to deal with accounts at their local bank or credit union. If they are buying a home, they might accelerate mortgage payoff. If their employer offers a 401(k) plan, there they have dozens of structural choices and hundreds of secondary choices, but few wrestle with any of them, choosing by default and choosing ignorance and sloth, going along with whatever recommendation is made to them by the plan's manager. This is how all the pension funds of Enron employees stayed wrapped up tight in Enron stock.

Mass-affluents have many more savings, investment, financial product and financial services choices available to them. With a self-directed IRA, for example, they can choose to broadly diversify the investment of their retirement funds, even into real estate, gold, and, in certain cases, businesses. With stocks, they can do it themselves and trade and manage their accounts online, use a traditional broker, let mutual fund managers pick the stocks, or put their money under management on a fee rather than per-trade commission basis. There are also choices to be made about types of stocks: the sectors, like tech or retail or pharmaceutical; U.S. or international; dividend or no dividend; degree of assessed risk, and more. Affluents have an even greater and more confusing array of choices. Ultra-affluents often have what is called a family office with a full-time CPA or money manager and family concierge. The myriad of money choices that come with having more money are especially troubling to many affluents, as errors in choice can have serious consequences; specialized knowledge and current, day-to-day watchdogging is necessary; and they are often ill equipped for the task, having focused all their efforts on the skills needed to make the money, not the skills needed to manage it.

But money is not the only place choice becomes mentally frustrating or overwhelming.

Consider something as simple as food. In Schwartz's book, he talked about finding 85 different brands and varieties of crackers on his supermarket shelf, some low in sodium, some fat free, some trans fat free, some in bite size, some normal size, some mundane and familiar like saltines, others exotic and expensive imports. There used to be one variety of Ritz® crackers. Today there are at least a dozen different Ritz® choices, some with extra herbs embedded, some in 100-calorie bags. Next to the crackers, Schwartz counted up 285 varieties of cookies. I'd guess now there are even more. When I was a kid there were Oreos,® period. Now there are double-stuffed Oreos,® mini-Oreos,® Oreos® dipped in chocolate fudge. If you are taking your health seriously and trying to choose the least-damaging foods to stock your frig and pantry with, you need to come to the supermarket with a reference manual, calculator, and a lot of time and patience. Further, the food manufacturers frankly make all this deliberately confusing, labeling things so they sound healthier than they are. Frustrated consumers look for shortcuts through the confusion and manufacturers know it, so putting the Weight Watchers® or Healthy Choice® brand on cookies or soup has real value in the marketplace—but beware: it is no guarantee whatsoever of a product less harmful to waistline or health than the one next to it on the shelf.

Government interference, incidentally, rarely helps. The more labeling requirements imposed on the food industry, the more confusing choices proliferate as manufacturers and restaurants seek to circumvent restrictions and offer the public what it really wants. Being told what you should choose by some authoritative source tends to breed defiance rather than compliance. Late in 2007, in a *USA Today* article, celebrated trend spotter Faith Popcorn noted and predicted expansion of a trend she's termed "pleasure revenge." This describes the behavior of consumers who are weary and annoyed at being told what to eat, what to drive, what light bulbs to put in their homes, and so forth and are rebelling, eating more red meat and fattening foods than ever, buying more gas guzzlers than ever. While consumers overwhelmed with choices and confusing information do seek shortcuts, a government or self-anointed moral authority is not a welcome one.

Affluents and ultra-affluents tend to deal with their over-whelming choices by delegating as many decisions as possible. Someone else does the grocery shopping, someone else manages the money. A personal shopper takes the list of people for whom gifts are needed and chooses the gifts, or at least narrows the choices. I recently wrote in my *No B.S. Marketing to the Mass-Affluent Letter* about the new profession of baby name coaches, who interview parents and then bring forward a narrowed number of name choices and, as necessary, mediate family disputes over the choice. Mass-affluents may not have the same opportunities and tendency to delegate the decisions of their lives, but, as I said, they look for shortcuts to simplify their decisions in other ways. Their two underlying questions are: *Won't somebody please just tell me what to buy? Whom can I trust to tell me?*

As I noted before, people do not actually trust the government and resist some daddy or nun-with-ruler type of self-manufactured authority figure, so they never look there for that somebody who can simplify their buying decisions.

This is why celebrity endorsements work and, yes, they do work no matter how far up the affluent ladder you go. The fact that Warren Buffett liked flying NetJets® so much he bought the company and Bill Gates is a client eliminates many others' need to shop around and consider other choices. The Trump name on a high-rise is persuasive and, itself, adds to price. Greg Norman driving a Land Rover® causes affluent car buyers to consider that brand—with more than 300 car models to choose from—when, without Norman in the ads, they might never have given it any thought. Attaching the right celebrity to just about any product

Recommended Resource

For assistance in finding, contacting, and securing celebrity spokespersons, endorsers, and speakers, check out www.CelebrityBlackBook.com as well as the Resource Directory for Glazer-Kennedy Insider's Circle™ Members at www.DanKennedy.com.

or service can provide buyers the shortcut they are looking for. People ultimately buy from people they like. A celebrity they like can be a personal bridge between an impersonal corporation and its customers.

So, let's drill down to specific ways in which you can profit from the confusion of choices confronting affluent buyers.

You need to simplify the competitive or comparable choices. When the affluent customer feels he has found the right person or place for customers like him, he will usually stop looking at other options. This is good news, providing you don't blow the first-impression opportunity. Anything and everything you can do to convey the impression that you are a match with customers like him is important. A short list of strategies follows.

- **Appropriate celebrity endorser(s), as mentioned.**
- **Social proof <u>clearly</u> from customers who match up with your prospect.** As example, as I was writing this chapter, a new piece of information came to light with regard to a $40,000.00 product that a company I own interest in sells

to dentists, with area exclusivity. In our marketing, we list all the areas in which a client exists and no other clients can be accepted. This is a form of social proof as well as urgency stimulation. But the newly realized fact is that nearly all of the 50 buyers to date are over age 50 to 60, with 20 to 30 years in private practice. I have immediately added each doctor's years in practice in parentheses after each taken city listed. This will tell the prospect that mature, experienced dentists just like him are enthused about the proposition.

- **Reassurance**. I happen to be a master at and advocate of using long copy, long sales letters, and plain-Jane marketing materials, and I alter that only slightly with especially affluent customers. With them, I also add at least one media piece that is very professional, classy, and elegant in appearance. If the customer comes to your place of business, then every little detail takes on huge importance—its look, its color themes, its cleanliness, its staff's appearance and language. A staff person using "downscale" language to upscale clients might as well be emitting a toxic odor and ringing an alarm bell. Your entire sales process either builds trust and reassures the customer he's in the right place for him—or it doesn't. At the end of this chapter, you'll find my colleague Sydney Barrows's report of her visits to two different auto dealerships (pages 380–386). Either one could have summarily ended her shopping had they gotten this reassurance right. Neither one did.
- **Expert status**, as discussed in Chapter 37.
- **Appropriate prices**. One very common mistake in marketing to the affluent is undermining the customer's confidence

by *under*pricing goods and services. One ad in my files has the headline "Reassuringly Expensive."

The goal is to make it easy and safe to choose you.

People are reluctant to choose and act out of fear. Fears vary. Fear of financial losses, fear of embarrassment, fear of a self-esteem wound by feeling stupid. For the affluent, fears of loss of status and self-concept are more significant than fears of wasting or losing money. But, basically, it can all be wrapped up as fear of regret.

Ironically, the mass-affluents and those a financial notch or two below them are much more likely to do extensive research online, in *Consumer Reports*, and elsewhere before making a significant purchase, like a car—or in many cases, even an insignificant one, like buying a countertop popcorn maker—to avoid regret than are affluent consumers, who are more time pressed and hurried.

Consequently, *trust* is the single most important factor in marketing to the affluent. Do not confuse this with ordinary or traditional credibility. This is not about how many years your firm has been in business or your grandfather's founding of the company. It is more about feelings than facts.

A FIELD TRIP TO THE DANGEROUS TERRITORY
OF AUTO DEALERSHIPS
By Sydney Biddle Barrows

"Why don't you check out both a luxury and a mid-range car dealership and write something for the *No B.S. Marketing to the Mass-Affluent Letter*," Dan asks me. The first thought that went through my head was, "Cars? I know as much about cars as I do about dog sleds." But then I remembered that "fresh eyes" and common sense are the two most important qualities we as consultants bring to the table. In-depth knowledge of the type of business in question is, for the most part, irrelevant and a good thing too, since I have never owned a car nor have ever had even the slightest interest in owning a car. New York City is one of the few places in the country where having a car is not only unnecessary, it is a serious financial hazard. Garage spaces start around $800.00 a month and trying to find a free space on the street with any degree of regularity is extremely time-consuming, a guaranteed exercise in frustration and, at times, utterly futile. This is why God invented taxicabs.

My first choice for luxury cars was Mercedes,® but their showroom is inconveniently located and closes at 4:00 P.M. on Fridays, a sure sign that their target customer has a place in the country and is on their way there by 4:00 P.M. on a Friday afternoon. I set off for 11th Avenue and 57th Street where there are a cluster of car dealerships. I spy a Lexus® sign on the far right corner.

You couldn't miss the entrance. There was a red carpet leading from the sidewalk to the front door with velvet ropes on each

A FIELD TRIP, CONTINUED

side, a not-so-subtle reference to the ubiquitous velvet ropes which separate the hoi polloi from favored guests on "the list" at all New York City night clubs. Upon opening the large smoky glass door, the first thing you see is a very large, polished black granite desk with the word CONCIERGE emblazoned on the front. There is a large screen behind it with changing pictures of various cars on it as well as an Armani-clad salesman, who gives me a courteous welcome and asks how he might help me. "I'm interested in buying a car," I tell him, adding that this is the first time I have ever bought a car. **He doesn't seem terribly interested in what type of car I want,** so I volunteer that I am looking for something on the small side with four doors, and am offered coffee or a soft drink, which I decline.

He leads me to what appears to be the smallest car on the floor and **launches into a sales presentation,** which consists of more than I want to know and certainly more than I could ever possibly hope to understand about this vehicle. The only subject not addressed in this **monologue** is its appearance, no doubt due to the fact that it is ugly. I found myself musing that should I be tempted to make this purchase, I would be forced to perform the vehicular equivalent of putting a paper bag over its head every time before driving it. After sitting in it for a couple of minutes and asking a few questions, I allowed as how I would like to think about it and thanked him for taking the time to work with me. He gave me his card, **never asked for mine,** and that was the end of it.

A FIELD TRIP, CONTINUED

The bold-faced sentences in the above paragraphs are symptoms of a flawed and failing sales process. Lexus® and this dealer spend untold sums on advertising to get a customer like me through the doors, and a substantial investment has been made in the physical facility, to make the appropriate first impression. But then a lazy, pre-judgmental or poorly scripted and managed salesperson wastes all that investment. His mistakes: no diagnostic questions to determine which product to present and how to present it. No personal connection made, such as inquiring why I'm a first-time car buyer, why I'm interested in a car. Expressing no interest in the customer is a pretty significant turn-off. Next, a canned monologue rather than a carefully orchestrated dialogue. Finally, even though I had clearly identified myself as someone interested in buying, my contact information was never requested, so there would be no follow-up.

As luck would have it, one block down was a Buick® dealership—who knew they still made them? I sang the "Wouldn't you really rather have a Buick®?" song to myself as I crossed the street. No red carpet, no CONCIERGE desk, but there was a desk with a woman behind it sporting a beehive hairdo, apparently channeling her inner lead singer from a '60s girl group. She also asked how she could help me and I told her I was looking to buy a car and that I had never been in a car dealership before. Smiling sympathetically, she handed me off to a fellow who was standing expectantly nearby. He led me to his desk, **a rather shopworn affair** among several just like it, at the back of the showroom. First there

A FIELD TRIP, CONTINUED

was personal information gathering, all captured on a form that had been photocopied so many times the background was gray and grainy. Then we had a lengthy discussion about all the ways there were to pay for a car, including leasing it, and which would be the most appropriate for me. It was extremely informative and very thorough, even if it felt a bit premature. I was there for 35 minutes before we actually started to look at cars. The dozen or so spiffy and shiny cars on the showroom floor were apparently not in my price range (this dealership sold several kinds of cars, not just Buicks®) so we took the elevator to the second floor which turned out to be a sort of covered open-air garage where the cars were anything but spiffy and shiny. Wrapping my skirt tightly in order to keep it from becoming filthy, we snaked our way through the lot, stopping at several vehicles he seemed to feel might be "right" for me. After sitting in at least half a dozen of them, I came to the inescapable conclusion that the pricier they are, the more comfortable they are.

Back at his desk, we narrowed it down to the two most likely suspects and he worked out exactly how much it might cost per month before applying any special deals or discounts. And since it was the last day of the month the deals and discounts were substantially more than they would be the next day. I told him I'd have to think about it and left feeling very guilty that I had taken up so much of his time and exploited his good nature. It's two weeks later and he has phoned twice to follow up. Good for him!

A FIELD TRIP, CONTINUED

It is difficult to know whether the Lexus® salesman decided I wasn't really ever going to be a buyer and therefore didn't bother to get my name or number or make an apparent effort to sell me a car, or whether the low-key approach is how they do things. They certainly went out of their way to visually create an exclusive ambience; the offer of a beverage was a nice touch too. Perhaps they believe that people buy a Lexus® simply because it's a Lexus® and if you need to talk about how you might pay for it, you probably can't afford it. Conclusion: the luxury car business is so good that (a) they don't care if you purchase one of their cars or not, (b) their feigned lack of interest is a legitimate, proven sales technique, or (c) they don't know what the hell they're doing and need my SalesDesign® Program! Dan Kennedy, a betting man, told me he'd place his wager on (c).

The Buick® guy may have been operating in a less-than-glamorous (not to mention clean) setting, but for the mid-range, i.e., mass-affluent customer, his approach seems appropriate. First you address their concern that a new car is very possibly beyond their financial means by proving to them they can, in fact, afford one. Once you've overcome that hurdle, it's just a matter of helping them choose which one they want. It's an interesting, presumably tested strategy that could work for any number of high-ticket items being sold to mass-affluent customers. However, physical environment does matter. In fact, Dan and I talk about the "five sense impact" of every selling environment. Customers are affected, positively or negatively, by input of all five senses: sight,

A FIELD TRIP, CONTINUED

sound, touch, taste, smell. Being served a fresh-made latte with a scent of cinnamon in a china cup has different influence than ordinary coffee in a Styrofoam™ cup. Being shown cars in a dusty, dirty environment, with the customer focused on avoiding ruining his or her clothes rather than on the automobiles or what the salesman is saying matters. It also suggests something about how the customer can expect to be treated after the sale, perhaps in the service department.

Those who sell certain luxury products only to the affluent may prefer to maintain the "if you are concerned with how you are going to pay for it, you probably can't afford it" position. If availability is limited, as with Lamborghini® or Maybach®, maintaining an air of exclusivity makes sense. But if you have plenty of product, expensive though it may be, you could sell a lot more of it if prospective customers for whom money is somewhat of an issue feel assured in advance they will be able to pay for it in what for them is a manageable way. But no matter what you are selling, never immediately assume that someone who is not particularly well-dressed, or is of a certain gender not usually known for purchasing whatever it is you are selling, is not a buyer. Certainly such persons need to be further qualified, but not written off from the get-go, as I suspect I was by the Lexus® salesman.

When I do on-site "mystery shopping" followed by on-premises, in-the-business observation and analysis of sales processes, language and Sales Choreography® (the "handling" of the customer),

A FIELD TRIP, CONTINUED

I always find a myriad of small sins to significant inconsistencies that, if repaired, offer great opportunity to increase sales and profits. Most businesses have what I call "broken bridges" between their advertising and marketing promises and their sales practices. In too many cases, the business owners simply leave the selling up to the salespeople, abdicating too much authority. Both of these auto dealerships have different things working for them, different things working against them, and different opportunities—but they both do have opportunities. Your business undoubtedly has opportunities too, in the careful analysis and improvement of your selling process.

SYDNEY BIDDLE BARROWS is the author of the *XXX-Rated Selling Secrets* (audio) and a forthcoming book by that same title, to be published by Entrepreneur Press. She periodically conducts a ten-week telecoaching program for business owners on her Sales Design® and Sales Choreography® strategies, featuring interviews with a number of experts including famous restaurant entrepreneur Danny Meyer, author of *Setting the Table*; Arnold Taubman, author of *Threshold Resistance*; and Dan Kennedy. She is available for speaking engagements and consulting assignments, and provides a two-day business analysis incorporating personal mystery shopping, diagnostics, and recommendations on sales process improvement, optionally supported by customized staff training. Information is available at www.SydneyBarrows.com.

CHAPTER 43

Personal Confidence

"No one can make you feel inferior without your consent."

—ELEANOR ROOSEVELT

Many marketers and sales professionals suffer **from affluent sales reluctance.** They unconsciously if not consciously avoid marketing or selling to the affluent because they, themselves, feel like fish out of water in dealing with them or feel inferior to them, even fearing exposure as pretenders to their world through some faux pas. George Dudley and Shannon Goodson, authors of *The Psychology of Sales Call Reluctance: Earning What You're Worth,* define social self-consciousness in salespeople as shunning prospects of wealth, prestige, power, education, or social standing.

As an extreme example, my friend Glenn W. Turner, who became famous or infamous, as you prefer for the heavily prosecuted Koscot and Dare To Be Great, two pyramid marketing companies' of the 1970s, grew up in stark poverty and began his door-to-door sales career burdened with a harelip and severe speech impediment. He deliberately chose to work in the poorest black neighborhoods in the South, where he felt his awkwardness, poor dress, and impaired speech would not be looked down on. It would seem ironic to most unfamiliar with the secret psychology of super-achievers that Turner went from there to becoming one of the most powerful motivational speakers of his time, attracting some 500,000 people to his companies, barnstorming the country with his own fleet of company jets, and turning thousands and thousands of others too shy to give silent prayer into incredibly persuasive salespeople and speakers. Even at the peak of his popularity, celebrity, influence, and affluence, though, he preferred the company of people who had risen up from poor backgrounds and of little education, and he chose to direct his companies' marketing to the non-affluent rather than the affluent. Dare To Be Great was designed and promoted as part self-improvement program, part mass movement, and part business opportunity to uplift the working men and women, not as a means of the already-affluent sales professional or entrepreneur to experience even greater success. I have chosen to be in the latter business. Turner chose the former.

Dudley and Goodson point out that such self-determined downgrading by sales professionals is not usually so obvious. "One reason that social self-consciousness is such a dangerous form of sales call reluctance is that it flies well under the radar of all but one salesperson selection [hiring] test. [And] only one form of prospecting becomes impaired. All other forms are left unbothered. Their other prospecting skills may dazzle recruiters." In other words, sales managers as well as the salespeople themselves may not detect or diagnose this avoidance.

Matt Oechsli, author of *The Art of Selling to the Affluent*, says that "no one is born with social self-conscious call reluctance—it is learned. Often it is confused with low self-esteem and low assertiveness, but it is more specific. The issue is the amount of emotional stress you experience when contacting or thinking about contacting someone of wealth or power; the issue is not how successful a salesperson you are in general."

I believe the very same reluctance extends to marketers, not just salespeople. Many, given all the information in this book, encouraged to learn more from additional sources, and possessing products or services easily adapted to appeal to the affluent, will fail to do anything to pursue these opportunities and instead choose to avoid targeting the affluent. Their choice will most likely be expressed in terms of excuses rather than admission of reluctance, but it will nonetheless be choice.

I own racehorses and can give you a strange handicapping and wagering tip. Racehorses *understand* class. A horse can move up in class, that race can go slower than the lower-class race he won the week before, but the newly promoted horse will actually slow himself down and fail to win, out of recognition of class, the sense he is *not supposed to* beat these *better* horses. This is why fastest speed rarely predicts race outcome. Most professional race handicappers rank class movement, up or down, as one of the top five factors to consider. It is my experience that businesspeople fear moving up in class of prospects and clients just as horses do. So, marketers of every stripe stay with the type and level of customer affluence they are most comfortable with—often mirroring their own status or even a notch lower.

Matt Oechsli lists as a key symptom of this move-up reluctance as "exaggerating the power, prestige and fame of affluent individuals, in your own thinking and verbally to others." I observe this constantly; the enunciated or evidenced belief that the affluent clients are somehow out of reach to somebody because of their superior intelligence or education, power, prestige, or status. Having had countless opportunities to work with, do business with, associate with, socialize with, and closely observe such intimidating-to-many individuals, including Hollywood celebrities, champion athletes, bestselling authors, Fortune 500 CEOs and multi-millionaire entrepreneurs and investors, I can absolutely assure you they are far from superior in any respect except their bank account balances or fame. Further, perhaps ironically, I've always found it easier to sell to people higher up in corporations and organizations or in affluence. There's less competition because of this common reluctance and avoidance.

Many people are reluctant to attempt marketing or selling to clients they believe or know to be considerably more successful or affluent than themselves, yet the financial services and investment businesses are proliferate with wealthy clients doing business with and served by agents and advisors of far lesser wealth. While it is true that successful people generally prefer dealing with successful people, the definition of successful need not be narrowed to or judged simply and solely in monetary terms. Extensive research from multiple sources indicates that 38% to 44% of all affluent buyers list the following as their top two concerns regarding any vendor: (1) that he understands their unique needs, desires, pressures, and lifestyle, and (2) that he can be counted on for exceptional after-sale service.

These are sought-after virtues that can be evidenced even when you have previously been selling to less affluent customers and when you are personally (temporarily!) significantly less affluent than your clientele.

I started out selling business opportunity while still in my teens to significantly older, more experienced, and more affluent individuals. Today, I am often selling my services to people considerably less affluent than I am. My sales practices have changed little. What worked, works.

The way around some of your reluctance is to focus on deeply and accurately understanding what is important to your targeted customers, then crafting your offered products and services to match, and demonstrating and documenting your personal attributes, expertise, and track record of meeting those needs. Your own level of affluence may be assumed, but will rarely come into question. You can derive your confidence from what you know and what you do, not from what size home you live in (vs. theirs).

The other way sales professionals and marketers erect obstacles between themselves and affluent clientele is with their personal Wealth Inhibition, which I discuss in-depth in another of my books in this series, *No B.S. Wealth ATTRACTION for Entrepreneurs.* Just as many people feel inappropriate in marketing to the affluent, an equal number feel undeserving of rapid and dramatic increases in income and affluence. Their relationship with money is not a healthy one. As with affluent sales reluctance, this is an unconscious rather than conscious reality, which tends to be denied when I first suggest it. Forced to confront their own

Recommended Resource

My Rich Dad, Poor Dad, Same Dad experience and other instructive personal experiences are collected in my Renegade Millionaire book, *Unfinished Business: Autobiographical Essays*, available exclusively at www.RenegadeMillionaire.com. The *No B.S. Wealth ATTRACTION for Entrepreneurs* book is available at Amazon.com, BN.com, and all fine booksellers.

attitudes, feelings, and beliefs about money, many of my clients and coaching members realize that they are, in fact, inhibited rather than welcoming toward wealth, and by making some deliberate changes in their thinking and self-talk about money, they very quickly experience positive changes in their incomes.

I had the interesting experience of having Rich Dad, Poor Dad, Same Dad. When I was very young, our family was very affluent, and my parents had a thriving homebased business. What I then heard at the top of the stairs was very positive about money and success. Later, when in my teens, the family had a profound reversal of fortunes and we were grindingly, desperately poor. What my much younger brothers heard as kids at the top of the stairs was very different dialogue. I believe what I heard made enormous contribution to my ultimate business and financial success. I believe what they heard has made major contribution to their comparative lack of success and difficulties experienced in life. In exploring the "What did you hear at the top of the stairs?" question with hundreds and hundreds of exceptionally successful people, I've discovered some very conscious of it, others relatively unconscious until prompted to ponder it; some very aware it produced considerable self-confidence, others very aware they had to work at overcoming it to develop self-confidence, others unaware of how adversely it was influencing them until deliberate change seemed to spark a sudden fireworks of progress and prosperity. This is one of a number of causes of Wealth Inhibition that can be identified and either erased or at least managed.

Failure or refusal to confront your own Wealth Inhibition or affluent sales reluctance effectively neuters the power of all the information and strategies provided in this book and forever guarantees that stepping up will be difficult rather than easy.

In my book, *Zero Resistance Selling*, based on the 30-million-copy bestselling self-improvement book *Psycho-Cybernetics*, I included a chapter titled "Selling Successfully When You're In Over Your Head," in which I voiced the silent, self-doubting dialogue too often going on in a sales professional's head:

> *You've worked very hard to get this opportunity, but this morning, as you looked at yourself in the mirror, the reality of what you are up against really hit home. Maybe it would be better for one of the more experienced account execs to handle this presentation. After all, what makes YOU think YOU'RE up to this, anyway? You've never landed an account even half this size. The conference room you'll be meeting in will probably be as big as your whole apartment! The prospect's custom-made suit worth more than half the furniture in your apartment! You*

*feel your planned and rehearsed comments disappearing from
memory, your anxiety rising. The face in the mirror says:
buddy, it looks like you've bitten off more than you can chew.*

Been there myself, years ago. Many salespeople are there, as
they begin dealing with more affluent and successful customers.

In *Zero Resistance Selling*, I go on to lay out prescriptions for
conquering stage fright, selling up anxiety, and other mental
impediments to peak performance. I think you need to honestly
assess your own feelings about this, and then develop a regimen
for replacing your anxieties and doubts with confidence. And I
recommend Dr. Maltz's Psycho-Cybernetics techniques for
doing so.

CHAPTER 44

Political Commentary, In
Defense of the Affluent

*"The American economy cannot be revived without
someone getting rich. Why not me?"*

—Rush Limbaugh

I can't finish a book about marketing to the affluent—
and, in part by doing so, becoming affluent—without com-
menting on the political implications of the explosive growth
of the mass-affluent and affluent segments of the population. In
January 2008, on his HBO television program, Bill Maher spoke
about American history as a series of gilded ages that were out of
control, when too much wealth was concentrated into too few
hands, then periods when that control was wrested away by liberal movements, resulting in appropriate redistribution of
wealth. He believes we are in such a gilded age now, in urgent
and desperate need of having the government interfere and

forcibly take wealth away from selected people and companies. Taking away more than it already does. This one-sided view of history ignores the fact that virtually all social, cultural, even political progress has been and is fueled by the wealthy.

On the day my wife and I took our grandkids to see Disney's® *Lion King*, we were joined by hundreds of middle-income and modest-income families who brought their kids downtown to the Cleveland Playhouse to see the touring Broadway production live theater, on stage right before their eyes. At, as I recall, about $20 a ticket. That cultural experience possible only because I and hundreds of other patrons of that playhouse each donate upwards of $25,000.00 a year to keep it afloat. Without us affluent patrons, tickets at $2,000.00 each, or, more likely, no theater at all. Would everybody live without seeing *The Lion King*? Of course. But consider the libraries, the wings of hospitals, the medical research, the charities and their works, the Boys and Girls Clubs,® the free dental care provided by the Smile Train,® the college scholarships, the free transport of ill children across country to hospitals on ultra-affluents' private jets, the book-length list of civic, cultural, charitable, and educational institutions and programs that exist solely thanks to the affluent.

Millions of jobs exist today at companies that would never have been birthed were it not for hundreds of millions of dollars *put at risk* on unproven ideas by ultra-affluent and affluent investors, who then paid capital gains taxes on the rewards, even though the dollars invested had already been taxed once before when earned as income. Much is written about the "excessive" profits of private equity investors and CEO pay, but nothing is written about the risks taken and losses incurred by these investors or the decades spent climbing the corporate ladder to the lofty CEO suites. Every paycheck other than those issued by the government has been made possible by an affluent person investing in business—or a person starting a business and becoming affluent in the process. If all the affluent took just one month off from investing and spending, the economy would crash and millions would find themselves unemployed. If Ayn Rand's fictional labor strike by much-criticized CEOs and entrepreneurs ever occurs, Bill Maher and everybody else employed by HBO and pretty much everybody else employed everywhere else will be immediately thrown to unemployment lines, and soon thereafter, the lights will dim nationwide.

A millionaire friend of mine said, "You and I have a big responsibility and a heavy burden. We have to keep finding enough stuff to buy to keep the economy going." While he was roundly criticized for it, President Bush was realistic when he suggested the best thing all Americans could do to support the war effort was to go shopping. Our entire economy and society is dependent on consumer spending.

It is popular to resent the rich. There is argument that too much wealth is concentrated in too few hands, that the rich get richer while the poor get poorer (as if that were cause and effect; it is not), that the widened wage gap between CEOs and broom pushers is evil conspiracy reflecting only greed (not value). And so on. When I was a child, I was chastised for wasting food and urged to eat everything on my plate because "children are starving in China," as if my eating or not eating tonight's peas would somehow starve or save some skinny urchin in a distant land. Similarly, the affluent are reviled for "wasting" money (which they rightfully earned) on outrageously overpriced trifles like jewelry or yachts or $5,000.00 bottles of wine when there are working poor unable to make their mortgage payments, as if not buying the yacht would magically erase the poor sod's mortgage across town. Actually, the affluent not buying the wine, jewelry, and yachts would only wind up making the plight of the poor worse, as the economy would slow, the lowest-pay commodity jobs cut first. If the only goods sold and bought in America were functional necessities and all obscenely unnecessary luxury goods were outlawed, how many jobs do you imagine would disappear overnight? 10%? 25%? 50%?

If You Eat the Rich, You Will Soon Starve

Let's assume we take $1 billion away from the wealthy and redistribute it to the working poor, the below-middle-class families struggling to make ends meet. This will result in each family getting, let's say, a hundred bucks. What will each family do with this windfall from the Socialists' confiscation and redistribution of wealth? Will they rush to Wall Street to invest it in ways that create venture capital to launch new businesses and support new product invention, thus creating jobs and exportable goods that help to balance trade? Will they run out and use it to buy investment real estate? Will they fund medical research or universities? They will not. Because they invest little, spend virtually all the income they get on necessities, and are in debt, their hundred-dollar windfall will disappear into that debt or into necessity purchases—or perhaps the luxury of a night out. **It will _not_ be planted as seeds** to grow in ways that enhance the economy and its ability to provide jobs, better jobs, health care, or community development, nor will it be invested in ways that make a difference in the individual family's life. That is the cold, harsh reality.

It is undeniable. And it does not even take into account the vigorish skimmed off its top by our incredibly wasteful, piggish government. Money confiscated by government has a nasty habit of disappearing altogether.

In January 2008, *USA Today* ran a front-page story I had been following for months, since my own visit to Katrina-ravaged New Orleans. Federal, Louisiana state, and city government bureaucracies all so hamstrung by mismanagement, incompetence, stupidity, red tape, conflict, and corruption; billions of dollars confiscated from taxpayers and long ago approved and furnished by the U.S. government for rehab of homes, public housing, businesses, and infrastructure sitting idle and unused. The money was taken from you and me by taxation, yet it has not been deployed for its purpose. However, private investors from Donald Trump to countless individual entrepreneurs, and private individuals like Brad Pitt and Angelina Jolie, have been getting things done and are having positive impact—with private money.

Taking money away from the rich accomplishes nothing positive for anybody. Leave those same billion dollars in the hands of the wealthy, and most will get invested, some will be put at risk, in ways that do create or expand businesses, fund medical research, hospitals, and universities, create jobs, create better jobs, and, in countless ways, benefit everybody. Because the affluent already have their needs met, additional money placed in their hands tends to be, in large part, invested, in other part, spent on goods and services. Money passing through affluent hands is jet fuel for the economy.

The three major, across-the-board income tax cuts in American history—John F. Kennedy's, Ronald Reagan's, and

George W. Bush's—ALL resulted in increased tax dollars collected in immediately subsequent years, meaning more (not less) money to the government plus measurable economic stimulus. This makes every one of the many who insist that taking away the Bush tax cuts and imposing additional taxes on the rich is the way to fund universal or free health care, college, and preschool either an imbecile or a liar. The facts are the facts: lower taxes provide more revenue with which to do those things; tax increases provide less revenue. Not that it is a good idea, but the fastest and surest way to put more tax dollars into the government's coffers would be to further slash income tax rates, lower or eliminate capital gains taxes, and eliminate the death tax. Those who claim otherwise are, by ignorance and stupidity or deceit, denying the facts of history just as if they denied the Holocaust or the landing of astronauts on the moon—and they should be viewed similarly. As loony birds.

Simply put, any and all attempts to punish the rich, confiscate from the rich, or limit the ability of the rich to get richer backfires, punishing the less-rich more and the poor most. This can be argued by Socialists with fervor, but not with facts.

How to Set the American Economy Back to the Stone Age Almost Overnight

Here are the most popular attack-the-affluent plans that have been proposed in 2007 and 2008 by Socialist members of Congress and presidential candidates, including that "man of the people" living in his 26,000-square-foot mansion, he of the $400.00 haircut, private jets, and million-dollar "salary" from a hedge fund.

❖ Eliminate the Bush tax cuts and let tax cuts expire, taking the top rate from 2008's 35% to 39.6%.

❖ Impose a surcharge on the rich, yet another add-on income tax—proposed, an extra 4% on those earning more than $150,000.00, 4.6% on those above $200,000.00 . . . taking the top, combined federal rate to 44.2%, plus state and local income taxes.

❖ Equalize capital gains taxes with earned income taxes, so same tax is paid on investment yield—scheduled to begin in 2011. This takes dollars already taxed once as income and taxes them again at the same rate when they are invested.

❖ Raise capital gains taxes on the rich while waiving them for "middle-income" investors.

❖ Create new, additional taxes on the rich to fund (1) wars, (2) universal health care, (3) universal preschool and day care, (4) universal college.

❖ Eliminate the $97,000.00 ceiling on Social Security payments. A self-employed person currently making $250,000.00 a year now pays $12,125.00 in Social Security taxes. If the ceiling is removed, that tax jumps a whopping 250% to $31,250.00.

❖ Tax partnership dividends (i.e., investments for which you currently receive a K-1) at the 35% corporate tax rate instead of the current 15% capital gains rate.

These goofy proposals have prompted numerous investment advisors to suggest selling off all appreciated assets well ahead of the 2011 punishing tax change, dumping all dividend-paying stocks, and, basically, preparing to stockpile and sit on cash. The results of enacting any several of these proposals would be simultaneous loss of value in the stock market and in real estate of 20% to 50%, massive cutbacks in investment in business startups or expansion, double-digit unemployment, and an enormous wave of affluent boomers now working or running businesses opting for retirement. Since THE MAJORITY of Americans are now invested in the stock market through their 401(k) plans, IRAs, and other pensions and are invested in real estate, the devastation will cut a very wide swath. In short, a depression that will make 1929 look trivial by comparison.

The ultra-affluent will do just what they did during the Great Depression: hole up in their mansions, wait for everything to hit rock bottom, buy it all at dirt-cheap costs, and patiently wait—ultimately winding up far richer than before. The suddenly, massively unemployed middle class and the retirees with pensions suddenly gone will join the poor in the bread lines.

Politicians act as if you can attack the affluent without consequence. This is the highest form of stupidity and arrogance. It defies history, economics, and basic natural law of consequences for every action. The assault on the affluent currently being planned and proposed is extreme, so it can produce only extreme consequences.

Refuse to Be "Played" with Guilt by the Socialists

I urge you to read everything I have to say about refusing to think guiltily about your entrepreneurship, marketing, success, and prosperity in my book *No B.S. Wealth ATTRACTION for Entrepreneurs.* Here, in briefest form, I tell you that the single biggest obstacle to you fully capitalizing on all the information I've provided here and all the opportunity I've presented here is other people—those around you, the media, Socialist political demagogues—who burden you with undeserved, unwarranted guilt about doing exceptionally well. To the exceptional achiever, exceptional risk taker, exceptionally hard worker, exceptionally diligent student, exceptionally astute user of the free-enterprise system and its markets *should* go the spoils. And in America, and in many other nations, there is no bouncer at the rope line letting only certain, arbitrarily selected people through to these paths to prosperity. The "Make Yourself Exceptional" door has no guard, no lock; it's wide open. You should have no guilt—none, nada, zero—for choosing to go through that door, nor need you have much sympathy for those who choose not to.

BOOK FOUR

Resources

Sources of Information in This Book and Other Resources of Interest

This section contains the key sources of information utilized in the research and preparation for this book and used on a continual basis in advising my clients and developing and presenting important marketing advice and strategies to Glazer-Kennedy Insider's Circle™ Members via the *No B.S. Marketing Letter* and the *No B.S. Marketing to the Affluent Letter* (see page 429). Also in this section are experts, vendors, and other resources I recommend.

www.AffluenceResearch.org. The American Affluence Research Center. Conducts a bi-annual survey of the affluent, publishes survey highlights and other research, and consults on marketing to the affluent with clients like Four Seasons Hotels and Resorts, *Town & Country* magazine, Silversea® Cruises, Ferragamo, Moen, and Condé Nast.

www.Automotive.com. Includes a blog about luxury and exotic cars; up-to-date information on luxury automobiles.

www.Concierge.com. Includes a wide range of information on luxury hotels, resorts, and travel.

www.LuxuryHousingTrends.com. Information about luxury home and patio furnishings, products for the home, gourmet kitchen products, and so forth.

www.EPMcom.com. EPM Communications, publisher of *ResearchAlert* and other specialized newsletters and reports on marketing to women, marketing to seniors, and marketing to other groups.

www.InternationalListings.com. Portal to the top 100 luxury blogs, covering art, automobiles, fashion, food and wine, gadgets, real estate, social networks, travel, and so on.

Spotlight Listing

www.UnityMarketing.com. By Pamela Danziger, author of *Let Them Eat Cake* and *Shopping: Why We Love It & How Retailers Can Create the Ultimate Shopping Experience*. Publisher of the Luxury Tracking Study, a $12,500.00-per-year subscription to quarterly reporting on affluent consumers' purchasing, a year-end summary of luxury goods and services trends, and other research. Danziger is the leading authority on the marketing of luxury goods and services and is available for speaking and consulting engagements.

---

www.JoeVitale.com. Vitale is a true marketing, sales, and promotion genius. He was kind enough to write the Foreword to this book. You may have seen him in *The Secret*. By far, my favorite of all his books is *There's a Customer Born Every Minute*, about P.T. Barnum and strategies for Barnumizing any business.

www.CraigProctor.com. Craig Proctor, mentioned in Chapter 36, is a leading business and marketing coach to real estate brokers and agents.

Dean Killingbeck at New Customers Now. For assistance with targeted direct mail and tested, proven mailing campaigns reaching people having birthdays per month, new movers, and other select groups. For information, fax (517) 546-2815.

www.SRDS.com. The source of information about commercially available mailing lists.

www.CatalogSuccess.com. Source of information on mailing lists, catalog companies' lists, and the catalog industry.

Spotlight Listing

INFUSION SOFTWARE. The solution to totally organized direct and target marketing and comprehensive customer follow-up for any business, small or large. Most businesses struggle with patchwork quilts of different software programs and different systems, each inadequate in some way, and often incompatible with each other. Only INFUSION was designed from the ground up to integrate multi-step, multi-media marketing campaigns' automation with customer relationship management, highly sophisticated yet easily understandable results tracking, and online and offline capabilities. Infusion is not just another software provider, either; the company's principals fully understand the kind of marketing described in this book and work with business owners to—simply—make a lot more money with less time and frustration. Free online demonstrations and introductory classes and other information are available at: www.Renegade MillionaireSoftware.com.

---

www.CelebrityBlackBook.com. Jordan McAuley provides an annual contact directory, online search, and other services for securing celebrity spokespersons, endorsers, and speakers.

www.bgsmarketing.com. Bill Glazer's marketing systems have been embraced and are used profitably by well over 5,000 retailers in home furnishings, jewelry, men's and women's apparel and other marketing-to-the-affluent categories. His free report *How to Discover the Hidden Wealth Buried in Your Business* is available on request.

www.Forbes.com. I rate *Forbes* as the best business magazine currently published, and I particularly urge you to study the annual *Forbes 400* issue, from which information for Chapter 2 of this book came.

www.504Experts.com/DanKennedyMarketingToTheAffluentBookSpecial. From Chris Hurn's company; an interview with Hurn appears immediately after Chapter 7.

www.MotorcyclesForWomen.com. See "The Martha Stewart of Motorcycles" immediately after Chapter 18.

www.Zappos.com. See "Zappos.com: A Global Shoe Store" immediately after Chapter 28.

www.jpeterman.com. See "The Catalog that Started a Cult" immediately after Chapter 32.

---

www.CosmeticSxProfits.com. See "Price May Be in the Eye of the Beholder, But Is in the Control of the Provider" immediately after Chapter 39

www.info-marketing. org. Site of the Information Marketing Association, the trade organization of authors, newsletter publishers, speakers, consultants, life and business coaches, direct-marketing entrepreneurs involved with information products, publicists, and other related professionals. Novices are welcome, and instructional courses for beginners in this field are offered.

Spotlight Listing

www.SydneyBarrows.com. See "A Field Trip to the Dangerous Territory of Auto Dealerships" immediately after Chapter 42. Sydney offers a short-term teleseminar/telecoaching program on SalesDesign® and SalesChoreography,® and is available for speaking and consulting engagements. Her expertise is particularly relevant to businesses attracting affluent clients. Sydney is also co-author with me of a new book from Entrepreneur Press, *XXX-Rated Selling Secrets*. Sydney's unusual, diverse background goes back some 20 years, when she developed, operated, and was ultimately prosecuted for running New York's most elite and expensive escort service, for which she was dubbed the Mayflower Madam. Her tell-all book about her experiences in this business was courageously ranked by *Fortune* magazine as one of the ten best business books of the year. Sydney has since been involved in sales consulting in a variety of fields, from cosmetic surgery and dentistry to fashion. Her sizzling XXX-rated examples help business owners and sales professionals see their own businesses from a radically different perspective, enabling selling on a more sophisticated level, with emphasis on experiences and desire fulfillment rather than commoditized products and services.

Websites about Boomers

www.BoomerProject.com. Newsletter and special reports.

www.MaryFurlong.com. Author of *Turning Silver into Gold*. Furlong's company conducts annual summits and conferences on boomer business.

www.AgeWave.com. Dr. Ken Dychtwald, in my opinion, the preeminent expert on age-related behavior, buying behavior, and trends.

www.BoomerMarketAdvisor.com. Mentioned in Chapter 6, this is a source of information for professional financial advisors, Certified Financial Planners, insurance agents, and marketers of investment products and services.

www.DennisTubbergen.com. Leading advisor, consultant, and coach to financial advisors and investment professionals. Among many services, Tubbergen's companies are expert in creating and marketing investment seminars to affluent boomers.

Magazines to Read—To Better Understand the Affluent

Elite Traveler

Forbes

Fortune

Millionaire

Robb Report

Town & Country

Trump

Upscale

Worth

TV to Watch

High Net Worth—CNBC

Forbes on Fox—FOX

Places to Go—To Better Understand the Affluent

Classic car shows, such as Barrett-Jackson®

Boat shows

Boca Raton, Florida

Scottsdale, Arizona

Bridgeport, Connecticut

Jackson Hole, Wyoming

Resources to Better Understand the Philosophy of the Affluent
Books

Atlas Shrugged by Ayn Rand

Think and Grow Rich by Napoleon Hill

Websites

www.RenegadeMillionaire.com

www.RushLimbaugh.com

Reference Books

The Paradox of Choice: Why More Is Less by Barry Schwartz

The Millionaire Next Door: The Surprising Secrets of America's Wealthy by Dr. Thomas Stanley

Marketing to the Affluent by Dr. Thomas Stanley

Richistan: A Journey through the American Wealth Boom and the Lines of the New Rich by Robert Frank

Trading Up: Why Consumers Want New Luxury Goods by Michael Silverstein

Shopping: Why We Love It & How Retailers Can Create the Ultimate Consumer Experience by Pamela Danziger

Let Them Eat Cake: Marketing Luxury to the Masses—as Well as the Classes by Pamela Danziger

The Art of Selling to the Affluent: How to Attract, Service, and Retain Wealthy Customers and Clients for Life by Matt Oechsli

Peterman Rides Again: Adventures Continue with the Real "J. Peterman" through Life and the Catalog Business by John Peterman

Rich Buyer, Rich Seller: The Real Estate Agent's Guide to Marketing Luxury Homes by Laurie Moore-Moore

Mass Affluence: Seven New Rules of Marketing to Today's Consumer by Paul Nunes and Brian Johnson

The Official Get Rich Guide to Information Marketing: Build a Million Dollar Business within 12 Months by the Information Marketing Association, Robert Skrob, Bill Glazer, and Dan Kennedy

Other Books by Dan S. Kennedy
Titles in the No B.S. Series
Published by Entrepreneur Press

No B.S. BUSINESS Success
21 Eternal Business Truths; How Entrepreneurs Really Make Big Money; How to Create Sales and Marketing Breakthroughs; Staying Sane in an Insane World

> *"Dan has written a book you can use immediately to get better, faster results . . . his approach is direct, his ideas are controversial, his ability to get results for his clients unchallenged. When you read, learn, and apply what you discover in these pages, your business life and your income will change forever."*
>
> —BRIAN TRACY

No B.S. SALES Success
33 Strategies; Positive Power of Negative Preparation; How to Stop Prospecting Once and for All; 6-Step Sales Process that (Almost) Never Fails; Takeaway Selling

> *"Dan has literally eliminated the B.S. in explaining great ways to make more sales."*
>
> —TOM HOPKINS

No B.S. TIME MANAGEMENT for Entrepreneurs

9 Time Truths; Dan's Personal Strategies for Peak Productivity; The Care, Feeding, and Slaughter of Time Vampires; How to Turn Time into Wealth; The Magic Power that Makes You Unstoppable; How to Accurately Value Your Time.

No B.S. DIRECT MARKETING for NON-Direct Marketing Businesses
(With Audio CD)

The 10 Rules; The Results Triangle; Making the Switch From Ineffective, Unaccountable Image/Brand and Big, Dumb Company Advertising/Marketing to Direct Response; Nine Comprehensive Case Histories Covering Every Type of Business; Putting an Iron Cage Around Your Customers

No B.S. WEALTH ATTRACTION for Entrepreneurs
(With "Live Seminar" Audio CD)

How to Stop Chasing Money and Let It Chase You; Overcoming Wealth Inhibition; Personal and Business Wealth Magnets; Converting Ordinary Businesses to Extraordinary Wealth Attraction Machines. (Based on Dan's Most Popular One-Day Seminar)

FREE INFORMATION, SAMPLE CHAPTERS and VIDEO DISCUSSIONS WITH DAN KENNEDY AND KRISTI FRANK FROM *THE APPRENTICE* AVAILABLE AT:

www.NoBSBooks.com

About the Author

DAN KENNEDY is a serial entrepreneur who has started, bought, built, and sold businesses of varied types and sizes. He is a highly sought after and outrageously well-paid direct-marketing consultant and direct-response copywriter, coach to groups of entrepreneurs, nearly retired professional speaker, author, equal opportunity annoyer, provocateur, and professional harness racing driver. He lives with his second and third wife (same woman) and a small dog in Ohio and Virginia. His office that he never visits is in Phoenix.

He welcomes your comments and can be reached directly only by fax at (602) 269-3113 or by mail at Kennedy Inner Circle, Inc., 5818 N. 7th Street #103, Phoenix, AZ 85014. (Do NOT e-mail him via any of the websites presenting his information and publications. He does not use e-mail.)

He is occasionally available for interesting speaking engagements and very rarely accepts new consulting clients. Inquiries should be directed to the above office.

All information about his newsletters, how-to products, other resources, and Glazer-Kennedy Insider's Circle™ annual Marketing and Moneymaking SuperConferences and annual Info-Summit™ at which Dan appears, can be accessed online at www.Dan Kennedy.com, and by click-link, the online catalog and web store. A Directory of local Glazer-Kennedy Insider's Circle™ Chapters offering networking meetings, seminars, and Kennedy Study Groups in more than 80 cities can also be accessed at www.DanKennedy.com. If you enjoyed this book, you'll enjoy getting together with other business owners in your area applying Kennedy strategies! Other websites of interest: <u>www.Renegade Millionaire.com</u> and <u>www.NoBSBooks.com</u>. Dan's horse racing activities can be seen at www.NorthfieldPark.com.

Partial List of Authors, Business Leaders, Celebrities, etc. with Whom Dan Has Appeared on Programs with as a Speaker

Legendary Entrepreneurs
Donald Trump
Jim McCann, CEO, 1-800-Flowers*
Joe Sugarman, Blu-Blockers*
Debbi Fields, Founder, Mrs. Fields Cookies*
Mark McCormack, Founder, IMG Sports Management*

Authors and Speakers
Zig Ziglar*
Brian Tracy*
Jim Rohn*
Tom Hopkins*
Mark Victor Hansen (Chicken Soup for the Soul)*
Tony Robbins*

Political and World Leaders
Presidents Ford, Reagan, and Bush #1*
Gen. Norman Schwarzkopf*
Secretary Colin Powell*
Lady Margaret Thatcher*
Mikhail Gorbachev*

Broadcasters
Larry King*
Paul Harvey*

Hollywood Personalities
Bill Cosby*
Christopher Reeve*
Mary Tyler Moore*
Johnny Cash
The Smothers Brothers

Sports Personalities
George Foreman*
Joe Montana*
Peyton Manning*
Coaches Tom Landry*, Jimmy Johnson*, Lou Holtz*
Olympians Mary Lou Retton* and Bonnie Blair*

*Indicates repeated appearances on same platform.

Index

Special Offer For No B.S. Marketing To The Affluent Readers

The Most Incredible FREE Gift Ever

$613.91 Of Pure Money-Making Information

_____ I want to *test drive* Dan Kennedy's & Bill Glazer's MOST INCREDIBLE FREE GIFT EVER and receive a steady stream of millionaire maker information which includes:

- **Glazer-Kennedy University: Series of 3 Webinars (Value = $387.00)**
  Webinar #1: The "10 BIG" Breakthroughs in Business Life, with Dan Kennedy
  Webinar #2: The ESSENTIALS to Writing Million Dollar Ads & Sales Letters BOTH <u>Online</u> & <u>Offline</u> with Bill Glazer
  Webinar #3: The ESSENTIALS of Productivity and Implementation for Entrepreneurs, with Lee Milteer

- **'Elite' Gold Insider's Circle™ Membership (Two Month Value = $99.94):**
  - o Two Issues Of The NO B.S. MARKETING LETTER
  - o Two CDs Of The EXCLUSIVE GOLD AUDIO INTERVIEWS

- **The New Member No B.S. Income Explosion Guide (Value = $29.97)**

- **Income Explosion FAST START Tele-Seminar (Value = $97.00)**

There is a one-time charge of $19.95 in North America <u>or</u> $39.95 International to cover postage for 2 issues of the FREE Gold Membership. You will automatically continue at the <u>lowest</u> Gold Member price of $49.97 per month ($59.97 outside North America). Should you decide to cancel your membership, you can do so at any time by calling Glazer-Kennedy Insider's Circle™ at 410-825-8600 or faxing a cancellation note to 410-825-3301 (Monday through Friday 9am – 5pm). Remember, your credit card will NOT be charged the low monthly membership fee until the beginning of the 3rd month, which means you will receive 2 full issues to read, test, and **profit from all of the powerful techniques and strategies you get from being an Insider's Circle™ Gold Member.** And of course, it's impossible for you to lose, because if you don't absolutely LOVE everything you get, you can simply cancel your membership after the second free issue and never get billed a single penny for membership.

***EMAIL REQUIRED IN ORDER TO NOTIFY YOU ABOUT THE
GLAZER-KENNEDY UNIVERSITY WEBINARS AND FAST START TELESEMINAR***

Name _____ Business Name _____

Address _____

City _____ State _____ Zip _____ e-mail* _____

Phone _____ Fax_____

Credit Card: ____Visa ____MasterCard ____ American Express _____ Discover

Credit Card Number _____ Exp. Date _____

Signature _____ Date _____
Providing this information constitutes your permission for Glazer-Kennedy Insider's Circle™ to contact you regarding related information via mail, e-mail, fax, and phone.

FAX BACK TO 410-825-3301
Or mail to: 401 Jefferson Ave., Towson, MD 21286